IDENTITY AND INDUSTRY

Identity and Industry

Making Media Multicultural in Canada

MARK HAYWARD

McGill-Queen's University Press
Montreal & Kingston • London • Chicago

© McGill-Queen's University Press 2019

ISBN 978-0-7735-5877-9 (cloth)
ISBN 978-0-7735-5878-6 (paper)
ISBN 978-0-2280-0010-5 (ePDF)
ISBN 978-0-2280-0011-2 (ePUB)

Legal deposit fourth quarter 2019
Bibliothèque nationale du Québec

Printed in Canada on acid-free paper that is 100% ancient forest free (100% post-consumer recycled), processed chlorine free

This book has been published with the help of a grant from the Canadian Federation for the Humanities and Social Sciences, through the Awards to Scholarly Publications Program, using funds provided by the Social Sciences and Humanities Research Council of Canada.

We acknowledge the support of the Canada Council for the Arts.
Nous remercions le Conseil des arts du Canada de son soutien.

Library and Archives Canada Cataloguing in Publication

Title: Identity and industry : making media multicultural in Canada / Mark Hayward.
Names: Hayward, Mark, 1975– author.
Description: Includes bibliographical references and index.
Identifiers: Canadiana (print) 20190190965 | Canadiana (ebook) 20190191031
 | ISBN 9780773558779 (hardcover) | ISBN 9780773558786 (softcover) | ISBN 9780228000105 (ePDF) | ISBN 9780228000112 (ePUB)
Subjects: LCSH: Ethnic mass media—Canada. | LCSH: Minorities in the mass media industry—Canada. | LCSH: Mass media and minorities—Canada. | LCSH: Mass media and ethnic relations—Canada. | LCSH: Ethnicity in mass media. | LCSH: Minorities in mass media.
Classification: LCC P94.5.M552 C24 2019 | DDC 302.23089/00971—dc23

This book was typeset in 10.5/13 Sabon.

Contents

Figures vii

Acknowledgments ix

Introduction: Multiculturalism, Media, and Infrastructure 3

1 Space: Movie-Going in the Multicultural City 32

2 Autonomy: Governing the Ethnic Press in Cold War Canada 67

3 Format: Inventing Multilingual Radio in Canada 106

4 Scale: Remaking the Spatial Logics of Third-Language Television 141

Conclusion: Post-Digital? Post-Multicultural? 169

Notes 173

Bibliography 203

Index 215

Figures

I.1 Image of woman in front of Bulletin Board. *Toronto Telegram*, 1955. York University Libraries, Clara Thomas Archives and Special Collections, *Toronto Telegram* Fonds, ASC12916. Photo by Reg Towers. 6

1.1 Spanish-language advertisement for *The Godfather/El Padrino*. *El Popular*, 4 April 1973, 7. 34

1.2 Newsstand. York University Libraries, Clara Thomas Archives and Special Collections, *Toronto Telegram* Fonds, ASC12915. Photo by Peter Dunlop. 42

1.3 Studio Theatre Marquee. York University Libraries, Clara Thomas Archives and Special Collections, *Toronto Telegram* Fonds, ASC12908. Photo by Peter Dunlop. 50

1.4 Naaz Marquee. Courtesy of the *Toronto Star*. Photographer: Dick Darrell. 51

1.5 "Thousands Pay $12.50 to see Cup TV," *Globe and Mail* article covering the 1978 World Cup. *Globe and Mail*, 12 June 1978. 55

1.6 Strike at the Lansdowne Theatre. York University Libraries, Clara Thomas Archives and Special Collections, *Toronto Telegram* Fonds, ASC 52273. Photo by Dave Cooper. 57

1.7 1970s Advertisements for Portuguese barbershops in Montreal. *Tribuna Portuguesa*, 12 April 1974. 59

2.1 "Ethnic Press Meets Cabinet." Courtesy of the *Toronto Star*. Photographer: Boris Spremo. 71

2.2 Lindal and Massey, 1955. University of Manitoba Archives and Special Collections, *Winnipeg Tribune* Fonds. PC 18, A.81-12. 77

2.3 New Canadian advertisement published in the *Globe and Mail*, 26 April 1957. 89

3.1 Cover. *Canadian Broadcaster and Telescreen*, 17 August 1955. 117

3.2 Cover of *Percy Faith Plays Continental Music*. Columbia, 1953. 120

3.3 Johnny Lombardi in Smock Coat. Courtesy of the *Toronto Star*. Photographer: Reg Innell. 126

3.4 Picnic advertisement. *Globe and Mail*, 18 July 1968. 135

4.1 Pasqualino Carpino. Courtesy of the *Toronto Star*. Photographer: Ron Bull. 148

4.2 Francis Cheung. Courtesy of the *Toronto Star*. Photographer: Ron Bull. 158

4.3 TLN program guide cover, 1985. Courtesy of Telelatino. 161

Acknowledgments

This book would not have been possible without support from the Canadian Social Science and Humanities Research Council. It provided funding that made possible much of the archival research gathered in this publication. Additional support was received from the Bibliothèque et Archives nationales du Québec (BAnQ), which provided me with a bursary to conduct research in its extensive collection of third-language newspapers published in that province. Finally, the York University minor research grant allowed me to conduct and transcribe some of the interviews that formed the basis of this project.

In writing the book, I was supported by an excellent team of research assistants, including: Maria Clara Casasfranco, Heather Gibb, Jade Guthrie, David Hibbs, Anna Lytvynova, Daniela Sanzone, Faye Spathara, Alice Wang, and Jason Wang. They were essential in allowing me to complete much of the work with primary sources.

I am grateful for support from my former colleagues in the Department of Communication Studies at Wilfrid Laurier University and my current colleagues in the Department of Communication Studies at York University. Ira Wagman and John Montesano read parts of the manuscript while it was in preparation. I presented some parts of this manuscript as talks at Carleton University and at the Canadian Communication Association. I am grateful for the response I received from attentive listeners in both venues.

The origins of this project lay in my dissertation at the University of North Carolina-Chapel Hill. While a very different project, this book is informed by the same questions of identity, belonging, and institutions that were at the centre of my dissertation. I would like to thank my advisor, Lawrence Grossberg, for his continued support. At McGill-Queen's University Press, Jonathan Crago has been an endless source of excellent editorial suggestions and support, as were the two anonymous reviewers.

I am thankful for the opportunity to speak with some of the key players in the history of minority and third-language media in Canada, including Olumide Adewumi, Justine Bizzocchi, Aldo Di Felice, Wayne Fromm, Rocco Mastrangelo, and Madeline Ziniak. They provided me with insights that were not otherwise available from printed sources.

The years writing this book have witnessed many moves, several floods, births, and deaths. I would especially like to thank my family. My mother, Phyllis, who is not here to see the book completed, was a formative influence on its subject matter and pretty much everything else about me.

Finally, Sara and Leo deserve particular acknowledgment for having put up with the excessive amount of time and paper involved in completing this project.

IDENTITY AND INDUSTRY

INTRODUCTION

Multiculturalism, Media, and Infrastructure

In a 2017 interview about the lack of diversity on Canadian screens, the actor, writer, and director Sarah Polley observed that "Canadian film and TV doesn't look like the Canada I live in — when I'm walking down the street or on the subway or in a hospital waiting room, that's so rarely what I see reflected on screen. If that's offensive to me, I can't imagine how deeply offensive it must be to someone who is unrepresented."[1] Polley's comparison of Canadian media to streets, subways, and hospital waiting rooms is a way of talking about forms of discrimination in media that make visible the absences that cannot by definition be seen on screen. Comparing media to public infrastructure is not unique to Polley, although the connection is often made in passing.[2] Gary Pieters, a Canadian teacher involved in anti-racism education, makes a similar connection between media and public infrastructure. He proposes "attending cultural events, riding on public transit, talking to people, watching multi-cultural shows on TV, picking up papers that are in a different language to English" as ways of exposing children to cultural diversity.[3] "Riding on public transit" may seem to be an outlier on this list as the other activities Pieters mentions all explicitly involve sharing culture and experience. However, its inclusion in his list suggests that he sees using public transit as sharing something with others, even if we rarely seek out direct social interaction with our fellow passengers.

These comparisons between media and public infrastructure belong to a long tradition of thinking about communication – a tradition that moves beyond examining how we exchange information interpersonally or by means of media technologies to view communication as a way of being together.[4] Of course, these comments offer a far from comprehensive account of the insights and/or actions that might result from such a comparison. Both comments overlook, probably for rhetorical effect and clarity, the complexity of the public spaces and services proposed as models for media to follow. Sidewalks, subways, and hospitals are not exempt from the same forms of discrimination and exclusion that Polley sees in the images on Canadian screens. However, I argue that there is a great deal that can be learned by thinking in infrastructural terms about the history of cultural and linguistic diversity in Canadian media. Given the space to more fully develop the complex terrain on which any movement towards Polley's and Pieters' ideal of more accessible media would take place, the history outlined here traces the negotiation between inclusion and exclusion that characterizes the transformation of media as part of the social, political, and cultural project of multiculturalism in Canada.

As a first step, we might acknowledge that this comparison is not just a metaphor: media *are* infrastructure. Communication media play an essential role in contemporary society alongside roads and power lines. The most significant of these functions involves coordinating interactions between large numbers of people, but they extend to education and entertainment. They also provide community and emotional support by connecting individuals with each other across distances both great and small. However, there is another way to think about this comparison. This requires recognizing that media themselves require infrastructure. This infrastructure supports and organizes how media operate. It includes the technical infrastructure of media systems: cables, broadcast towers, and so on. But it also involves a cultural and political infrastructure made up of generic norms, policies, and rules of social address. The way that media infrastructure develop is far from spontaneous, being the product of both individual and collective projects to realize particular forms of agency and to encourage specific forms of community. I am interested in infrastructure as "civic" rather than as "civil" engineering.

A number of questions follow from this starting point. If there is a general consensus that an important function of media is to inform and to connect individuals with each other whether one-to-one or as mediated by processes of identification with a group or community, what are the kinds of connection that have been (or should be or could be) developed and why have these been favoured? If an analysis of media finds its ethical and political orientation by drawing examples from other kinds of public infrastructure, which model provides the best map for understanding how media infrastructure are organized? And for understanding how they should be organized in order to make the desired connections and communities possible? Are media most productively compared to a network of roads (reticular and open, although mostly individualized since the rise of the personal automobile), or to healthcare (in which centralized distribution points like hospitals and medical offices serve individual members of a community), or to public transit (in which large groups of people are served by a common service)?

It is tempting to answer to these questions in ways that are primarily determined by technology. However, political, cultural, and economic factors play an equally significant role. A good example of what an emphasis on technology obscures can be seen in an image of a woman standing in front of a bulletin board outside a shop on College Street in Toronto (figure I.1). The photo belongs to a series taken in 1955 for the *Toronto Telegram*'s reporting on how new immigrants to the city were building homes for themselves. Its appeal at the time likely derived from showing a world unknown to the average *Telegram* reader, but it also archives an often-overlooked scene of media consumption. While newer forms of media usually attract the most attention, the complexity and significance of the moment captured in the photograph for the history of Canadian media should not be ignored. It shows the very old, but still effective, technology of public posters integrated with a broader media economy of publications and live performance. The posters and the events they publicize are in multiple languages, but none is in English. Looking at the image with an eye only for technological innovation allows us to see only posters; it ignores the cultural and social innovations that are inscribed in the image and that are evidence of the complex ecology of media and cultural activities emerging from the new ways of sharing space being explored by the large numbers of immigrants settling in Canada over the course of the twentieth century.

In the broadest terms, this book is a contribution to a better understanding of the historical development of ethnocultural media in relation to a context that has been simultaneously supportive and stifling. This is a history in which every person living in Canada participates, although for many their main contribution is indifference. Like people who pass each other without acknowledgment on the sidewalk mentioned by Sarah Polley, ethnocultural media are

Figure I.1 Unidentified woman reading postings for publications in multiple languages on Toronto's College Street, 1955.

often invisible in accounts of the development of Canadian media and culture. However, *Identity and Industry* is not "the history" of something called multicultural media, nor does it claim to document all of the enterprises and individuals who produced and distributed media for minority, migrant, or diasporic audiences in Canada. The parameters of such a project would be overwhelming, vague, and would risk contributing to the further marginalization of such media. Bringing together media across time periods, languages, cultures, and contexts of production and reception in an over-simplified manner runs contrary to the very notion of a more fully realized diversity that must lie at the heart of any truly open and democratic form of cultural diversity. As many critics of media and multiculturalism have noted, over-simplistic and careless media producers and critics alike risk advocating forms of recognition and inclusion that reduce social and cultural complexity to stereotypes.[5]

I agree with such critiques and acknowledge the damage that such an approach can cause. Yet I also show that an emphasis on ethnocultural or linguistic difference as the primary way of categorizing media risks overlooking the institutions and industrial practices that, for decades, have been shared across different media, languages, and communities in Canada. My claim is not that minority media possess the characteristics, or fulfill the functions, of infrastructure because *all* media function as infrastructure. Rather, I examine and analyze the institutions, organizations, norms, and regulations that served as the infrastructure supporting, monitoring, organizing, and managing the production and distribution of media serving minority communities, many of which were in languages other than English or French, over the course of the second half of the twentieth century and up to the present day.

It should already be apparent that I do not believe that to be attentive to media infrastructure is to claim that technology produces meaning or significance – as in McLuhan's aphorism "the medium is the message"; rather, I show how the mobility of films, music, or television programs through a complex of legal, technological, and cultural networks contributes to their meaning and significance for specific audiences. One way of thinking about this is to view it as drawing on the catalogue of media's logistical effects, which Harold Innis analyzes in his research on the relationship between social order and information distribution, but without the broader civilizational narrative within which his analyses are situated. Another, more modest, way to describe this approach is to view it as an example of what Will Straw describes as the "anti-interpretive" tendency in media studies, which he proposes as an alternative to approaches in which the interpretation of texts takes centre stage.[6] Rather than look at what texts mean in isolation from industries or audiences, I focus on how the mobility of media across social and technological networks produces particular kinds of meaning and significance that may not be found in the words, sounds, or images we experience.[7]

Because it is the path taken by media from other parts of the world that often contributes to their meaning for audiences and individuals, the mobility of media is particularly important when studying its production and use in migrant and diasporic communities. A focus on the movement of media does not negate the fact that people make sense of films, newspapers, radio, and television programs, but it recognizes that an awareness of, and affective investment in, the ways that these texts have crossed cultural and political borders is built into how they are interpreted. Taking such an approach highlights the literal and symbolic participation in the media infrastructure that, through media, allows individuals and communities to bridge the distance between one's present surroundings and an actual or imagined home. While influenced by research into media production belonging to the tradition of political economy in media studies, my attention to the overlapping relationship between symbolic and economic registers of media production is more accurately described in terms of "cultural studies of media industries."[8] Returning to the distinction made above between technical and cultural media infrastructures, this approach provides a framework for considering how these two forms of infrastructure influence each other in ways that are often overlooked by frameworks that emphasize a more rigid definition of the economy.

However, as I discuss later in this introduction, infrastructures are often conceptually and empirically obscure. Sometimes they can only be observed through the effects and affordances of their operation rather than as discrete objects on their own. Reflecting this, *Identity and Industry* is organized into four chapters that document different characteristics of Canada's minority and multilingual media industry as the product of a particular configuration of the nation's media infrastructure. The chapters are organized around the following four concepts, which might also be described as functions or products of media infrastructure:

- *Space,* or how media distribution contributes to the creation of common spaces in Canadian cities in which many different languages and cultures flourished;
- *Autonomy,* or how the relationship between minority media and state is represented, organized, and managed;
- *Format,* or the relationship between language, culture, and different ways of structuring media texts in relation to political and economic exigencies; and
- *Scale,* or the role media plays in discussions about the relationship between the local, national, and global movement of information.

Each of the chapters focuses on a different medium, discussing film, print, radio, and television, respectively. The themes of space, autonomy, format, and scale raised in relation to one medium are, to varying degrees, relevant to all of these media.

The decision to adopt this structure is strategic in that it will, I hope, allow readers less familiar with media history to better understand the factors that have shaped the institutionalization of cultural and linguistic diversity in Canadian media since the middle of the twentieth century. The conclusion extends this argument up to the present day, briefly sketching how a changing regulatory environment, the rise of digital media, and new cultural dynamics have fundamentally transformed media and cultural infrastructures that were established in the previous century. It argues for a new understanding of the nation's media infrastructure – one that might better support Canada's cultural and linguistic diversity in relation to contemporary forms of communication.

In each of the chapters, I explore the intersection between a range of interests and agendas. The most prominent of these include the government's interest in using media as tools for encouraging the cultural, political, and economic integration and assimilation of immigrants; the desire of media entrepreneurs to make a profit; and the broader popular desire of individuals and communities to create media in which they can see and hear their own cultures and languages. Like many debates about infrastructure – from the building of roads and public transit services to the management of hospitals – the consensus that results from the encounter between conflicting agendas is often an unhappy compromise. The institutions and social networks contributing to the media infrastructure that serves cultural and linguistic minorities has yet to (and may never) fully realize their potential contribution to an equal and just society. On the contrary, I present many examples of how they have not even fulfilled the more modest goals of media producers, let alone the hopes and aspirations of the wide range of people who rely on these media for information and entertainment. For this reason, recognition of the persistent forms of systemic social and institutional discrimination necessarily complicates any celebration of the successes experienced by media producers in establishing platforms and services that contributed to the creation of space for diverse voices in Canadian public life.

Despite expansive gestures towards inclusion found in statements about multiculturalism made by representatives of the Canadian state, the nation has struggled with the institutional and quotidian realities of discrimination and racism. At many points in this book, I note how the implementation of Canadian multiculturalism lapses into programs supporting more restricted notions of multilingualism. The significance and effects of this slippage are developed to a much greater extent by Eve Haque in her analysis of the Royal Commission on Bilingualism and Biculturalism. As Haque argues, this movement from multiculturalism to multilingualism enables the institutions of Canadian civil society as well as the Canadian government to avoid a direct engagement with the persistence of race as a mechanism of exclusion in the nation's history.[9] The complicity of multicultural policy with the logics of racial exclusion and associated practices of marginalization must not be explained away or minimized as unfortunate accidents or oversights. The failure to engage with the complexity of multiculturalism would ignore what Augie Fleras describes as the "paradox of multiculturalism," which is "progressively inclusive yet potentially exclusionary" in so far as it overlooks both "multicultural racism" (thus failing to address the complexity of identity and existing forms of discrimination) and forms of "racist multiculturalism" (thus serving to preserve existing forms of racial discrimination).[10]

The possibilities and limitations of the realization of the goals of multiculturalism in Canada have been addressed in research across a number of fields, and how to assess this history remains a matter of debate. As Rinaldo Walcott writes, "it might be argued that the only consensus on Canadian multiculturalism in the last thirty-plus years is that it has become a fundamental Canadian entity, but consensus on what it means and how it should work continues to elude us. Ideas and practices of multiculturalism remain contested sites and so they should be."[11] It is my intention to make a modest contribution to how multiculturalism is discussed and debated by developing a more nuanced understanding of the historical development of the relationship between media industries, the state, and various configurations of the public. The remainder of this introduction elaborates the justification for making the theoretical and methodological shift away from an analysis of the relationship between representation, identity, and community and towards the infrastructural perspective taken here, which emphasizes the industrial structures and systems through which media are made available to the public.

In what follows I first provide a brief discussion about the meaning, relevance, and limitations of what Charles Taylor has called "the politics of recognition." Taking up Taylor's work on the "politics of recognition," I pay particular attention to the role he assigns to media and communication. I argue that many discussions about cultural and political recognition influenced by Taylor rely on over-simplified models of how media distribution and production take place. In the remainder of the introduction I examine how an engagement with the concept of infrastructure might orient an analysis of media and cultural diversity that productively remedies this shortcoming in a way that bridges theoretical debates about identity and belonging by providing a more grounded analysis of how media is produced and distributed.

THE "MEDIA" IN MULTICULTURALISM

Media is a common starting point for talking about questions of identity, community, and belonging. In all but the most abstract discussions of multiculturalism, there is some reference made to communication media as an important factor in the formation of identity and maintenance of relations within, and between, cultural and linguistic communities. In many cases, these are references to "the media" as an undifferentiated social institution whose primary role is the distribution of information. One of the contributions of *Identity and Industry* is that it does more than just argue that "the media" matter in an analysis of Canadian multiculturalism: it shows that it is important to bring the significant insights into media industries found in media and communication studies to bear upon debates about how multiculturalism has taken shape, and continues to evolve, in Canada. My intention here is to elaborate upon some of the problems that emerge when the complexity of "the media" is left unexamined.

Charles Taylor's writings on multiculturalism and diversity are significant in relation to my concerns for two reasons: (1) their prominence as a touchstone for many discussions about cultural diversity and (2) the central role Taylor gives to mediation in his theorization of "the politics of recognition." Given that the politics of recognition was developed in the context of Taylor's broader project of exploring the foundations and limitations of liberal democracy, it is perhaps not surprising that media do not figure explicitly in his discussion of it. Yet his emphasis on "exchange," "encounters," "dialogue," and "interaction" between different individuals and groups within a society as part of the formation of identity implies that communication plays a significant role in how such phenomena might play out in a more concrete fashion.[12]

However, the most detailed discussions of media in Taylor's writings come not when he is considering the complexities of recognition between different groups but, rather, when he is attempting to elaborate an understanding of the public sphere within which such recognition might take place. In *Modern Social Imaginaries*, he writes: "The public sphere is a common space in which the members of society are deemed to meet through a variety of media: print, electronic, and also face-to-face encounters; to discuss matters of common interest; and thus to be able to form a common mind about these. I say 'a common space' because although the media are multiple, as are the exchanges that take place in them, they are deemed to be in principle inter-communicating. The discussion we're having on television now takes account of what was said in the newspaper this morning, which in turn reports on the radio debate yesterday and so on."[13] Taylor's description of the interconnection between different forms of media feels like an apt description for the time in which he wrote this passage (and echoes other well-known formulations, such as Newcomb and Hirsch's seminal discussion of television's role as a "cultural forum"). However, such an understanding of "inter-communication" is difficult to sustain when looking at the history of media serving cultural and linguistic minorities since it overlooks the disjunction between mainstream media and minority media in terms of language, cultural values, tone, subject matter, and accessibility.

This is a theme that has been taken up by a number of researchers who have shown that the model of the public sphere, most frequently associated with the work of Habermas and, in the above passage, explicitly connected to media by Taylor, is better understood in a more fragmented way both as a result of culturally heterogeneous populations and in response to the emergence of media infrastructure that does not simply broadcast messages to the undifferentiated masses.[14] In this, Taylor's understanding of the media can be seen as overly simplified even for the time when he wrote his essay (1990). His claim that media contribute to the social development of a society seems intuitively true, but he pays very little attention to the complexities of how these media are actually organized or received by people. A more conceptual and schematic way of describing his approach is to note that, effectively, this discussion of media assimilates contemporary media technology into a more generalized and de-historicized understanding of mediation. As Richard Day writes, critiquing Taylor's ideas by means of the metaphor of media: "Taylor's dream thus might seem rather black and white, or perhaps even radio."[15]

In contrast to his more philosophical work, in *Building the Future: A Time for Reconciliation* Taylor offers a more nuanced understanding of the role that different media play in shaping opinions about cultural and linguistic minorities. This report, co-authored with Gerard Bouchard, on cultural difference and accommodation in Quebec, develops a more complete rendering of the complexity with which media producers as well as audiences take up issues related to diversity, recognition, and inclusion.[16] The report was commissioned by the government of Quebec in response to "public discontent concerning reasonable accommodation" of cultural and linguistic minorities in the province. While providing a more detailed account of media production and consumption, the Bouchard-Taylor report focuses almost exclusively on the way that mainstream media – meaning media in French and English – addresses issues around cultural and linguistic accommodation in response to a populist movement against migrants and minorities in Quebec.[17] In the report, the media are portrayed as a complex social institution consisting of different voices and competing interests that are subject to a wide range of interpretations. However, one set of voices is mostly absent from the report: minority and community media. Although the report recommends that "members of the ethnic minorities must do more to make themselves seen and heard," there is little attention given to community media originating in minority communities in the province, despite Quebec's being home to some of the oldest minority publications and broadcasters in the country.[18]

My goal in addressing the place given to media in the work of Charles Taylor is not to discredit his contributions but, rather, to draw attention to the peculiar role played by media (and, one could say by extension, media studies) in discussions of the "politics of recognition." They are at once ubiquitous and overlooked; they are recognized as being among the most powerful and significant social institutions even as the complexity of their organization, operation, and reception are ignored. The absence of engagement with the complexity of media is similarly true of many of the critics who have taken issue with Taylor's elaboration of "recognition." Media, as a conduit for representations, is a powerful tool that can be used to stoke feelings of resentment and intolerance towards minorities as well as to provide a platform for raising awareness about the lived experiences of members of minority communities. However, the context within which media production takes place remains unexplored.

This might appear to be a minor issue given the scope of Taylor's broader philosophical and political project, but it is significant in so far as it might allow us to address the limits that he himself sees in his analysis of diversity. The essay on the politics of recognition ends with a discussion of the importance (and perhaps the impossibility) of determining the comparative value of cultures or, as he writes, "a willingness to be open to comparative cultural study."[19] The result of this comparative study would displace and transform the values of any and all cultural systems, even though it would not provide an "ultimate horizon from which the relative worth of different cultures might be evident."[20] Taylor's essay ends with the open question: What are the proper ethical and political terms upon which another culture can be encountered and interpreted?

Taylor's presentation of this dilemma suggests that it is not a question to be answered; rather, it is a recognition of the aporia at the centre of the attempt to reconcile difference and inclusion. However, anti-colonial and Indigenous scholars have argued that the pragmatics of the politics of recognition rarely maintain Taylor's commitment to openness for very long. Writing of the relationship between Canada and Indigenous peoples, Glenn Coulthard draws on the writings of Frantz Fanon to argue that this is an encounter in which there are "*asymmetrical* and *non-reciprocal* forms of recognition either imposed on or granted to them by the settler state and society."[21] Coulthard's critique elaborates the distinction between the ideal and the actual in the recognition of cultural and linguistic difference. Taking up a similar set of concerns in relation to multiculturalism, Rinaldo Walcott argues that the history of multiculturalism cannot be understood outside of the context of European modernity and its attendant logics of racialization.[22]

Following the need to situate the promise of inclusion in relation to the pragmatics of recognition, the following chapters develop an analysis of how media infrastructure in Canada evolved not only to accommodate but also to manage, contain, and even erase cultural and linguistic difference. In this approach the political, technological, and cultural factors that contributed to the configuration of a "multicultural" media infrastructure is a site in which Taylor's aporia has been addressed and "resolved" in practical terms. Taking up media infrastructure in this way requires blurring the line between political philosophy and cultural production; it draws attention to how even the most pragmatic approaches to the production of media are not independent from a more general understanding of what is and is not possible in a given context – which is to say that it is an analysis of and response to existing power relations.

MEDIA INFRASTRUCTURES

To better understand what is at stake in translating Taylor's philosophical problem into the more prosaic register of infrastructural concerns, it is necessary to begin by examining the often overlooked conceptual and material complexity of infrastructure itself. "Infrastructure" is a concept that has received renewed attention across the humanities and social sciences in recent years.[23] This interest has coincided with the broader public's interest in infrastructure and the importance of infrastructural development and maintenance. While the objects of these debates may seem very concrete (e.g., roads, bridges, communication networks, hospitals, and so on), what is at stake in these discussions often leads to an engagement with the scale and complexity of modernity. In a passage that brings concrete concerns together with their wide-ranging importance, Bowker and Leigh Starr write: "In the past 100 years, people in all lines of work have jointly constructed an incredible, interlocking set of categories, standards, and means for inter-operating infrastructural technologies. We hardly know what we have built. No one is in control of infrastructure; no one has the power centrally to change it. To the extent that we live in, on, and around this new infrastructure, it helps form the shape of our moral, scientific and aesthetic choices. Infrastructure is now the great inner space."[24]

Despite the attention the topic of infrastructure has garnered, the term remains difficult to define. Brian Larkin notes that infrastructures are "conceptually unruly."[25] John Durham Peters observes that "infrastructures are generally thought to be bulky and boring systems that are hard to carry, such as airports, highways, electrical grids, or aqueducts."[26] Yet he goes on to note that there can be "hard and soft infrastructures" and that there "can be lightweight and portable as well as heavy and fixed infrastructures."[27] Yet it would be a mistake to view the unruliness of the term as a weakness. On the contrary, the fuzziness accompanying definitions of infrastructure is better understood as indicative of the peculiar nature of infrastructural systems. Larkin touches upon this in his attempt to define the ontology of infrastructures. Building on the very general definition that "infrastructures are matter that enable the movement of other matter," he goes on to explain: "Their peculiar ontology lies in the facts that they are things and also the relation between things. As things they are present to the senses, yet they are also displaced in the focus on the matter they move around."[28]

Lisa Parks also draws attention to the continuum between intelligibility and concealment along which all infrastructure sits. She writes, "While some infrastructure sites are celebrated as sites of technological spectacle and wonder, others are hidden beyond thick green shrubs or buried deep underground."[29] These intentional efforts at camouflage supplement the operational obscurity of infrastructure that results from greater attention being given to the activities and interactions it makes possible than to the infrastructure itself. Accordingly, the turn towards infrastructure requires a reorientation of how media have usually been analyzed in media and communication studies. Parks and Starosielski argue that "a focus on infrastructure foregrounds *processes of distribution* that have taken a backseat in humanities-based research on media culture, which until recently has tended to prioritize processes of production and consumption, encoding and decoding and textual interpretation."[30] Along similar lines, John Durham Peters describes those theories and methods that recognize the importance of infrastructure ("infrastructuralism," he calls it) as providing "a new way of understanding the work of media as fundamentally logistical. Logistical media have the job of ordering fundamental terms and units."[31]

Looking at "processes of distribution" and media as "fundamentally logistical" moves media studies away from established concerns with meaning and representation towards problems of coordination. How problems of coordination are resolved is a frequent theme throughout the following chapters, whether with regard to how professional organizations have functioned, broadcast formats, or the regulation of television distribution. Yet coordination is a fraught process. Projects involved in the ordering and structuring of "fundamental terms and units" within a communication system quickly take on a more threatening air, particularly when discussing identity and self-expression. Foregrounding the protocols and formats that emerge through the functioning of media infrastructures calls to mind the concerns about standardization that, for nearly a century, have circulated in relation to media and the industrialization of culture.[32]

I argue that Canada's multicultural and multilingual media infrastructure should be recognized as one of the most significant outcomes of the manifold struggles, during the second part of the twentieth century, to include individuals and groups who did not identify linguistically or culturally with the country's two dominant settler communities. However, arguing for the significance of this media infrastructure is not the same as offering unqualified praise. Tracing the development of a media infrastructure designed to support multiple languages and cultures brings to light many of the ways that multiculturalism as a social, cultural, and political project has enabled both (1) improved access to Canadian media for marginalized communities and (2) the expansion of modes of state surveillance and control that exclude those same communities.

There is a sizeable body of work within media studies, communication studies, anthropology, sociology, cultural studies, and political science that takes up the role media play in relation to cultural and linguistic diversity in Canadian society. Yet surprisingly little of this focuses on the industrial and infrastructural formation of minority media, instead choosing to emphasize representation or consumption. However, the work of Catherine Murray and Lorna Roth, in particular, has contributed essential insights into the industrial organizations that constitute minority media as they are shaped by political and economic factors. While her work on the evolution of Canadian policy regarding cultural and linguistic minorities remains a significant contribution in a field with too few pieces of general scholarship, Lorna Roth's account of the founding and evolution of the Aboriginal People's Television Network is a model of the kind of detailed, mixed-method scholarly work to which this book aspires.[33]

Due to its scope and detail, Catherine Murray's analysis of ethnic media in British Columbia is a similarly important contribution. More important, it must be noted that *Industry and Identity*'s key claim regarding the importance of examining media as infrastructure for the development of multiculturalism in Canada is inspired in part by Murray's examination of ethnic media as infrastructure.[34] In a short essay on media infrastructure and multiculturalism, she writes: "Next to family and personal networks, the infrastructure most important in immigrant adaptation to the adopted country is the depth and breadth of ethnocultural networks (including immigrant-serving organizations and religious or cultural groups) and the availability of media in their language of choice."[35] Murray's work in this article and elsewhere develops a set of concerns that is similar to that outlined in the British context by Charles Husband's argument that media infrastructure is an essential component of a multi-ethnic public sphere. As he explains, a multi-ethnic public sphere would entail "both a media infrastructure that can address and reflect the interests of specific ethnic communities, and media which facilitate dialogue and engagement across ethnic boundaries."[36]

However, there is a significant difference between Murray's approach to media infrastructure and the one taken here. Both approaches look at the norms, institutions, and regulations that shape how media operate. However, Murray's consideration of how minority media are organized places the emphasis squarely on policy. The question she poses for herself is: "How can policy improve the integration process?"[37] I am not opposed to intervention in policy as one of the possible outcomes of scholarly research, but it must be recognized that the turn to policy orients the structure and tone of a research project in ways that align with the task of governance. Such an approach may foreclose a more expansive engagement with the historical developments that contributed to the constitution of contemporary media institutions. Murray is not unaware of this, writing that "the major story about ethnic media in Canada is their autonomous development."[38] However, she remains focused on questions of policy. The historical approach taken here does not valorize history for its own sake but shows how a careful analysis of the historical development of ethnic media is essential for acknowledging the extra-institutional, unofficial, and informal activities and interactions that constitute an important part of culture and cultural production.

Although it is not the only means through which to take up these aspects of culture and media, a historical approach is one way of avoiding the risks of naturalizing as structural determinants the activities of the members of elites who were able to marshal the financial and social capital required to establish and operate media outlets. It would be a mistake to believe that the processes through which specific media producers were "chosen" to speak for the community via print, radio, or television were democratic, even though they sometimes describe themselves as "community media." As is noted at the beginning of this introduction, infrastructure is as much a product of the unequal distribution of power and resources as anything else. Thus, the infrastructures discussed in the chapters that follow are not simply the spontaneous, yet optimal, institutional and organizational products of different cultural groups coming together: they track the ways in which these institutions and organizations have formalized inequality and exclusion.

CANADIAN ARCHIVES AND GLOBAL MEDIA

The importance of history to understanding the cultural context within which minority and ethnocultural media develops is particularly important because, in Canada, there is comparatively little work dedicated to it. A handful of publications on historical topics were produced in the years immediately following the adoption of official multiculturalism in 1971, made possible in part by the funds that accompanied that announcement. Many of these consist of organizational commemorations, recognizing significant anniversaries in the lives of individual publications or professional organizations. While such publications are useful, they rarely engage in rigorous historical analysis. Other monographs, such as Victor Turek's *The Polish Language Press in Canada* or Angelo Principe's *The Darkest Side of Fascism*, have provided histories of media within particular communities, most often focusing on newspapers and other print media. The organizational history of media has also appeared in historical studies of integration and national identity. For example, Fujiwara's comparative study of ethnic elites in Canada during the first decades of the twentieth century gives some attention to the role played by newspapers editors.[39] There is, however, significantly less material that looks at more recent developments in ethnocultural media from a historical perspective.

The period covered here concentrates on the years since the end of the Second World War, with particular emphasis on the period between 1950 and 2000. There are a number of reasons for choosing this period. Primary among them is that it was during these years that, due to the actions of the government, media producers, and the public at large, ethnocultural media expanded significantly. It is also a period that saw extraordinary changes in the technologies that people used to communicate both with each other and when seeking information and entertainment. To put this in perspective: television was still a new and experimental medium in Canada in 1950; by the year 2000 it was already becoming clear that broadcast television would eventually be displaced by digital forms of distribution. As becomes apparent in the chapters that follow, the emergence of multiculturalism and changes in media technology intersected and influenced each other in important ways and continue to do so.

Because of the pervasiveness of the cultural and technological changes taking place in the period covered here, there are a number of practical and methodological issues related to studying ethnocultural media from a historical perspective that must be elaborated upon if the reader is to understand the grounds upon which the claims made in this book rest. Some of these issues result from a fundamental reality of historical research focusing on media in Canada – namely, that the most comprehensive (and widely accessible) archives in Canada are those compiled and maintained by the state. It is important to recognize that these archives often suffer from particular kinds of absences and biases. These relate to three areas, each of which particularly affects ethnocultural media. The first area concerns the predominance of materials related to public media over materials related to privately owned media services; the second concerns the linguistic bias that is often inscribed in these archives and that favours official over non-official languages; and the third concerns the complications associated with media that circulate across multiple national contexts. While it is not possible to address each of these issues exhaustively, it is important to provide a general overview of each as well as to address some of the strategies that I use to account for, and, I hope, to overcome, the biases of the archives.

The difficulties encountered when researching privately owned media in Canada are apparent in published research in the field. Compared to public media institutions, there is comparatively little research on private broadcasting in Canada. This may reflect the interests of researchers, many of whom are committed to the kind of social democratic project that public broadcasters like the CBC are often taken to represent. But it is also a matter of the ways in which archival materials have been preserved and made available. There is no widely accessible archive of materials that concerns the operations of many private media companies. Newspapers have been the most cooperative media producers, while television and film companies have been slow to make their internal archives available to the public.

In the case of television, this has led to a particularly dire circumstance in which it is not just corporate materials that are kept private but also the programs that these broadcasters have produced (if they are preserved at all). Internal corporate archives and libraries may exist, but many companies are reluctant to grant access to researchers. Two factors in particular have led to this situation: first, the absence of resources (and supporting policies) that would lead to the creation of a public archive of privately owned media in Canada and, second, the increasingly expansive and aggressive application of intellectual property law, which has led many media companies to restrict access in the hope of protecting future prospects for revenue. In the case of media serving cultural and linguistic minorities, this situation is further complicated by the fact that many of the organizations did not have the resources to preserve historical materials themselves, meaning that they never created institutional archives. This is complicated yet again when it comes to small organizations that no longer exist. The result, when it comes to minority media, is a variety of collections with varying degrees of consistency and accessibility. Two examples drawn from my experience researching this book are indicative of some of the problems encountered by the researcher looking for historical materials.

The story of how I came to gain access to a collection of materials concerning the creation of Telelatino, which started broadcasting in Spanish and Italian in 1984, is a telling example of the effects of the absence of resources and policies designed to encourage the preservation of the activities of multicultural media. I first became aware of the Telelatino materials when I was contacted by the president of the network about a "closet full of stuff." Having worked for the network many years before as a documentary producer, he wondered if there might be something that I might find of interest before they disposed of the material. It turns out that the contents of the tattered boxes included many of the early documents associated with the network, which, while Telelatino was unable to keep them due to limited space and resources, were certainly of historical interest to myself and to other scholars. That these papers were preserved was very much a case of good timing and a little bit of luck. However, it is not a stretch to imagine that there have been a number of other occasions on which scholars and archivists have not been present to rescue such materials from the dumpster.

Another example, which highlights issues of access rather than preservation, is the case of the collection of programs produced during the early years of CFMT, a multilingual broadcaster based in Toronto that later became part of Rogers Communication. For reasons that are unclear to the archivists, a collection of about one hundred hours of programming produced in the years following the launch of CFMT in 1978 was deposited in the Archives of Ontario. While a finding aid was produced shortly after their deposit in the archive, it became clear when my research assistant first inquired about the material that the collection had not been looked at in some time as it was stored in the obsolete half-inch tape format. Thankfully the archivists were able to digitize some of the materials. However, when I asked them to make some of these materials available (even for screening in a class), I was informed that their copyright was still held by the producers. The ownership of the broadcasts, often produced by third-party production companies, was a complex tangle of rights and permissions effectively removing from easy public access a significant document pertaining to multicultural media in Canada.

Thankfully, this is not always the case. Sometimes materials have been kept due to the efforts of individuals pushing for the preservation of important historical materials. Such is the case with the collection of the episodes of the program *Ethnicity*, a weekly program documenting minority communities in Canada that was produced by CFMT in Toronto in the 1980s and is now held as part of the collection at Library and Archives Canada. Their preservation is a result of the efforts of the program's producer, Madelaine Ziniak. And the situation is not equally dire across all media. Indeed, there are a number of comprehensive archives of newspapers produced by many different communities in many different languages. The policies mandating the deposit of publications that were put in place by both national and provincial archives have contributed to the creation of a significant historical resource.

As a result of these gaps in the archive, it has often been necessary to read across media, relying upon newspaper reports of television programs and film screenings when other documentation does not exist. At times, I have turned to the numerous government filings for regulatory bodies, which are also the public face of the minority and third-language media industry. An entire section of chapter 2 concerns how newspapers published in languages other than English or French participated in public hearings related to mass media, bilingualism, and cultural diversity along with other official public forums debating multiculturalism. For television and film, such records often include the variety of licensing and regulatory filings that are required in order to continue operating in Canada. In the case of television, transcripts of government hearings often include many details about the history of third-language broadcasting that are not readily available in other locations. Another source of information comes from the various kinds of data collected by government agencies. For example, part of the chapter on film distribution draws on the database of film exhibition licences that were issued to films shown in British Columbia and Ontario between 1945 and 2000.

It is, however, important to recognize the extent to which these records are not entirely reliable or complete. One of the limitations of this archive is that such documents often represent an organization putting its best face forward and, thus, may not provide an accurate picture of the day-to-day operations of a particular company. And this does not address the extent to which diasporic and minority media occasionally function within "grey" markets. Many kinds of media were distributed in ways that exploited the areas left unaddressed by the guidelines and directives of Canada's media and cultural policy. The arrival of home video is particularly illustrative in this regard as there are numerous documents in government archives querying the legal status, in relation to both copyright and content rating, of the materials being rented or sold.

If the archive as it has been constituted is far from complete, the issue of language further complicates the ways in which the documents related to minority media have been preserved. While minority media speak in dozens of languages and are connected to even more cultural groups, Canada's official archives function primarily in the two official languages of the nation. The effect of this is that documents tracing the activities of media serving linguistic and cultural minorities often involve an unacknowledged process of translation. For example, the records regarding the licensing of film distribution and exhibition are perhaps the most comprehensive source on the distribution and exhibition of films in languages other than English or French. Yet they also bear the marks of an encounter between an institution speaking a different language from the businesses and individuals that are being regulated. The titles of the films themselves change as they are translated into English or French, a process affected by the presumed expectations of film censorship boards; these titles may even differ in different provinces, depending on the preferred strategies of film distributors for dealing with local regulatory authorities.

The final way that the complex position occupied by minority media often exceeds the logic of the archive speaks to the complexities of cultural and political borders. In this book, the focus is primarily on how cultural diversity has been incorporated into the cultural and political fabric of Canada over the past fifty years. It is a decidedly "national" framing of this topic. And yet this national framing of minority media necessarily obscures the ways in which the communities that are being discussed are connected with other communities in other parts of the world, whether these other groups are also in diaspora or "back home." In researching the history of multicultural media in Canada, there is often a point at which it is difficult to determine where it bleeds into the transnational history of media of different cultural and linguistic groups.

This is an issue that I engage with in detail in chapter 4, which looks at the period in which the possibility for global distribution of media content to domestic audiences made possible by digital media led to a number of questions about influence from media and political organizations outside of Canada. In other words, there is a point at which the Canadian archives end, having reached the limit of the nation's interests, even though this is not the end of the story. There are a variety of ways in which the transnational nature of these media industries has been made manifest. Claims regarding the right to distribute materials have been made based upon laws of other countries, an indirect challenge to the jurisdiction of Canadian intellectual property laws. At other times, questions have been raised regarding the national origin of capital behind owners of newspapers or broadcasters, linking them to companies or governments outside of Canada. Here, the history of multiculturalism overlaps with the history of other nations' relations with emigrants and diaspora. In some cases, this has required exploring not just the activities of multicultural media in Canada but also the position of these media producers and distributors in the context of the global cultural or linguistic market in which they operate. It is here that the narratives of cultural integration and assimilation intersect with, and are sometimes contested by, the unmooring of the institutions of the nation-state from territory – an unmooring that has accelerated over the past fifty years.

Each of these issues raises methodological problems and questions. As already mentioned, *Identity and Industry* does not attempt to document every publication, cinema, and broadcaster. Given all I have said about the constitution of the archive at hand, the folly of such an attempt cannot be denied. I freely admit such limitations and hope that they serve as a starting point for further research into the history of minority media in Canada. That being said, the following chapters provide a useful overview of some of the dynamics that define the development of the media that serve cultural and linguistic minorities in Canada. The turn towards infrastructure is a way of acknowledging that the processes through which ethnocultural media are inscribed within the archive speak to the categories, institutions, networks, and cultural forms that made their existence legible within the context of the Canadian nation-state. Thus, the primary focus of this book is not to reveal the cultural truths behind these processes of translation and engagement but, rather, to analyze these processes themselves as constituting the infrastructure that made cultural and linguistic diversity possible in Canadian media.

CHAPTER OUTLINE

While each of the chapters examines a particular medium – film, newspapers, radio, or television – the focus is on a specific affordance of media infrastructure rather than on a particular medium. For this reason, the reader is cautioned against assimilating the historical narratives presented here into mainstream histories of Canadian media. It is important to be attentive to the divergent periodization of dominant media forms in minority communities, which are indicative of the different configuration of media infrastructure being discussed. Failure to do this consigns third-language and minority media to what Dipesh Chakrabarty describes as the "waiting room of history," implying that members of linguistic and cultural minorities follow mainstream progress but are always one step behind. The approach taken here is intended to disrupt any simplistic linear and universal understanding of the history of media in Canada in order to bring to light the distinct technological, cultural, and economic contexts within which ethnocultural media in Canada evolved and to which they have contributed.

Chapter 1 documents the expansion of movie theatres catering to cultural and linguistic minorities. The decision to start with this discussion of theatres as common spaces is not based upon chronology but, rather, on an attempt to emphasize the collective social energies upon which any democratic multiculturalism must be built. While access to institutional power is an important goal for many involved in ethnocultural media in Canada, such gains cannot legitimately take place in isolation from the expansion of the symbolic and material capacities of individuals to come together. This chapter describes the opening up of film theatres to more diverse offerings and audiences that followed the decline of the film industry after the arrival of television in the 1950s and 1960s. Thanks to the radical restructuring of media in Canada, a number of new spaces for the distribution and sharing of culture became available in many Canadian cities.

Chapter 1 looks at these theatres from two perspectives. First, they are examined as places in which people could gather. Throughout their existence, these theatres became important places for members of minority communities, often marginalized within the mainstream public sphere, to encounter one another. Theatres were not only used to show films but also to host labour meetings, religious gatherings, live music, and charity events. However, of equal importance was their role as spaces within which different communities could encounter one another. Only a few theatres were dedicated to a single cultural or linguistic group, most often a number of different groups shared the use of one theatre. In the years that followed, alongside their social significance, the economic viability of these theatres also played an important role in structuring the multicultural media industry. Film distribution and exhibition, as much as print journalism, proved to be an important training ground for the media entrepreneurs who, over the following decades, transitioned to television.

Chapter 2 focuses on the relationship between the ethnic press and the Canadian state. The history of the multilingual press in Canada is one that dates back to the eighteenth century, but the chapter focuses on the period immediately following the Second World War. Throughout the nation's history, but particularly in the twentieth century, the government has viewed newspapers serving linguistic and cultural minorities with a mixture of suspicion and interest. In the years prior to the Second World War, the Canadian government had forced many ethnic papers to cease publication because of their perceived risk to national security. However, the period documented in this chapter differs from those earlier periods in that, rather than enforcing silence, the government and members of the press now worked together in an attempt to integrate minority cultures into Canadian society.

Chapter 2 documents the emergence of organizations through which the Canadian political and cultural establishment reached out to linguistic and cultural minorities through newspapers. This involved the creation of "ethnic press federations" in a number of Canadian provinces as well as a national group. The earliest of these groups was established in 1942 in Winnipeg, and its goal was to encourage ethnic newspapers to contribute to the war effort. However, this group did not disband at the end of the war. Indeed, a number of similar organizations took shape over the course of the 1950s with the Cold War and the communist threat as their primary focus. Over time, these groups engaged with the Canadian government in a number of ways, from publishing government-produced articles to providing lobbying efforts on the part of editors and publishers. Alongside the emergence of ethnic press federations across the country, there was also the creation of the Canadian Scene news agency, an organization founded and supported by members of the Imperial Order Daughters of the Empire that provided material for publication in dozens of languages. Finally, at the beginning of the 1960s, there was the arrival of advertising agencies that centralized and managed the sale of ad space in the vast majority of Canada's minority newspapers. Chapter 2 shows how, at the beginning of the 1950s, these organizations formed an industrial infrastructure that was shared by a number of newspapers published in non-official languages and how, by means of this infrastructure, the Canadian government was able to interact with minority media. While these events all took place prior to the adoption of official multiculturalism in 1971, it can be argued that these organizations laid the foundations for the kinds of relations between media and the state that would characterize multicultural policy in the 1970s and beyond.

Chapters 3 and 4 focus on the history of broadcasting serving linguistic and cultural minorities. Focusing on radio and television broadcasts between the late 1960s through to the early 1980s, these chapters explore how established media players in Canada as well as government agencies restructured policy frameworks and business models to accommodate third-language broadcasting. Chapter 3 looks at the evolution of third-language radio, tracing its history from its origins with independent radio producers in the 1950s through to the licensing of dedicated multicultural broadcasters such as Montreal's CFMB, Toronto's CHIN, and Vancouver's CJVB. It documents this history as the evolution of a broadcast format. This is in line with trends in the radio industry generally, which was being reorganized around the adoption of programming formats that entailed guidelines covering the kind of music programmed and the kind of commentary permitted from DJs. The motivations behind the formatting of the industry were primarily economic, the goal being to permit stations to more efficiently serve as a conduit for delivering particular audiences to advertisers. Chapter 3 argues that the emergence of cultural and linguistic diversity in Canadian radio is the history of a format as much as it is the history of individual broadcasters. This format is the fruit of a long series of debates about the purpose of multilingual and multicultural radio services, which outlined such features of the new broadcasters as the ratio of different languages spoken, the kind of music played, and the identity of the station in general.

Yet the formatting of programming for these stations was only part of the story. The context within which these developments in the radio industry at large took place was defined by a broader process of economic rationalization that included the introduction and standardization of audience metrics. Simply put, stations were standardized in ways that aligned with the new and increasingly formalized ways of measuring audiences. Multilingual radio, however, did not easily fit into this process, and chapter 3 also traces how radio served as the testing ground for establishing alternative ways of displaying the size of audiences. In ways that harken back to the kinds of community and sociality discussed in chapter 1, chapter 3 discusses how street fairs and picnics came to play an important role in showing prospective sponsors what wasn't immediately visible in the quarterly audience ratings reports. These alternative methods of engaging audiences were important in that they displayed audiences to advertisers, and they also spoke to the relationship between broadcasters and audiences – a relationship that resulted in what is perhaps the most distinctive characteristic of the multicultural broadcast format as it developed in Canada: the for-profit model of community broadcasting.

Chapter 4 focuses on third-language television, in the context of long history of televisual media practices in Canada. Having discussed some of these practices in previous chapters (e.g., chapter 1 discusses the use of theatres to show sporting events), in this chapter I argue that one of recurrent problems in the history of minority and third-language broadcasting is that of the relationship between scale and identity. While it is often argued that migrant and diasporic media are global by definition, I contend that the history of multicultural media in Canada is one that has consistently involved aligning cultural diversity with localism. From site-specific events like sports telecasts in the 1970s through to the licensing of the first multicultural television station – Toronto's CFMT – multicultural broadcasting was positioned in ways that saw it as operating at a smaller scale than what was allowed for in the nationalizing logics of English- and French-language broadcast policy. Even the establishment of national third-language services in 1984 – Telelatino (originally Latinovision) and Chinavision (later Fairchild Broadcasting) – was premised on the presumption that the techniques and aims of national cultural policy would take precedence over the necessarily global scale at which these broadcasters operated.

In chapter 4, I argue that cable television was the first, and probably last, medium in which the state and the organization of the medium would coincide to promote a multicultural agenda. The chapter concludes by exploring a series of debates, both in the media and between broadcasters and regulators, regarding the status of Canadian versus non-Canadian broadcasters. These debates were brought to public attention by the transition from analogue cable distribution of television to digital distribution, which allowed for the inclusion of a dramatically increased number of third-language offerings. These debates, taking place towards the end of the 1990s and into the early 2000s, raised questions about both the nationalist orientation of Canadian policy concerning media industries as well as long-standing concerns about the political loyalties of international broadcasters. The most well-known example of these discussions involved the licensing of the Canadian service for the Qatar-based Al-Jazeera, but a number of other services (such as Italy's RAI International) also featured in these discussions about the tensions between multiculturalism and the international political economy of media and culture.

The conclusion brings together some of the general themes of the book and also brings the discussion of media infrastructure and multiculturalism up to the present. I argue that proclamations and lamentations about the "death of multiculturalism" cannot be understood in isolation from the new forms of information distribution and access made possible by increasingly distributed forms of media production and individualized modes of access. In light of the preceding chapters, I argue that the modes of governance as well as the forms of popular media engagement that have informed both ideas about, and the practical implementation of, the media infrastructure of multiculturalism have come under stress with the new political and informational context in which we find ourselves. The new informational, spatial, and social logics of media require a reconsideration that, in the eyes of some critics, constitutes the death of multiculturalism. Here, however, I offer a less absolutist view, along with a number of suggestions about possible ways that the project of multiculturalism, understood in its broadest democratic and universally inclusive form, might be – and, indeed, must be – renewed for the contemporary moment.

It is my hope that this book will provide a brief and useful history of the multicultural media industry in Canada. Its brevity is the result of a desire to produce a book that is both informative and accessible to the broadest possible cross-section of readers. It is not intended to be a definitive statement on the depth or complexity of the history of media produced by cultural and linguistic minorities in Canada since the 1950s. Indeed, I hope that *Identity and Industry* will encourage those who played a role in making media as well as my fellow researchers to expand upon, clarify, and correct its claims.

My aspirations towards utility when writing this book may fall victim to the fraught process of translating insights gleaned in the archive into the field of practice and pragmatics. However, *Identity and Industry* is a response to the peculiar status that multiculturalism has achieved in Canadian political life, being both of central importance to a particular view of the nation and recognized as being insufficient for the realization of a more equitable and open society. My intention is to recover some of the important historical details concerning the development of minority media in Canada with an eye towards how this might help us better address the limits of contemporary media. Taking an approach that is selective rather than encyclopaedic, *Identity and Industry* does not aspire to provide a neutral document of events but, rather, focuses on those chapters in the history of minority media that speak to the limitations of Canada's multiculturalism as it actually exists while also drawing attention to the experiments and achievements of media producers that hold promise for the development of a more open and democratic society.

I

Space: Movie-Going in the Multicultural City

On Sunday, 7 April 1974, a few hundred people braved the cold and rain typical of early spring in Toronto to attend a screening at the Centre Theatre on Dundas Street West of *Argentinísima II*, a film featuring performances by folk musicians from Argentina.[1] The Centre was one of many independent theatres located in cities and small towns across the country that struggled to fill seats when the introduction of television and the growth of the suburbs caused ticket sales to nosedive. The screening took place thanks to the efforts of a film promoter named David Tenuto who, beginning around 1972, leased the theatre from Leonard Fromm, who, along with his wife Miki, had been co-owner of the Centre since the 1950s.[2] Tenuto followed a "mixed bag" programming policy, attempting to sell tickets to the different immigrant communities that called the surrounding neighbourhoods home. Alongside films in Italian, *Argentinísima II* was programmed in recognition of the growing Spanish-speaking community that had settled around the nearby intersection of College and Bathurst Streets. Tenuto's multilingual policy was not a complete departure from previous years at the Centre. The theatre, originally known as the Duchess when it first opened in the 1920s, had long programmed films with an eye to attracting recent immigrants from nearby neighbourhoods such as Kensington Market and College Street's Little Italy.[3] However, the films shown at the Centre prior to Tenuto's tenure were usually Hollywood blockbusters that were long on action and spectacle, making fluency in English unnecessary for following the plot.[4]

The turn to films in other languages was a short-lived experiment at the Centre. In 1975, the theatre returned to art house eclecticism, targeting students from nearby University of Toronto with ninety-nine-cent tickets. "The Centre for film buffs" was the theatre's pitch in its final years.[5] Yet an article published in *El Popular* – Toronto's only Spanish-language newspaper at the time – two days after the screening of *Argentinísima II* claimed that more than a thousand spectators had crowded into the theatre that night.[6] The exaggerated estimate of the size of the audience – according to its licence, the Centre had fewer than 450 seats – is perhaps best taken as an indication of the enthusiasm such events could generate.[7] Further emphasizing the importance of audience excitement, the article was accompanied by a photograph showing the theatre filled to capacity.

The article in *El Popular* praised the evening as the beginning of a new era for Latin American culture in the city. This, however, is a more complex declaration than it might initially seem. In terms of "Latin American" culture, the screening of *Argentinísima II* at the Centre was not without precedent. Throughout the mid-1970s, every month one could find one or two Spanish-language titles among the twenty or so non-English-language films to be found in Toronto theatres, with some of these coming from Central America and South America. The Centre and another nearby theatre – the Kensington on College Street – had scheduled Spanish-language nights since at least 1973.[8] The Pylon, also on College Street and operating under the name Cinema Colon, would later join the Kensington after the Centre switched back to primarily English-language films and before the team who ran the Colon moved to Montreal.[9] However, *Argentinísima II* was the first Argentinian film to be shown in Toronto. The excitement this film generated highlights the complex intersection between culture, language, and nationality that was unfolding in Canadian theatres at the time.

Speaking to this complexity, the Spanish-language films shown in Canada during the 1970s were a mix of dubbed versions of Hollywood hits, children's cartoons, productions from Spain, and others from across Latin America.[10] The variety of films imported into Canada reflects both the global hegemony of Hollywood and the make-up of the Spanish-speaking community in Toronto at the time, which was comprised mostly of Spanish immigrants who had been arriving since the 1950s and a more recent wave of immigrants from Central and South America beginning in the 1970s.[11] In the 1970s, the Mexican-produced comedies of Cantinflas (best known to English-language audiences for his performance as Passepartout

Figure 1.1 Advertisement for Spanish-language screening of *The Godfather* with Portuguese subtitles, at the Kensington Theatre, published in the Spanish-language newspaper *El Popular*, 4 April 1973.

in *Around the World in 80 Days* [1956]) were shown regularly. The decision to program *Argentinísima II* was a timely departure from the usual Spanish-language films shown at the Centre, and it appealed to Argentinian immigrants who had recently settled in the city after fleeing their home country's economic and political instability.[12]

It is not possible to determine with any degree of accuracy who attended these films. An advertisement for a Spanish-language screening of *The Godfather* (1972) with Portuguese subtitles suggests that theatre owners hoped that there would be some cross-language attendance. Yet Wayne Fromm, son of the theatre's owners and general manager of the theatre for two years before it closed in 1977, recalls that Tenuto's programming strategy was not entirely successful because audiences had trouble figuring out which language would be featured on any given night.[13] However, the "mixed bag" programming policy pursued at the Centre during these years does bring to light the constantly changing context within which film screenings in languages other than English or French took place across Canada between the 1950s and 1980s. Even though most theatres were not like the Centre, where the language on screen changed depending on the day of the week, there was little stability in the emergent circuit of theatres showing "foreign" films.[14]

This chapter is not primarily a history of the films that were shown or even the communities that gathered to view them, although it touches on both of these topics. Rather, in keeping with the ideas about media infrastructure laid out in the introduction, it focuses on the spaces where "foreign" or "ethnic" films were shown – mostly, but not always, theatres – in order to draw attention to their role in providing places where communities could gather. It explores the history of these venues as an entry point for thinking about the role media infrastructure plays in supporting the development of a cultural milieu.

By emphasizing the overlapping cultural, spatial, and economic circuits within which the internationalization of Canadian cinemas took place following the Second World War, this chapter documents the complex relations between sites of media distribution and space, which is sometimes overlooked in the analysis of identity, economy, and community. Take, for example, the literature on ethnic economies.[15] As a conceptual framework bringing together economics, geography, and sociology, it offers a way of understanding the role that cultural identity plays in shaping economic activities within minority communities. It proposes using the language or cultural identity shared among business owners, employees, and customers as a way of analyzing how communities organize themselves within industrial, mostly urban, social contexts. "An *ethnic economy*," write Light and Gold, "consists of co-ethnic self-employed and employers and their co-ethnic employees."[16] Theatres, like other "ethnic" businesses, might be assumed to fit within this definition of ethnic economy. However, the complexities of ownership and patronage discussed in this chapter highlight the limitations of using such a rigid definition of identity to map the borders of the social, cultural, and economic circuits that made up film distribution and exhibition in languages other the English or French in the second half of the twentieth century.

With regard to ownership, theatres were sometimes owned and operated by community members. In many other cases, though, the situation was more complicated. Owners, managers, and programmers might see themselves as members of different ethnic groups. Audiences might be linguistically and culturally diverse as well. Theatres like the Centre do not fit easily into such systems of categorization. However, it would be difficult to argue that the Centre was less important as a venue for Spanish-language cinema, or Latin American culture in Canada generally, because it was owned by the Fromm family or programmed by David Tenuto, neither of whom identified with many of the cultural and/or linguistics communities to which they catered. The complex relationship between the identities of audiences and theatre operators makes it clear that a much more flexible understanding of the relationship between community and identity is required in order to understand the variable rhythms of individual movement and the associated performances of collective belonging that took place in movie theatres.

Calling for a more flexible and open understanding of the relationship between identity, community, and space is not to suggest that these theatres should be seen as spaces hosting only random and fleeting encounters. Their physically stable nature as buildings of bricks and mortar, their relationship to a number of different legal and economic regimes regulating both the buildings and the activities they hosted, contrasts with the ephemeral experiences of audience members who passed nightly through their doors. Bridging the divide that separates the different registers at which media contribute to the formation and maintenance of community is an important reminder of the relevance of the concept of infrastructure. Emphasizing affordances over events, infrastructure balances the different rhythms that characterize the cultural and economic aspects of urban life in a way that is equally attentive to both the slower rate of change in the built environment and the brevity of gatherings that last only a few hours on a single evening.

The first part of this chapter documents the increase in the distribution and exhibition of films in languages other than English or French in Canada following the Second World War. It situates these changes in relation to the fundamental restructuring of the entertainment economy that took place during the 1950s.[17] The increased number of theatres in Canadian cities showing films in minority languages was made possible due to a variety of factors that undermined movie-going as a common practice for most Canadians. The fundamental shift in the geographic distribution of the Canadian population as the suburbs expanded thanks to the widespread adoption of cars complemented the introduction of television to encourage individuals to stay home rather than to venture out in search of an evening's entertainment. The smaller, "sub-run" venues that were unable to attract mainstream audiences in the postwar cultural landscape turned to new kinds of films hoping to attract new kinds of audiences.

The second part of this chapter explores how these theatres were situated within the social life of those who frequented them. Describing them as quasi-public spaces, theatres sit alongside churches, community halls, and restaurants: all of these are venues that allowed people to be together in ways that were defined by a shared identity and varying degrees of anonymity. The conclusion explores the demise of theatres with the coming of home video, addressing both the economic and social changes resulting from the further domestication of media consumption as well as the continuities with film exhibition. While the cultural significance of the theatre diminished, the professional expertise developed by film distributors continued to play an important role in the development of ethnocultural media in Canada as individuals adapted to the growth of multilingual television programs and home video rental.

In recounting the history of these venues, it must be remembered that, at the time, relatively little attention was paid to the significance of these spaces. This is certainly an example of infrastructural concealment in action. Their subsequent disappearance from the urban landscape following successive waves of theatre closures has further dimmed contemporary awareness of their importance as the buildings that once held them have been converted to gyms, churches, or condominiums (if not demolished entirely). If this chapter is tinged with nostalgia, it is because I recognize that the radical spatial and socio-economic changes that have taken place in Canadian cities during recent decades have depleted both the physical and psychic resources that support conviviality.

Yet, in looking back on what has since been lost, I take care not to suggest that the past offers some pure, uncorrupted form of community and connection. While these theatres offered infrastructural support for what could be described as multiculturalism "from below," this remained a project that was defined as much by its possibilities as by the obstacles that it encountered. I do not provide an account of the Edenic moment during which true community was achieved only to be later corrupted through its encounter with government, capital, or subsequent media technologies; rather, I describe a series of spaces and institutions in which the possibility of communal media consumption intersected with cultural and legal contexts that afforded – most often thanks to indifference on the part of government officials – the potential for community.

THE TELEVISION AGE?

The history of the exhibition of international films from countries other than the United States has not received a great deal of attention from historians of Canadian film and culture.[18] Most of the research that examines the development of "ethnic theatres" focuses on the United States and is defined by that country's history of immigration.[19] In the US context, the emphasis has been on the development of these theatres prior to the Second World War and their subsequent decline in the postwar period. Douglas Gomery's widely cited research on the subject is representative in this regard. Gomery documents the emergence and decline of ethnic theatres in conjunction with the rise of Art House theatres, with the Second World War as the turning point marking the decline of the former and the rise of the latter.[20] The exodus of European immigrants and their children from the urban ethnic enclaves of the prewar period into the suburbs precedes the shift in programming of some small and mid-size theatres, which had previously catered to cultural and linguistic minorities, towards the cosmopolitan interests of theatregoers who saw cinema as an art form.[21] With regard to the years following the Second World War, there are a number of excellent studies of the "art house" movement and the "foreign film renaissance in the United States." However, these works often relegate "ethnic theatres" to the margins of the story.[22]

Given the prominence of research concentrating on the United States, it is not surprising that there is an emphasis on the importance of cinema as an urban amusement among immigrants during the early twentieth century.[23] There is evidence of similar activities in Canadian cities before the Second World War, particularly in relation to the production and screening of Ukrainian films in Winnipeg, occasional screenings of Chinese films in Vancouver, and the exhibition of Yiddish films in Winnipeg, Toronto, and Montreal during the 1930s.[24] However, there is a more significant expansion of alternative theatres in Canada that begins in the 1950s, including many that showed films in languages other than English or French in the hope of attracting an audience from among recent arrivals.

It is this fundamental difference in the technological and cultural context that distinguishes the expansion of cultural and linguistic diversity in Canadian movie theatres from similar trends in its neighbour to the south. This is simply to point out the obvious, but unavoidable, fact that the west end of Toronto in 1960 or the north end of Montreal in 1970 – both areas that were home to multiple theatres that programmed films primarily for communities in which languages other than English or French were spoken – cannot be equated with New York's Lower East Side in the 1920s without significantly distorting the social and technological contexts of both.

Recognizing the significant differences between the two national contexts requires a detailed account of the Canadian context. The pages of the annual *Yearbook of the Canadian Motion Picture Industry*, published by the industry magazine *Canadian Film Weekly*, provides short but detailed accounts of the far-reaching transformations in the Canadian film industry during these years.[25] While most of the yearbooks' pages are taken up with a directory of producers, distributors, and exhibitors from across the country, their short summaries – usually written by the magazine's publisher, Nathan A. Taylor, a theatre owner himself – document the events of the previous year in the industry. The annual resumés of "Our Business" discuss the prospects, both good and bad, facing the film business in Canada. By the end of the 1950s, the news was mostly bad. A number of new forms of entertainment threatened the film industry's place as the dominant form of mass entertainment; in his resumés, Taylor gave special mention to both television and bingo.[26]

Frequently, these reports attempt to put a positive spin on an industry in crisis. In the 1958–59 edition of "Our Business," Taylor writes: "Theatres continue to close and very few new ones are being built ... The period of change and metamorphosis continues. The principal victims of the new era have been the sub-run theatres in large centres and those in very small towns."[27] The following year, in recognition of the changing times, the series was renamed *Yearbook of the Canadian Motion Picture Industry with Television Section*. That year, with a hint of optimism, Taylor notes in his comments in "Our Business" that, "while one cannot conclude that theatres will stop closing[,] the rate has slowed down and again it is the antiquated and obsolete which are being shuttered."[28]

The ups and downs of the industry that Taylor documents in the 1950s is a reminder that the challenges faced by the film business did not result in the immediate closure of theatres across the country. Rather, the 1950s and early 1960s witnessed a number of attempts to fill seats even as box office revenues declined and theatres closed. Among the more spectacular experiments tried by theatre owners were new projection technologies such as Cinerama (introduced in 1963) and outrageous theatre gimmicks like "smell-o-vision" pioneered by B-movie impresario William Castle.[29] Recognizing that the threat posed by television would not be overcome by improving the cinematic experience alone, theatre owners across Canada also lobbied local authorities for permission to operate on Sundays or to allow children to attend screenings in jurisdictions where such activities were banned.[30] Some theatres turned to burlesque and other erotic offerings looking to entice a reliable, if potentially rowdier, audience through their doors as families stayed home.[31] Others venues started to program a selection of American and European films defined by aesthetic sophistication and narrative complexity with the aim of attracting people bored by what they perceived as the low-brow distractions found on television.[32]

Less frequently mentioned in accounts of the period, and completely overlooked by Taylor in his annual reports, is the increase in the number of theatres programming films from around the world and, occasionally, Hollywood films dubbed into languages other than English or French. These theatres saw the rapidly growing communities of new immigrants settling in Canadian cities as their primary audience.[33] This is a surprising oversight as Taylor's publishing partner at *Canadian Film Weekly*, Hye Bossin, had grown up among the Yiddish vaudeville and movie theatres along Toronto's Spadina Avenue in the 1930s; Bossin was also the author of *Stars of David*, a history of Jewish contributions to the Canadian film industry.[34] The decision to exclude these theatres from the annual overviews is perhaps a reflection of the view that the internationalization of Canadian screens was a local, rather than a national, phenomenon only taking place in major cities. Nonetheless, their emergence fits within the broader changes in the industry that Taylor documented as many of these "new" theatres took over venues that had previously operated as the "antiquated and obsolete" second-run movie houses he described as having fallen on hard times. With few exceptions, these new "Foreign language" theatres were mostly the small- and middle-sized urban venues with between three hundred and five hundred seats collectively known as "the nabes," shorthand for the neighbourhood theatres that had come into existence during the years when film dominated popular entertainment.[35] A survey of the records documenting the interactions between provincial safety inspectors and theatre owners in Ontario testify to the poor state that these venues were in by the time they started to program films in language other than English.[36] The inspectors regularly made note of broken boilers, poorly lit exits and concession counters, as well as issues with broken or dirty washrooms.[37]

Geographically, the venues that converted to foreign language houses were located in the midst of other businesses providing goods and services tailored to the needs of newly immigrated communities. Their location situated them both spatially and socially within networks that distributed both local and international information in non-official languages, a network that included bookstores, newsstands, live musical venues, and, later on, radio and television broadcasters. It is, however, necessary to recognize the complex cultural geography that characterized life in Canada's largest cities, particularly those areas that served as the "arrival cities" where most recent immigrants settled.[38] In recognition of the linguistic and cultural diversity of neighbourhoods, businesses that distributed information and entertainment media frequently served a number of different communities. This is apparent in both the image of a

Figure 1.2 Newsstand on Toronto's College Street with publications in German, Polish, Italian, and English on display, ca. 1955.

bulletin board discussed in the introduction (see figure I.1) and a photo (taken at the same time) of a newsstand showing publications in multiple languages, both local and foreign (figure 1.2).

Similarly, many of these venues did not operate as fixed entities "belonging" permanently to a single group defined by a shared culture or language; rather, there existed a spectrum of relationships between venues, programming, and audiences. At one end, there were a small number of venues that programmed films from a single country or in a single language over an extended period of time, and, at the other end, there were thousands of occasional screenings at which a film would be shown for a single night only, sometimes as part of regular or semi-regular events in the same language that would occur throughout the year. The pattern and frequency of film screenings was determined by the size of the local audience and the supply of films available. Only those parts of the world that had large film industries and that were also able to draw upon large local audiences were able to survive. In Toronto, this included Italian films beginning in the 1950s, Chinese and Indian films from the late 1960s onward, and Greek films from the mid-1960s to the mid-1970s. In Vancouver it included Indian and Chinese films beginning in the 1960s. In Montreal it included Italian films from the 1950s, Spanish-language films in 1970s, and Chinese films beginning in the early 1980s.[39]

In terms of stable venues, the Cinema Riviera in Montreal, which converted to showing Italian-language films in the late 1950s, was one of the few venues in the country that was able to stay in operation for a lengthy period of time without significant changes in its programming. Built in 1955, the theatre operated under the management of Palmina Puliafito, whose image featured prominently above the weekly advertisements she ran in the local Italian papers. Puliafito started out promoting Italian-language live theatre in Montreal and moved into film once she took over the Riviera. The theatre remained in operation until the early 1980s, when it transitioned to screening adult films.[40] In Toronto, the St Clair Theatre – which started showing Italian films in the early 1960s – served the local Italian community until the 1980s, when competition from home video put it out of business.[41] The Naaz Theatre on Gerard Street in Toronto and the York Theatre (later known as the Raja) on Commercial Drive in Vancouver both screened Bollywood films beginning in the 1970s and continued operation into the 1980s.[42] A few other venues found a path to sustainability by bringing together films from a broader geographic or linguistic region. Such was the case with the Brighton Theatre on Roncesvalles Avenue in Toronto, where films from across Eastern Europe were shown.

However, the majority of theatres were economically precarious and survived only as long as they were responsive to the cultural and demographic shifts resulting from the flows of people in and out of the surrounding area.[43] Rather than fixed points in the cultural infrastructure of a community, these theatres are more accurately viewed in relation to the ongoing cultural recoding of space within Canadian cities. Theatres changed their programming and were given new names as owners and managers left or went bankrupt. Thus, in thinking about the temporalities of cultural hybridization, it is perhaps helpful to see many of these venues as functioning more like newsstands selling a range of publications in many different languages – some local, others from around the world – than as newspapers that operated in a single language and perhaps included some English or French. The persistence of the buildings gave the appearance of stability despite the economic turbulence that forced owners or managers quit or move on.

Given the difficult economic circumstances of the movie business during these years, this rate of turnover does not seem out of the ordinary as it reflects the broader dynamics in the industry. Indeed, it is important to note that the venues that programmed for migrant and diasporic communities were not isolated from trends in the industry at large. By the 1970s, a venue that made its business programming films for recent immigrants might just as quickly turn to showing counter-cultural or pornographic films as move on to showing films in another minority language. In some cases, the emergence of the circuit for international films overlapped with the circuit for art house theatres. Such was the case, for example, with Winnipeg's Cinema 3 (previously known as Mac's Theatre), whose audience was described in a satirical 1979 profile as "granola," yet which often programmed more popular films that were leased from the film distributors in Toronto after their run at the theatres in that city's Little Italy.[44]

Finally, there were a number of film exhibition practices that pushed the volatility of the theatrical market to its extreme. Some theatres adopted a flexible programming policy with the aim of selling as many tickets as possible through the week. I began this chapter with the example of the Centre Theatre in Toronto, but it was not unique in offering a "mixed bag" approach to scheduling. In the same week that *El Popular* published its article about the screening of *Argentinísima II* at the Centre, the paper also ran an advertisement for a double-bill featuring Russ Meyer's *Vixen* and *Faster Pussycat Kill! Kill!* in English at the Cine Kensington, a nearby theatre that, only a few weeks before, had advertised an evening of Spanish melodramas.[45] The Olympia Theatre at the corner of Hastings and Nanaimo in Vancouver pursued a similarly varied approach to programming. That theatre – demolished to make way for a bank in 1985 – was located in an area that was initially the centre of the city's Italian community but that subsequently welcomed Chinese immigrants.[46] Managed by the Martinellis, who lived in the apartment above the theatre, the venue also programmed a mix of underground films (which were advertised to students at the University of British Columbia on the pages of the *Ubyssey*), Italian films, and, beginning in the late 1960s, semi-regular screenings of films from India and Hong Kong.[47]

An important complement to the adoption of variable programming strategies on the part of theatre managers and owners were screenings arranged by community organizations. In Vancouver, there emerged a number of groups that leased theatres for Chinese-language screenings in the 1960s prior to the opening of dedicated Chinese-language venues in the following decade. The first of these groups was the Cultural Film Association, later joined by the Chinese Art and Film Society under the leadership of Quon H. Wong, who held screenings at the Lux, Majestic, and Avon Theatres through the 1950s and 1960s. Both of these organizations had connections with community performing arts groups that sponsored Vancouver dates for Chinese opera companies that toured North America. Similarly, Indian films were shown on an occasional basis in both leased theatres and non-theatrical venues. A key figure in introducing Indian film to Vancouver was Janki Shori. As Shori's daughter recalls: "She was the first person and only woman to bring movies from India to entertain the East Indian society in the Lower Mainland ... She showed [them] in the old theatre in Vancouver at the Kingcrest Theatre, at the York Theatre, the Rio and at the Lux."[48] She was later joined in promoting films by Avtar Bains and Arjan Dhaliwal who rented out the Olympia and, later on, the Queen Elizabeth Playhouse.[49]

IMPORTING FILM INTO CANADA

Using the records of films licensed in Ontario and British Columbia, it is possible to gain a more systematic perspective on the volume and range of films that were available in two of the country's largest and most diverse provinces.[50] Records show that there is a steady increase in the number of international films that were licensed in Canadian cities through the 1960s and 1970s before the sharp decrease in the 1980s following the arrival of home video.[51] Aggregate data, however, only give a very general sense of the growth and decline of different kinds of international films in Canada in relation to demographic changes, geopolitical and economic factors, and/or the introduction of new technologies. A more detailed analysis of film licensing data reveals that there is a great deal of variation in the distribution in countries from which films were imported and that each follows a slightly different cycle of growth and reduction. Similar to claims that Canada is the "most" multicultural country in the world, the records suggest that the diversity of films – with titles identified as coming from more than ninety countries/regions between 1947 and 2000 – obscures the fact that only a handful of communities had regular access to film.[52] Chinese, Italian, and Indian films constitute a little more than half of the non-Hollywood films licensed for distribution in Ontario between 1950 and 2000. During these years, smaller but still significant numbers of films arrived from Greece (enough to support two Greek-language theatres in the east end of Toronto during the 1970s), the Soviet Union and Eastern Europe (typically shown at the Brighton in Toronto), as well as Latin America. Chinese-language films – identified as originating in China, Hong Kong, or Taiwan – are by far the most numerous, constituting two to three times as many more films than were imported from any other country throughout the 1970s.

Recognizing the dangers of over-estimating the significance of these data, there are still a handful of claims that can be made based on what it shows. Most important, these data provide insight into the rhythms of exhibition for international cinema in Canada. They show that the uneven distribution of films imported from different parts of the world during the 1960s and 1970s produced two very different kinds of ephemerality. For the three most frequent countries of origin for film (India, "China," and Italy), the velocity with which films passed through theatres was shaped by the limited number of screens available at any given time. The multi-tiered structure of the mainstream film market meant that there was considerable variation in the duration of the theatrical runs for films released in English or French. The most popular films would survive in theatres for months, while in some cities less popular films would play for as little as a few days if at all. Given the limited number of screens showing films in the three most popular minority languages (usually one or two screens and never more than seven in any city at any given time), the duration of theatrical runs for many international films was greatly reduced. Most films were shown for a week and in many cases for only a single weekend.[53]

Combining licensing information with newspaper advertisements, it can be concluded that the majority of the other screenings are best described as occasional, which refers to both the duration of the run and to the relationship between venues and presumed audiences. The development of these screenings differs between Ontario and British Columbia and is indicative of the differences in the history of immigration in these two provinces. In Ontario, these intermittent films make up a minority of films – a little less than 40 percent of the total number of non-pornographic international films licensed for exhibition in Ontario between 1950 and 2000 – but they cover a much wider variety of countries than are represented by permanent venues. For this reason, their significance should not be underestimated as they constituted one of the only ways for many recent arrivals to gain access to entertainment from back home. In British Columbia, where the establishment of permanent venues did not occur until the 1970s, there is a longer period in which there are only occasional screenings.

However, this should not be taken as suggesting that there is a common lifecycle for such screenings across languages, cultures, and locations. Montreal, where a variety of factors stemming from the city's unique bilingual media infrastructure limited the number of theatres that transitioned to multilingual films, follows a different trajectory with regard to the arrival and growth of multilingual film than do Toronto or Vancouver. Dozens of film screenings were held for films from India, although a dedicated theatre was never established likely due to the comparatively small size of the city's South Asian community. Many of the Indian films shown in Montreal during the late 1960s and early 1970s were organized and hosted by the South Asian Student Association of McGill University and, later, by the efforts of local entrepreneur C.B Singh.[54] Some of the screenings were held at the university's student centre even though the audience for these films certainly extended beyond students. The case of Portuguese film in Montreal is similarly instructive as it shows how a limited supply of films can shape exhibition practices. The very few Portuguese films imported to Canada, reflecting the smaller scale of Lusophone cinema, were screened at the school auditorium at the École Jeanne-Mance on Rue Rachel and the Arena Paul-Sauvé on Avenue Beaubien. These films were often combined with live musical and theatrical performances or personal appearances by celebrities visiting from Portugal. Their location was likely chosen due to their proximity to the centre of commerce for the city's Portuguese community, which settled along St Laurent Boulevard.

Supporting these screenings was a unique distribution and exhibition network that, while divided among the three or four largest minority language groups in the country, functioned more or less autonomously from the mainstream film industry, which was dominated by major US film studios. A common feature across all of these screenings was the close relationship between distribution and exhibition, with many theatres themselves submitting films for licensing to the provincial bodies tasked with rating and censorship. A survey of government licences for "film exchanges" in Ontario – the province with the largest number of theatres in operation throughout the second half of the twentieth century – shows that there were about a dozen such distributors operating in the 1950s and that this number would increase significantly over the course of the following decades as the number of theatres programming international films increased. Records show that Cine Europa, Films of Italy, Italian Film Importers, Radio City Film Exchange, and Roma Film were all licensed to distribute Italian films in Ontario during the 1950s. The paperwork for Cine Europe Films, based in Montreal, and Radio City Film Exchange show that they were owned by theatre owners A. Angelozzi and V. Simone, respectively. The All Nations Film and Book Service, distributing films in German and, later, German and Hungarian, occupied the same address as the All Nations Book Store on College Street in Toronto's west end, with most of these films being show at the Melody Theatre next door. Also in Toronto, the Brighton Theatre licensed films in Russian and Polish; the China Theatre and the Pagoda Theatre licensed large numbers of films from China and Hong Kong through the 1970s and 1980s; and the Naaz Theatre licensed hundreds of Bollywood films.

SAME ADDRESS, MANY NAMES

These high-level descriptions of the film industry provide only a very partial view of the cultural and spatial networks within which these theatres were situated. The King/Kino/Studio Theatre on College

Street in Toronto is a good example of the ongoing changes in the cultural geography of the city as it was being reorganized in tandem with the new media landscape that was emerging at the time. Having opened in the 1910s, the theatre was owned by the Lester family. Robert Lester, whose parents owned the theatre and who later became an important executive with Famous Players Theatres, described the audiences at the King during the 1920s and 1930s as Jewish, with "particular tastes which included musicals and the films of Al Jolson, but a dislike for Westerns and the comedies of Hope and Crosby."[55] In September 1946, the theatre was renamed the Kino Theatre (a rather cost-effective rebranding that required changing only a single letter on the marquee), and its operation was taken over by Leo Clavir. Clavir was the Canadian representative of the Soviet film distribution company Artkino, and his arrival coincided with the venue's turn to films from the Soviet Union and other socialist countries in Eastern Europe.[56]

The decline of the Soviet film industry in the late 1940s (following Stalin's rise to power and the dawn of the Cold War) saw the return of the Lester family, who changed direction once more. Renamed the Studio Theatre, beginning in 1951, the venue programmed Italian-language films in response to the demographic shifts taking place in the neighbourhood, which involved both the growth of the Italian community along College Street and the shrinking of the Jewish community centred in Kensington Market as it moved northward along Bathurst Street.[57] During the 1950s, the theatre also provided other services, such as receiving mail for labourers who were frequently moving between jobs in the region. An item from 1954 notes that the theatre, "which is in the centre of Toronto's cosmopolitan section, has become a little cultural centre and a favorite haunt of new Canadians since the films are in the native language with subtitles."[58] Years later, Robert Lester described the theatre as being a "community centre" not just a place to watch movies.[59] The theatre would go through a number of other incarnations before its closure, and eventual demolition, in the 1980s. During these later years, it continued to be known as the Studio before being renamed the Kensington – which frequently screened films in Spanish – and finally the Liberty.[60] In its final incarnation, it was known as the Shock Theatre, one of the city's first punk venues, which was managed by Bill "The Count" Cork (an important promoter in Toronto's underground scene who claimed to sleep in a crypt at Mount Pleasant Cemetery).[61]

Figure 1.3 The Studio Theatre Marquee, ca. 1955. The year before it had been described as "a little cultural centre and a favorite haunt of new Canadians" in Toronto's "cosmopolitan section."

A similar set of transformations to those that took place at the King/Studio Theatre can be mapped in the east end of Toronto, where the theatre originally known as the La Plaza, which opened as a cinema and vaudeville theatre in the 1930s, went through a number of changes in programming and name between the 1960s and the 1980s.[62] Speaking to its location at the border of areas with significant communities of both Greek and Chinese immigrants, it showed Greek-language and then Chinese-language films before opening as a live music venue. During this period, it was known by a number of different names, including the Acropolis, the Dundas, the Cinema Ellas, and the China Cinema before opening as the Opera House.[63] Further north, an article about the commercial centre of Toronto's Indian community along Gerard notes that "the Naaz" (named after its owner, Gian Naaz) had at various times in its history shown films in English, Greek, and Italian – known as the Eastwood Theatre at

Figure 1.4 Marquee of Naaz Theatre on Gerrard Street in Toronto, ca. 1980.

the time – before converting to a grocery store after the arrival of home video drastically reduced ticket sales.[64]

The space at 5380 St Laurent Avenue in Montreal also traverses the complex history of the city's changing inhabitants. It opened in 1956 as the Cinema Verdi, an Italian-language house, before being briefly renamed the Pagoda (which showed Chinese films) in the early 1970s. Subsequently, it hosted the Cinema Colon, which showed Spanish-language films for a brief period of time in 1979–80, having recently migrated to Montreal from Toronto.[65] It would later become an art theatre and performance space known as the New Yorker and Milieu before becoming a Spanish-language Pentecostal church in the 2000s. Sometime around 2014 it was demolished to make room for the New Yorker lofts, taking the name of one of the site's earlier incarnations. In western Canada, the transformation of venues did not follow precisely the same timeline because of the lower levels of immigration to the region in the 1950s. However, similar trends took place beginning in the 1960s. Vancouver's Majestic Theatre, having started life as part of the Pantages Theatre chain, started to show Chinese-language films regularly starting around 1960, following an unsuccessful attempt by the theatre's owners to revive vaudeville performances in 1958.[66] The Chinese films were successful enough to continue for many years, ending only when the theatre owners sold the venue in 1967 to make room for a parking lot.[67]

In tracing the cultural and linguistic transformations over the life of these theatres, it is important not to lose sight of the impact of broader transformations that affected film exhibition during these years. As the industry suffered with the rise of television, the new medium did not have the same effects on theatres showing international films. Indeed, the largest growth in foreign-language theatres took place during the years of television's ascendency. This was in part because restrictions on third-language television programming meant that the new medium was not significant competition, providing no more than a few hours of such programming at most for even the largest communities. Furthermore, these television programs tended to focus primarily on community events and news. Thus, the theatres programming international films catering to migrant and diasporic communities had become an established part of film exhibition in Montreal, Toronto, and Vancouver by the 1970s. It was not until the 1980s and the arrival of home video that the theatres encountered a period of significant difficulty, which led to the closure of many.

THE CURIOUS WORLD OF REAL FOREIGN FILMS

While the social aspects of film-going are often seen as secondary to the action on screen, the importance of the theatre as a site that made particular forms of sociality possible cannot be overlooked, and it comes to the forefront in accounts documenting the other uses to which these theatres were put. It is for this reason that the significance of these theatres to the transformation of Canadian cities resulting from the activities of new Canadians between the 1950s and 1980s cannot be reduced to movie-going. Such a claim would divorce the economy of international film in Canada from its broader cultural significance, which requires an analysis of the space occupied by the theatres themselves. Theatres were not simply conduits providing access to films from other parts of the world; rather, they also provided a place in which members of a community were able to interact with one another.

Period accounts published in mainstream newspapers often exoticized the communal aspect of movie-going while drawing on a host of ethnic stereotypes. In one such article in the *Toronto Star*, the reporter describes going to the St Clair Theatre as follows: "To enter an Italian audience is to enter an entirely different world – the world of marvelous, maddening Mediterranean volatility. On Sundays, family day, whole clans, from squawking babies to gentle grandmothers, troop in *en masse*. They don't seem to care *what* is playing. But for pure volubility, nothing can touch the Friday and Saturday night audiences – they're comprised of men: men of all sizes, shapes and ages ... And the boys don't just *watch* the movies. If they don't like what's happening on screen, they talk back to it. If they do like what's happening, they talk and *chuckle* over it among themselves."[68] Echoing the same fascination with the activities of audiences, a 1976 article from the *Toronto Star*, this one on Chinese films, notes, with a similar mixture of enthusiasm and confusion, that "Chinese movie-going is ... well ... different, to say the least ... Young mothers walked up and down the aisles soothing their babies to sleep and sighing over a romance called *He Loved One Too Many*. In a corner, several old men chatted. Children nudged each other and giggled over the love scenes."[69] Both of these articles compare an idealized vision of the audience as silent and attentive with the audiences they encountered during their visits to what one article described as "the curious world of *real* foreign films."[70] Such tensions were not limited to newspaper accounts as, in an interview, Wayne Fromm recalled the frictions between audience members at the Centre Theatre in Toronto, where the mostly silent viewing practices of students conflicted with the more engaged and interactive viewing habits of other audience members.[71]

Another significant example of the theatres supporting spaces in which communities could gather is the hosting of closed-circuit telecasts, usually of sporting events, beginning in the early 1970s.[72] The technical infrastructure for these events had been developed over the course of the 1950s and 1960s as what came to be known as "theatre television."[73] In Canada, the most popular use of this technology was the broadcasting of hockey games and boxing matches. The market for theatre television faded for most sports as television sets became a common fixture in many homes. However, boxing was a prominent exception, with championship fights being shown throughout the 1960s. Given the importance of such screenings for professional boxing and hockey, it is not surprising that the theatre television industry in Canada was dominated by All Canada Sports Promotions, which was co-owned by Irving Ungerman, who was also the manager of Canadian heavyweight champion George Chuvalo, and by Bobby Orr Entertainment, which was directed by Alan Eagleson.[74] Emilio Mascia, the owner of the Italian-language Playhouse Theatre in Hamilton and host of the weekly television show *Italian Journal*, partnered with Ungerman when he purchased the Canadian broadcast rights to the 1972 World Cup in order to make them available through CCTV in theatres and arenas across Ontario and Quebec.[75]

Unlike films, which often attracted audiences defined by language, sporting events brought a number of different nationalities together under one roof. The size of the events, growing to fill venues such as Toronto's Maple Leaf Gardens, attracted the attention of mainstream media, which discussed this phenomenon with surprise, given the low level of interest in soccer in mainstream Canadian culture. An article in the *Globe and Mail* noted the high level of engagement among audience members and condescendingly praised the well-behaved crowd (figure 1.5).[76] Accounts of these telecasts emphasize the communal and participatory aspects of events in theatres, drawing attention to the interaction between audiences through and around media rather than exclusively to the transmission of meaning and information.[77]

Figure 1.5 "Spectators were well behaved," notes an article describing closed-circuit broadcasts of World Cup games in Toronto for matches screened at the Coliseum and the Gardens. *Globe and Mail*, 12 June 1978.

More than just places of leisure, the theatres also provided labour organizations and workers groups with spaces in which to recruit and address members. During the 1930s, there were a number of workers' groups that used film as a way of attracting and engaging their members. The Ukrainian Labour-Farmer Temple in Winnipeg, for example, was not just the political gathering pace for the left-leaning members of the city's Ukrainian community: it was also a media and cultural centre.[78] A handful of newspapers and magazines as well as the city's largest Ukrainian-owned theatre, in which both live theatre and film screenings took place, called the temple home. In Toronto, Polish communists, with the support of the newspaper *Glos Pracy*, established a film distribution company for the purpose of importing

Polish-language films from the United States in the hope that they might effectively communicate the party's message to the masses.[79]

The connection between theatres and the labour movement did not stop with the rise of anti-communist anxieties following the Second World War. Anticipating the relationship between cinemas in neighbourhoods in which recent immigrants settled and labour struggles, a meeting took place at the Playhouse Theatre immediately preceding the strike against STELCO in 1946. Chosen in part because of its proximity to the STELCO plant, the Playhouse would come to show almost exclusively Italian-language films under the direction of its owner Emilio Mascia, who would later become the first president of the Italian-Spanish language television broadcaster Telelatino. Other examples highlight the potential of theatres to serve as spaces in which groups that saw themselves as excluded from the organizations that were supposed to represent their interests could gather. In both 1967 and 1968, labour meetings were held at the Lansdowne theatre. Meetings took place when it showed Italian and (later) Greek films (figure 1.6).[80] Many of these meetings were moved to theatres rather than to union facilities as they were organized by recent immigrants who felt that they were being discriminated against by the current executive.

Paying attention to these non-cinematic activities both complicates and expands the relationship between the public sphere and sites of media consumption. The contribution of diasporic and minority media to the creation and expansion of the public sphere has been the focus of a great deal of research in media and communication studies. Some of this material has developed more refined notions of the public sphere for describing how migrant and diasporic communities make use of media as a means of participating in a globally dispersed community.[81] This research has typically focused on post-broadcast media, with less attention being paid to older forms of media distribution such as theatres. An examination of the history of film exhibition in Canada in languages other than English or French reveals the multiple uses to which theatrical spaces were put, a reminder that theorizations of the public sphere must be explicitly discussed as a question of both communication and space. Spaces of media consumption are important counterparts, and in some cases antecedents, to the virtual and imagined communities assembled around media consumed individually or in domestic spaces, which is what has been the focus of more recent media research.

Figure 1.6 Italian construction workers on strike meet at the Lansdowne Theatre, a venue that, through the 1960s, would alternate between live theatre and films in Greek and Italian. *Toronto Telegram* Fonds, 1960.

In his discussion of theatres in Los Angeles' Chinatown, Brian Hu argues that theatres serving the city's Chinese community may be viewed as "semi-public" spaces.[82] He draws on Miriam Hansen's work on spectatorship in the early decades of cinema in North America. Hansen argues that, unlike closed communities defined by class or ethnicity, the cinema provided an "alternative public sphere" that offered a means of transitioning from "an ethnically separatist, inward-looking public sphere to a more inclusive, multiethnic one."[83] Hu, however, argues that Hansen's discussion does not extend to the social dynamics in operation in theatres identified with particular ethnic or linguistic groups. Describing them as "semi-private," he argues that the Chinese-language theatres he describes work as distinct public spheres "precisely [because of] their implied exclusionism to both insiders and outsiders."[84]

It would, of course, be a gross overstatement to claim that theatres were the only such sites where communities gathered. On the contrary, they belonged to a broader network of quasi-public venues in which individuals might encounter one another. These sites emerged in conjunction with the cultural recoding of Canadian cities during the postwar period. Places of worship and community halls are two other important categories of common spaces alongside theatres. However, there are yet other venues, including restaurants, barbershops, and beauty salons, that should not be forgotten. All of these locations incorporated media in some fashion, and they frequently did so in ways that supported community gathering and collective participation. The previously mentioned example of Janki Shori's efforts to program screenings of Indian films in the hall attached to her local temple is emblematic in this regard, highlighting the intersection and mobility of cultural practices and media forms across different kinds of space. But it is important not to allow such an example to obscure the broader range of venues through which media was distributed. Although they are often excluded from many discussions of ethnocultural media, religious groups often hosted screenings of religious films and educational documentaries that were promoted through the newsletters and bulletins these organizations published.[85] Halls owned by community groups hosted a variety of social events, from organizational meetings to dances, situating them within the circuits of live and recorded musical performance. There were also less obvious but no less important venues for the consumption and discussion of media; for example, throughout the 1970s Portuguese barbershops in Montreal included "newspapers and magazines" among the various services that might attract prospective clients (figure 1.7).[86]

Print media, and later broadcasting, allowed for the domestication of media consumption, even though there were many examples of semi-public modes of consumption, such as the barbershops in which newspapers were shared and sold. However, theatres, of necessity, involved participation in public life. At one level, the appeal of the theatres was a product of the access they granted to a scarce commodity: they were the only places where films in a particular language or from a particular country or region could be seen. But the theatres also created a particular kind of communal space – one that differed from other spaces in which individuals might encounter one another in that it was a quasi-private space. The term "quasi-private" is used to describe the intersection between the anonymity granted audience members and the mutual recognition of common interests (and

BARBEARIA CALDENSE

CASA ESPECIALIZADA EM CORTES MODERNOS

Secção de Jornais:
"O SECULO", "DIARIO DE NOTICIAS" "A BOLA", etc

66 Duluth E. - MONTREAL - Tel. 849-1047

BARBEARIA CENTRAL

A mais moderna Barbearia de Montrea

Agente e Distribuidor de todos os Jornais e Revistas Portuguesas

118 Pine Ave - Montreal - Tel. 843-5651

Figure 1.7 Advertisements from *Tribuna Portuguesa* announcing that "modern" haircuts and the latest newspapers and magazines from Portugal could be found at barbershops serving Montreal's Portuguese community (1974).

perhaps more). The importance of this quasi-privacy was increased by the theatres' walls, which protected audience members from the kinds of scrutiny that limited the ability of groups to gather in public spaces like parks, patios, or street corners.

It is important not to underestimate the difficulties encountered by theatre owners and patrons. The rundown nature of the theatres made encounters with government inspectors a fraught affair, but more particular to foreign language theatres were problems associated with translation. The required approval for almost all material associated with the screening of films, from advertisements to the films themselves, often implicitly created significant obstacles to the ability of theatres to operate profitably. Films as well as all promotional material needed to be submitted for review both in the original and in English translation (or French translation in the case of Quebec.) In some cases, this required film distributors either to commission translations or to remove films from consideration.

More widely commented on in the mainstream press was the scrutiny and harassment the theatres and theatre owners attracted. In Toronto, the Naaz Theatre was vandalized and its patrons were the object of racist harassment.[87] This, however, was only one manifestation of a broader anxiety relating to the theatres and the kinds of assembly they permitted – an anxiety that goes back decades A screening of *La Figlia Italiana*, starring Rita Pavone, is described as having caused a riot when theatre-goers amassed outside the St Clair Theatre. An article in the *Globe and Mail* describes "police reinforcements [and] a paddy wagon," along with a "fire truck ready to douse the crowd," and cites a similar incident that occurred the year before, when crowds were unruly before Pavone's performance at Maple Leaf Gardens.[88]

Despite the invocations of Canada's more conciliatory history of ethnic and racial relations, there is a long and troubling history of public space being policed in ways that would re-enforce the dominant racial and linguistic hierarchy. Sherene Razack has called for us to pay greater attention to how "the constitution of spaces reproduces racial hierarchies."[89] From the very founding of the nation, this requires an understanding of how social practice intersects with law to structure how individuals are permitted to gather and interact with one another in ways that confirm rather than disrupt established racist social forms. This entails both formal and informal constraints on the right to assemble in public spaces such as sidewalks and street corners as well as the ability to occupy semi-private spaces like patios, theatres, or private halls. It is only in relation to the application of laws regarding public assembly, noise control, and other euphemisms for maintaining racialized hegemony over space that the significance of theatres becomes apparent. As the records kept by provincial authorities make clear, these venues were frequently subject to inspection in ways that risked blurring the line between public safety and more pernicious forms of discrimination that singled out minorities. Yet, at the same time, theatres also provided spaces that could not be easily surveilled. This is a significant fact in a context within which, as the above examples show, the public assembly of some communities was viewed with suspicion.

CONCLUSION: DARK THEATRES AND GREY MARKETS

This chapter shows that theatres were important spaces in which communities could gather and that they were also highly versatile, serving a number of different communities. In doing this, they served as the infrastructure that supported a broad range of communal and collective activities. They stand alongside a number of other institutions that supported communal gathering and that were constructed by linguistic and cultural minorities, which included many different kinds of spaces for meeting that ranged from the social to the religious to the more explicitly commercial. Theatres can be described as media infrastructure because they made the viewing of films possible, but they also served a more general infrastructural role related to the maintenance of common spaces. They provided physical spaces in which communities that experienced obstacles in their attempts to gain access to public space were able to gather and participate in shared experiences. In the first part of this chapter, the contingent and variable identification of audiences with venues, along with the example of sport telecasts, further highlights the extent to which these cinemas served as points of intersection between communities. Chapter 2 looks at the press federations and other organizations that served newspapers across linguistic and cultural lines but whose activities were primarily limited to professionals. Theatres were open to a much broader portion of the community. For this reason, it is important to contrast the governmentalization of the ethnic press with the less predictable modes of sociality that took place within theatres. Of course, the cinemas' primary reason for existing was to provide a space in which audiences could watch films in their language of choice, but they also served a variety of other purposes in the lives of many cultural communities.

Of course I have neglected a great deal of information regarding the rhythms and organization of migrant and diasporic film culture in Canada so that I might highlight the ways in which theatres functioned as an essential part of the cultural infrastructure built and inhabited by cultural and linguistic minorities. I provide an opportunity to consider the complex of constraints and interactions that contributed to the formation of Canadian media culture for marginalized communities. Rather than islands only reaching towards "home," my goal is to bring attention to the interaction and overlap between the cultural milieus that took shape in multiple Canadian cities. This was a product of the common social and economic context within which the media entrepreneurs of the period were working. It is here that the overlap between international cinema and the burgeoning counterculture of the 1960s and 1970s is particularly important. For this reason, these theatres should be situated at the vanguard of an emergent cultural plurivocity in Canadian cities rather than presented as sites in which cultural identity and heritage were venerated in isolation from the new patterns of cultural circulation shaping the neighbourhoods beyond the box office window.

The connection between these theatres and the new forms of urban life taking shape in Canada beginning in the 1950s highlights the importance of grounding a vernacular multiculturalism in popular culture rather than in the petrified versions of folk culture that would later be given a prominent place in official multiculturalism. Furthermore, it makes clear that the temporalities of migration in the second part of the twentieth century exist somewhere between accounts that describe the temporal and spatial dislocation that characterized the experience of early twentieth-century migration and the perceived informational simultaneity of migration in the digital age. For this reason, it is important to situate the digital revolution of the past two decades within a continuum of evolving media practices among migrant and diasporic communities that has developed over decades rather than to treat it as a radical break.

The continued importance of the theatres was in part a response to the inability of many minority communities to gain access to other forms of media. Chapters 3 and 4 outline the establishment of broadcasting in languages other than English and French, telling the other side of how access to certain media was limited during this period. The characterization of these decades as the golden age of television needs to be qualified when speaking of many minority communities. This is not to say that television was absent from the experience of "New Canadians" in the 1960s and 1970s. Indeed, community newspapers published in most languages included advertisements for furniture and electronics stores selling television sets, with some stores entering the video rental business in the 1980s. There were programs being broadcast in languages other than English or French, but the limited amount of television broadcasting in minority languages remained constant into the twenty-first century. The prominence of theatres through the 1960s and 1970s is indicative of the disjuncture between mainstream Canadian culture and the everyday media consumption of minorities and recent immigrants.

The arrival of home video would bring the distribution of international film back into alignment with the dominant media technologies of mainstream media, and it would do so abruptly. Those searching for historical specificity when analyzing periods of transition in media history may be comforted to know that 1985 was the year in which the three-decade period that witnessed the growth and success of theatres programming international films was undone by the arrival of home video. Unlike the rise of television, which shrunk the market for English-language theatres and gave rise to the multilingual theatres profiled here, the effects of home video were felt across the industry regardless of language. Indeed, home video was perhaps even more significant for the ethnic theatres since a central factor in their success was the absence of significant competition from television. While the regulatory transition from film to home video was more or less seamless, its effects on the industry were profound as a cheaper and more convenient alternative to going to the theatre arrived on the scene. In many cases, the same distribution networks that brought films into the country for theatres also supplied the home video market.

The introduction of home video followed the emergence of a profoundly different geography and economy of immigrant settlement that was taking shape in Canadian cities. The compact urban ethnic enclaves that had shaped Canada's cities for much of the twentieth century gave way to more spatially dispersed suburban settlements. Not requiring any kind of critical mass of paying customers within a relatively short distance in order to survive, video stores could thrive in the strip malls that lined major suburban arteries. This was the final step in the integration of media distribution into general retail, as the sale of magazines and music had long since moved into groceries. This is a development that would, during the same years, find a parallel in the geography of third-language television production. While some of the older broadcasters' offices remained in the downtowns of the country's major cities, the cost of rent as well as the changing cultural geography of Canadian cities encouraged many of these companies to establish themselves on the outskirts in suburban industrial areas. Toronto's CHIN Radio and Television, with an office in the middle of the city's first Little Italy, was an outlier as other third-language broadcasters (Telelatino, Fairchild, and CFMT) all established themselves in less centrally located neighbourhoods.

However, the arrival of home video did not bring about a wholesale transformation in the economics of film; rather, different aspects of this economy came to be emphasized. If part of the significance of movie-going – and of movie theatres more generally – came from their capacity to support forms of community that were policed in more public spaces, the development of the video market highlighted the legal liminality of diasporic culture in Canada in a commercial rather than in a social register. Due in part to the complexities of navigating intellectual property laws in two jurisdictions, the rise of home video was supported through a rapid expansion of a "grey market" for films, meaning films that were not licensed for distribution in Canada yet for which the distributors had made some kind of arrangements with the company that held the copyright for the material in question. These kinds of arrangements were not previously possible given the high levels of government regulation for theatrical exhibition. Films needed to be licensed, venues needed to be inspected, and even advertisements needed to be submitted for approval in order to ensure that all of the legally necessary information – such as ratings – was available for the public.

Home videos were much less amenable to scrutiny as the promotion and operation of the video rental industry did not require the same forms of publicity (i.e., marquees or newspaper listings of show times) that facilitated government oversight and regulation. In this regard, the distribution of home videos resembled the market for publications and recorded music. Numerous stores across the country had emerged to distribute records, magazines, and books (as well as occasionally selling imported dry goods.) A survey of licensing data from Ontario shows a significant reduction in the number of films submitted for licensing beginning in the mid-1980s. Dropping from a high of 592 films submitted for licensing in 1975, there were fewer than two hundred hundred films in languages other than English that were submitted to the province in 1988 (a level that would remain more or less consistent throughout the 1990s.)

Documents held by the government of Quebec show that a significant number of the companies investigated by the Regis du Cinema in the 1980s for violating the province's regulations regarding the rating and licensing of home videos were involved in the distribution of films in languages other than English or French.[90] More anecdotally, Rocco Mastrangelo recalls the day he decided to close the St Clair Theatre arrived when he heard patrons complaining about the high cost of tickets given that the same film was available for rental at a store down the street.[91] A similar story is told by Gianni Naaz, owner of the Naaz Theatre in Toronto's Little India, regarding the inability of his theatre to compete with the convenience and price of home videos.[92] The movement of home video into the grey market makes it difficult to document the pace of the development of the home video market as there are simply no reliable data. But the effects of the transition were relatively swift, with most of the theatres that had opened in the 1960s and 1970s closing by the end of the 1980s. Some of the individuals involved in the theatres were able to make the transition, but others simply left the business. Rocco Mastrangelo, for example, began to sell video copies of the films he had previously exhibited in theatres across the country; the company took the name of one of his first theatres, Radio City Video.[93]

However, the importance of the theatre would continue as a metaphor to explain the importance of ethnocultural media to the communities they served. This is most notable in Emilio Mascia's decision to use the metaphor of the "electronic theatre" during his appearance before the Canadian Radio-television and Telecommunications Commission (CRTC) in February 1984, when he explained his hopes for what his proposed Italian- and Spanish-language station might contribute to Canadian society.[94] Using the example of the San Carlino Theatre, a venue for film and live performance he owned in the north end of Toronto, Mascia explained that the new service would provide a space in which a community might gather to be informed and entertained. Importantly, the aspect of the theatre that Mascia and Price, his lawyer at the hearings, emphasizes was what they called its non-commercial aspect. They clarified that this did not mean that the new service would be run as a non-profit but, rather, that the subscription model that they were proposing would be one that would separate the commercial aspect of the service from the programming itself.[95]

At one level, it is hard not to see this as a criticism of the close ties between sponsors and producers that had developed in third-language radio and television. Yet, lingering somewhere in the background of this metaphor, there is an invocation of the modes of sociality that these theatres made possible. In this way, the social life made possible by the theatres discussed in this chapter haunted the arrival of third-language television, providing at least some of the symbolic inspiration for the subsequent development of minority and third-language media in Canada, even though the theatres themselves would soon disappear.

2

Autonomy: Governing the Ethnic Press in Cold War Canada

Robert E. Park's *The Immigrant Press and Its Control* is the most extensive and widely circulated analysis of ethnocultural media in North America published in the first half of the twentieth century. The volume was commissioned by the Carnegie Institute in 1918 as part of its Americanization Studies series, one of the many initiatives in this period concerned with how immigrants adapted to life in the United States.[1] While Park recognizes the positive social and cultural contributions of immigrants, his book sees the press primarily as a tool supporting the integration of immigrants into American society leading ultimately to their assimilation. In this way, Park's analysis of ethnocultural media sits unambiguously within the goals of the project of Americanization, which the publisher of the reports describes as "the union of the native and foreign born in all the most fundamental relationships and activities of our national life."[2]

However, Park's study is not just an analysis of the role print media plays in the processes of assimilation. Perhaps more urgently, it outlines concerns that newspapers might exert foreign influence on recent immigrants. The final section of Park's text focuses on the "Control of the Press" and examines a number of notable cases in which newspapers were used to promote what were deemed to be anti-American ideas.[3] The conclusion of his book does not embrace an unfettered free press no matter the language but, rather, calls for the adoption of more effective strategies to ensure that newspapers serving the needs and interests of recent immigrants remain committed to a program of integration and assimilation. This is not surprising given the broader sociological framework within which Park was developing his research for *The Immigrant Press*, a framework which posited that "social control is the central fact and central problem of society."[4]

Park's analysis of the newspapers as social institutions can be read from an infrastructural perspective, recognizing how the ideological work of the newspaper is supported by means of a series of material and cultural networks. However, it is Park's insight into media, power, and social control in his discussions of the ethnocultural press rather than infrastructural concerns that make his text an appropriate starting point for this chapter. Questions of power have already been raised in chapter 1, drawing on Sherene Razack's discussion of how the production and policing of public space intersect with each other, and even Charles Taylor's elaboration of the aporia of the politics of recognition (as outlined in the introduction) recognizes that power relations shape the struggle to balance recognition with equality. This is not to say that Park outlines the problem in the most satisfactory or comprehensive manner: his appeal to nationalism and the invocation of a "natural" process of assimilation speak to the moment in which he wrote the project. However, his text does offer evidence of how the complexity of relations between the state, media, and ethnocultural minorities were already being addressed in the early twentieth century.

Similar discussions and debates were not uncommon in Canada at the time, but they developed in a somewhat different direction from those in the United States. Richard Day describes the approach that would become dominant in Canada as a "constrained emergence theory" in which ethnocultural difference was supported within constraints set by the institutions of government. He traces the origins of this line of thought to the early twentieth century, particularly to the writings of J.S. Woodsworth and the sociologist Robert England.[5] With the beginning of the Second World War, Day observes that "the constrained emergence theory was taken up by the Canadian state as a solution to the wartime problem of Europe Immigrant diversity."[6] This would set the stage for an approach to diversity that would ground the Canadian approach to governing identity within bureaucratically implemented programs aimed at managing diversity rather than through categorical exclusion or assimilation.

Questions of power are at the very centre of Day's account of the history of cultural diversity in Canada, but it is an account that primarily documents the voices of those in positions of influence. In this chapter I take a different approach to the dynamics he describes by documenting the role of organizations that served as intermediaries between "the ethnic press," the government of Canada, and the public during the 1950s and 1960s.[7] I argue that these intermediary organizations performed an infrastructural role: coordinating and structuring relations between newspapers and their readers, between minority newspapers themselves, and between newspapers and the institutions of government. They were not exclusively an exercise in state power or control; rather, they were created by the newspapers and state officials together, even if not always in complete cooperation.

Examining these intermediaries as emerging from the activities of the press itself alongside the actions of the state requires engaging with how infrastructure simultaneously enables and constrains autonomy. The production of autonomy is an important characteristic of infrastructure. Chapter 1 shows how the sites and systems designed to distribute film also served to support a wide variety of social interactions among individuals belonging to cultural and linguistic minorities. The usefulness of these spaces was determined by what they made possible through the establishment of parameters and norms, not through the centralized control of all the activities that took place within them. The relationship between individual and collective autonomy was constantly shaped by the constraints within which the theatres under discussion operated (censorship, the policing of public meetings, zoning, etc.) Building on this, my approach here does not presume that the freedom to act precedes attempts to manage and control action. Rather, the independence of newspapers after the Second World War developed in relation to institutions and frameworks capable of enforcing the strictest possible limits and restrictions: complete censorship. Indeed, both the First and Second World Wars provided occasions in which the exercise of these powers moved from the theoretical to the actual.

The onset of the Cold War is essential for understanding the constraints on the autonomy of the ethnic press. The anti-communist ideologies emerging as part of the Cold War's cultural front helped to organize and orient both efforts to welcome immigrants and anxieties about the new arrivals, providing criteria for separating the "good" from the "bad" in public debates about migration.[8] The stated goal of the government's engagement with the ethnic press during these years – the promotion of citizenship training and language education programs – was presented as free from political ideology or partisan agenda.[9] Yet both goals were promoted in ways that aligned them with the anti-communist consensus of the Cold War, which is what dominated Canadian culture at the time. However, my primary focus in this chapter is not exclusively the hidden ideological work of the Canadian government; rather, it analyzes how government efforts to control the ethnic press cannot be separated from strategies designed to protect the autonomy of minority newspapers.

There were concerns about the outcome of any proposal that involved either absolute censorship of minority media or its co-optation by government agencies. Despite the red scare, there were concerns that the appearance of government control over the press would undermine claims regarding the importance of free expression – claims that were loudly touted as foundational to democratic values and anti-communist ideology. Furthermore, many of the editors and publishers had recently immigrated from countries where state surveillance and control over the press had left them sceptical of any kind of direct state intervention. It was in response to this resistance that postwar relations between the government and the press differed from wartime efforts at monitoring and managing "foreign-language" newspapers. Rather than taking the lead, the government left the central role in organizing and coordinating the ethnic press to private organizations that frequently proclaimed their independence from the state. Operating at arm's length granted these intermediary organizations greater latitude to directly engage with minority communities than had been possible for state agencies prior to or during the war. In this way, the granting of autonomy to newspapers was indissociably linked with techniques of management and control.

What emerged during these years was an arrangement between publications, intermediaries, and government that coupled ideological guidance with financial support through the purchase of advertising. The appeals to follow the ideological guidance of the state were articulated using the language of patriotism and the public obligation of newspaper editors to the nation. By contrast, the financial support the industry organizations were able to organize was explicitly private in nature, even extending beyond government sponsorship to include major national companies whose executives were aligned with the political and cultural elite of the nation. Alongside these two roles, these organizations also took on the

Figure 2.1 Vladimir Mauko, president of the Ontario Ethnic Press Association, presents a group of Slovenia-Canadian musicians to Ontario premier John Robarts at an event at the Royal York in Toronto. The event was organized to thank the premier for supporting the association's activities over the years (1969).

responsibility of representing newspapers serving minority and immigrant communities to the nation as a whole, often speaking on behalf of "the ethnic press" in the media. These were the first formal attempts to establish organizations to represent the ethnic press to government and Canadian society more broadly. Thus, the activities of these intermediaries not only served the ethnic press but also played a role in defining it within Canadian political discourse in the second half of the twentieth century.[10]

The focus here is on three different types of organizations that contributed to the cultural infrastructure that mediated between the ethnic press and the government during these years: press associations, news agencies, and advertising agencies.[11] The earliest of these organizations to be established was the Canada Press Club (CPC), a group serving the ethnic press that was formed in June 1942 by editors and publishers in Winnipeg. Despite being a private professional organization, the CPC was associated with the network of government agencies that monitored and managed the "foreign language press" – as it was known during the war – in order to prevent the political subversion of the country's minority communities. After the war, a number of other organizations with similar mandates were founded across the country. The Ethnic Press Association of Ontario was established in 1951. The Canada Ethnic Press Federation was created in 1957. Further regional associations, serving British Columbia and Quebec, were formed in 1959 and 1962, respectively.[12] Alongside these new organizations representing the press, a news agency named Canadian Scene, which was dedicated to distributing material in translation, was established in 1951. That same year an advertising agency – New Canadian Publications – was founded in Toronto, and its primary focus was representing minority papers to large companies and government agencies. The ideological work of gatekeeping undertaken by these organizations and agencies as part of the Canadian government's Cold War project became inextricably linked with the reorganization and rationalization of the ethnic press as an industry.[13]

FEDERATING THE ETHNIC PRESS FROM WEST TO EAST

In 1950, the province of Manitoba, and the city of Winnipeg in particular, was home to the highest concentration of foreign language newspapers in the country. The largest of these publications were the German-language *Der Nordwesten*, the *Ukrayinskyi holos* (Ukrainian Voice), and *Dos Yiddishe Vort* (initially known as *Der Kanader Yid*), all three of which claimed to have a circulation of around ten thousand copies per issue through the 1920s.[14] Before communist political activities were banned nationally in 1940, Winnipeg had also been home to some of the most prominent socialist and radical newspapers published in Russian and Ukrainian, many of which were produced by the Workers Farmers Publishing Society housed in the Ukrainian Labour-Farmer Temple located on the corner of Pritchard Avenue and MacGregor Street.[15]

There is not adequate space here to document in detail the factors contributing to the development of the foreign language press in Winnipeg, but its place as the capital of foreign language papers dates back to the beginning of the twentieth century. Developing alongside the establishment of newspapers in English and French, there had been a handful of Canadian newspapers printed in other languages as far back as the eighteenth century. In the late nineteenth century, while some of these were located in major cities, many more operated in smaller towns across the country as part of the "Pioneer Press."[16] There was a significant consolidation of publications in urban areas in the first decades of the twentieth century. The centralization of the press, and the move to cities, followed trends in immigrant settlement. It also involved a strategy shift on the part of publishers that saw many newspapers come to view themselves as regional (and even national) publications rather than as local publications.[17]

Given its prominence as the Canadian capital of "foreign language" media in the first half of the twentieth century, it is not surprising that Winnipeg was the location of the first group claiming to represent the ethnic press across languages and cultures. On 5 June 1942, twenty-one editors and publishers from nineteen of Winnipeg's foreign language newspapers, along with representatives of the city's two liberal dailies, met in a dining room at the Fort Garry Hotel to formalize the creation of the Canada Press Club.[18] The meeting had been organized through the efforts of Walter Jacobson Lindal, a judge of Icelandic origin with ties to the provincial Liberal Party.[19] Lindal had recently published *Two Ways of Life: Freedom or Tyranny*, which laid out a staunch defence of Canadian values against the threat of fascism.[20] He was also known for well-received speaking engagements across the country in which he showed himself to be a fierce advocate for Canada's involvement in the Second World War.[21] The purpose of the club, as laid out at its inaugural meeting, echoed Lindal's beliefs regarding the importance of building solidarity at home in support of Canadian military activities overseas.

Documented in the preamble to the group's by-laws, the aims of the club are listed as follows:

1 To interpret the Canadian scene and its problems, thus striving to contribute to a more united and sounder Canadianism.
2 To promote a better understanding among the various national groups in Canada.

3 To study Canada's position in relation to the British Commonwealth, the United States, the United Nations, and any organization which may emerge out of the latter concept.
4 To disseminate information of the basic principles for which the United Nations are fighting and a clearer conception of the master-race theory on which the expansion programmes of Germany, Japan and Italy are based.
5 To study post-war problems in the light of the world situation as it develops from time to time.[22]

Recalling the formation of the club forty years later, Lindal would describe the meeting as an occasion on which the assembled members gave thought to "ways and means of combining their efforts which would enable them more effectively to contribute to the prosecution of the war and afterwards the building of the Canadian nation."[23] However, Lindal had been more frank in his assessment of the group's origins elsewhere, recalling that "the first purpose of the existence of the club, namely the prosecution of the War, was included because of a fear that there were national groups in Canada who had originated in enemy countries and would 'have to be watched.'"[24] The mixture of patriotism and anxiety that surrounded the Canada Press Club's founding connect it with the efforts of the Canadian government to monitor and regulate the foreign language press during these years and was symptomatic of what Whitaker and Marcuse call "the national insecurity state."[25]

While the group's executive was drawn from the ranks of editors and publishers in Winnipeg, the decision to name G.W. Simpson as the honorary vice-president of the group indicates the club's connection with the government's engagement with minority media. Simpson, an expert on Ukrainian history and chair of the Department of History at the University of Saskatchewan, had served as an advisor to the Public Information Bureau during the first years of the Second World War.[26] His naming as a patron of the group coincides with his brief tenure as chair of the Committee on Co-operation in Canadian Citizenship, a position from which he resigned in August 1942 due to illness. At the time the Press Club was formed, the official role of the committee was "to act as a link between the Canadian immigrant communities and the national government," but it would soon become the government body tasked with monitoring the foreign language press across Canada upon its transformation into the Nationalities Branch in October 1941.[27]

The Canada Press Club's activities were focused on showcasing the loyalty of the diverse communities making up the province of Manitoba. Its programs primarily consisted of arranging regular meetings that provided a venue at which prominent speakers, often government representatives, could share their pro-Canadian views with members of the foreign language press.[28] It also contributed to the development of stronger ties between minority and mainstream newspapers in Manitoba. The first indication of this connection was the publication of a series of editorials authored by editors of ethnic publications celebrating "Unity with Variety," which ran from 11 September 1943 until 26 February 1944 in the *Winnipeg Tribune*.[29]

This connection with the government's initiatives to monitor and regulate the ethnic press position the Press Club as a node within the network of information distribution and community mobilization activities in which the Canadian government engaged as the war effort expanded.[30] These activities included the production of the radio series titled *Canadians All*, which was broadcast on the CBC in the spring of 1941 (discussed in further detail in the next chapter); the distribution of editorial material under the direction of Vladimir J. Kaye at the Nationalities Branch; and a collaboration between the Nationalities Branch and the National Film Board that resulted in the production of the film *Peoples of Canada* (1941).[31] These propaganda efforts were supported by a long-standing program of government surveillance and regulation of foreign language newspapers dating back decades. At the end of the First World War, this program had even gone so far as to declare a publication ban on newspapers published in "enemy languages."[32]

However, the collegial patriotism that guided the activities of the Canada Press Club represented a new approach to the foreign language press on the part of the government. As Dreisziger writes of these years: "They mark a perceptible watershed between the age when 'ethnics' or 'ethnic populations' were generally ignored, and the post-war era when increasing attention was paid to them, not only at election time but on an ongoing basis."[33] While censorship was not wholly abandoned during the Second World War, its use was limited to the fascist, communist, and socialist publications monitored by the RCMP that were perceived as "radical."[34] Most publications were allowed to continue publishing with the caveat that they maintain pro-Canada editorial positions. In place of outright censorship there existed a workable, if not always stable, balance between government monitoring and self-censorship that ensured that publications adopted positions that were generally in line with the views of the Canadian government. Iacovetta describes this approach as "the tactics of close liaison," which is a phrase she borrows from Vladimir Kaye, one of the bureaucrats who was most active in engaging with the ethnic press.

The commitment to "Canadianism" found in the governing documents of the Canada Press Club is evidence of the ways in which papers that espoused different political and economic viewpoints, specifically the philo-fascist and socialist press, were expressly excluded from the mainstream of Canadian media and of Canadian society in general. The precarious political balance that came about with the Cold War meant that anxieties about foreign language newspapers would continue after the Second World War. After 1945, the Press Club continued its efforts to support "Canadian Unity" for all inhabitants of the country regardless of their cultural background. In line with this, its major activities included hosting notable political figures and educating new arrivals about the meaning and benefits of Canadian citizenship following the passing of the Citizenship Act, 1947 (figure 2.2). These efforts included the publication of articles in the *Winnipeg Free Press* over the course of 1946–47 discussing the importance of citizenship for recent immigrants as well as the publication of a short book by Walter Lindal entitled *Canadian Citizenship and Our Wider Loyalties*.[35]

At the same time as the Canada Press Club engaged in these efforts to promote Canadian citizenship, a broader systemic transformation was affecting the group's member publications. By the 1940s, the foreign language press in Winnipeg had achieved a level of maturity that meant that many of its publications had been in existence for more than three decades. Even as some of the more prominent members of the press were achieving political and cultural influence, several long-serving editors and publishers were coming to the end of their careers. While mostly known for the books he authored, Lindal himself was part of this generational transition. He sat on the editorial board of the *Icelandic Canadian*, a magazine published in English targeting second- and third-generation Canadians of Icelandic descent.[36] The Icelandic community was not unique

Figure 2.2 Charles Dojack welcomes Governor General Vincent Massey to a meeting of the Canada Press Club, with Walter Lindal looking on (1955).

in entering a period of transition as many established editors and publishers engaged in the process of passing the torch to a younger generation, and editorial policies shifted to reflect demographic transitions. Ben Cohen, who had founded Winnipeg's the *Jewish Post* in 1925 and served as its publisher until shortly before his death in 1953, transferred ownership to Leo Lezack and Mel Fenson.[37] Frank Dojacek, president of National Publications (which was responsible for *Der Nordwesten,* the Polish-language paper *Czas*, and *Canadian Farmer*), suffered a stroke in 1945, and his responsibilities were taken over by his son Charles Dojack upon his return from military service overseas in the Canadian army.[38]

Of perhaps greater long-term significance than the generational shift affecting existing publications in the west was the impact of new waves of immigrants, which started entering Canada after the relaxation of immigration limits after the Great Depression and the end of the war. While these new arrivals led to a period of renewal for some established titles, they also contributed to the creation of a number of new publications. Overall, the new arrivals moved the centre of the ethnic press eastward, with the result that the majority of new publications were based in Toronto. Indeed, some of the titles already established in the west relocated to Toronto after the war as part of the arrival of large number of migrants to that city. For example, two Japanese papers that initially operated out of Vancouver – the *New Canadian*, founded in 1938, and the *Continental News*, founded in 1907 – moved to Toronto in 1945 and 1948, respectively.

There was a much shorter period of time between the first appearance of these new publications in Ontario and the decision to create an organization to serve their interests. In October 1950, representatives of the ethnic press decided to found an organization similar to the Canada Press Club. This was initially known as the Ethnic Press Club of Toronto but, as its geographic scope expanded, was later renamed the Ethnic Press Association of Ontario. Its founding documents show that its goals were almost identical to those adopted by the Canada Press Club at the time of its establishment, with both groups committed to "a more united and a richer Canadianism."[39] The primary difference between the constitutions of these two organizations was that the newer one's language expressed a commitment to "freedom and democracy," to reflect the dominant discourses of the Cold War, while the older one's language expressed opposition to "master-race theory."[40]

There are differing recollections about the origins of the Ethnic Press Association of Ontario. Walter Lindal recalls a lunch meeting in May 1947 with Bruno Tenhunen, the first president of the Ontario association and a long-time editor of the Finnish weekly *Vapaa Sana*, that he claims eventually led to the creation of the Ontario association.[41] However, Vladimir Mauko, founder of the Slovenian National Federation and editor of the anti-communist *Slovenska Drzava*, credits the idea for the creation of the Ontario association to the initiative of Z.S. (Stan) Mokrzycki.[42] According to Mauko, Mokrzycki thought it important that the federation create a forum through which the different members of the ethnic press might join together to more effectively advocate for their needs.[43]

Mokrzycki was not an editor or publisher himself; rather, he was the director of New Canadian Publications, an advertising agency established in 1951 with the purpose of coordinating the purchase of advertisements in ethnic newspapers on the part of national companies and government agencies. The suggestion to found a group representing newspapers in Ontario can be seen as one that served his own business interests as much as it served the needs of the rapidly increasing number of ethnic newspapers based in Toronto. Of equal importance, however, is the venue at which Mokrzycki made his suggestion: a meeting hosted by the president of the news agency Canadian Scene. Canadian Scene, also formed in 1951, initially operated under the auspices of the Imperial Order Daughters of the Empire (although, on numerous occasions, the agency's founders would clarify that the two organizations acted independently of each other).[44]

The three Toronto-based organizations were ostensibly independent organizations financed privately through donations (in the case of Canadian Scene), member contributions (in the case of the Ethnic Press Association of Ontario), or sales commissions (in the case of New Canadian Publications).[45] However, a complex web of connections to the government's wartime engagement with foreign language newspapers persisted. Some of these involved formal ties, such as the presence of Charity Grant, Toronto liaison officer of the Citizenship Branch of the Department of Citizenship and Immigration, on the board of Canadian Scene.[46] However, other connections were less formally recognized. Such was the case with the role played by Steve Davidovich in the formation of the Ethnic Press Association of Ontario.[47] Davidovich was not an editor or a publisher, but, going back to the Second World War, he had worked for various international information agencies through which he came into contact with the Polish and Ukrainian press around the world. He also had a stint as the director of the Ukrainian National Information Service, an organization based in London, England, and he distributed information in support of Ukrainian independence before serving in the Canadian army beginning in 1941.[48] He took a position with the Citizenship Division in the Ministry of Citizenship and Immigration in 1948 before moving to similar positions with the province of Ontario. Frank Glogowski, who served as editor of the Polish weekly *Zwiazkowiec* and was active with the Ethnic Press Association of Ontario from its beginning, recalls that Davidovich played an important role in building relationships between Polish and Ukrainian newspapers in the years leading up to its creation. Glogowski also notes that it was Davidovich who worked to "marry" the ethnic press to Canadian Scene as a source of publishable material. Finally, it was Davidovich who suggested the term "Ethnic Press Association," which was widely lauded because it "fortunately at last wiped out the term 'Foreign Language Press.'"[49]

In 1957, the decision was made to pursue the formation of the Canada Ethnic Press Federation, a national organization that combined the members of the groups in Winnipeg and Toronto as well as publications in British Columbia and Quebec (although provincial organizations bringing together editors in these provinces would not be formed until 1959 and 1962, respectively).[50] The need for the national organization was increasingly apparent to the membership of the provincial groups given that many of the problems the papers faced – such as postal rates – were under the jurisdiction of the federal government. The government itself was in favour of the development of a national organization, although efforts were made to ensure that it did not simply appear to be a front for government propaganda. The minutes of the meeting in Ottawa, where the vote was taken to establish the national organization, notes that J.W. Pickersgill, in his capacity as minister of citizenship and immigration, spoke at the meeting and "stressed that the Government did not want to control papers. If the impression was created that the papers were 'a stooge' of the Government, the papers would lose their influence."[51] He further encouraged the group to support the motion, while ensuring that it retained its independence, by announcing that "it would be quite proper for him, if it was decided to form an association, to recommend a small annual grant to assist the association, not with a view to controlling the association, but as a supplementary item to help provide for annual meetings."[52] With that offer on the table, Pickersgill left the meeting to allow the assembled editors to vote their conscience free from the appearance of inappropriate influence.

The policy of supporting the Canada Ethnic Press Federation survived the defeat of the St Laurent government in June 1957 (and would continue until the mid-1960s.) At the group's first national conference, held in Ottawa on 8 March 1958, the new deputy minister of citizenship and immigration, Laval Fortier, spoke to the assembled membership and reiterated the government's support for the group and the importance of its independence: "If we have provided the means to support you, we are happy. There are no strings attached, you are absolutely free to decide anything you want."[53] Response to the formation of the national organization was not unanimously positive. Many in the mainstream press saw the organization, and the government-funded conference, as little more than an attempt to buy the votes of ethnic communities.[54]

Despite the involvement of government representatives in the early day-to-day operation of these organizations, the decision was made to bar government employees from taking on official roles as their doing so would appear to compromise both government impartiality and the legitimacy of the newspapers.[55] However, the informal ties between the government and these agencies remained in place. It was through these connections that the government sought to ensure that the ethnic press would remain within the ideological orbit of the Canadian political establishment. Canadian Scene was perhaps responsible for the most explicit efforts to shape the editorial agendas of the ethnic press. Its origins stem from the perceived obligations on the part of the patrician members of the Imperial Order Daughters of the Empire (IODE) towards recently arrived immigrants in the face of the threat posed by communist propaganda.[56] And, throughout the first decades of its existence, Canadian Scene remained an organization that was firmly rooted in the country's anglophone establishment. Members of the Eaton family, former prime minister Arthur Meighen, and heads of major Canadian corporations were members of its editorial board.[57] As already noted, the government's representative at the agency was Charity Grant, a member of a prominent Toronto family whose uncle was former Governor General Vincent Massey.[58]

An article in the *Globe and Mail* describes the origin of Canadian Scene among the nation's elite, recalling how a group of "public-spirited Canadians" gathered for a meeting of the IODE responded to the threat of communist subversion: "They resolved that some means must be taken to supplement the material gathered and printed by the small, democratic foreign language newspapers so that those who bought them and read them would be able to get a better picture of their new country and what it stood for."[59] Although officially independent of the IODE, Canadian Scene was managed by its members throughout the first three decades of its operation. Producing materials that could be used free of charge, it relied upon tax-deductible donations from corporations (particularly large retail chains, manufacturing firms, and oil companies) while receiving technical support from the *Toronto Telegram* and the *Globe and Mail*.[60]

Canadian Scene sent out bi-weekly packages that alternated in length between eight and six pages and that consisted of articles covering a variety of topics, with the shorter packages accompanied by two pages of pictures available for publication.[61] After one year of operation, it circulated material in translation to fifty-two newspapers and newsletters across the country in eleven languages.[62] This grew to sixty-four newspapers (out of an estimated 128 nationally) in thirteen languages by the end of its second year.[63] The articles that were distributed addressed a number of different topics, mostly focused on Canadian culture and the country's public institutions. Many of these dealt with highly practical matters, such as taxes and social benefits, while others dealt with topics related to Canadian political life more generally. In its first year, for example, articles such as "Democracy, Government and the Individual" and "Summer Theatre" were circulated along with shorter, more factual pieces such as "Canada Supplies Radar to European Allies."[64] An index published in 1960 divides articles into the following categories, giving further information on the kind of materials circulated to subscribers: Local, Cities of Canada, Government in Canada, Economic Subjects, Education, New Canadian Personalities, Regional Articles, Indians and Eskimos, Self-Help, Art and Culture, Canadiana and Holidays.[65]

In line with the mandate of the press associations, Canadian Scene described itself in terms that placed its anti-communism at the forefront of its activities. In the words of a press release announcing the establishment of Canadian Scene: "The primary function of Canadian Scene is to combat the Communist line by giving new Canadians a clear and interesting picture of what is going on in this country, emphasizing the institutions of democracy and inculcating a feeling of national pride."[66] While the government of the time was generally supportive of the efforts made by Canadian Scene, the exact nature of its relationship with the government is difficult to determine. Throughout its history, the agency went to great lengths to clarify that it was in no way connected to the Canadian government. Indeed, a brief written in preparation for the public hearings of the Royal Commission on Bilingualism and Biculturalism goes so far as to suggest that, even if offered, the group would not take support from the government as "it seems to take a great pride in its complete independence."[67] Yet, beginning shortly after its establishment, ongoing correspondence between Canadian Scene and representatives of the federal government, most frequently the Ministry for Citizenship and Immigration, makes it clear that the agency developed a number of connections with specific government agencies that might well call into question claims about its independence.

The generally positive attitude on the part of the government towards the work of the Canadian Scene meant that the agency's leadership felt it was able to ask for a variety of different kinds of information and support. Among the permissions granted was access to confidential materials listing and describing non-communist Canadian newspapers published in languages other than English or French, including the monthly press summaries (published between 1963 and 1966 in a publication called Ethnic Scene).[68] The editors of Canadian Scene would frequently rely upon information from government representatives for their articles, and, by 1954, they were willing to accept materials written by government agencies directly (which were then translated at Canadian Scene's expense).[69] Later on, Canadian Scene received reports from the staff of the *Foreign Language Press Review*, published by the Ministry of Citizenship and Immigration, regarding the accuracy of the translations of their articles across multiple languages.[70] Canadian Scene cooperated particularly closely with the Ministry of Citizenship and Immigration around the Hungarian refugee crisis in 1957, publishing special issues for distribution in Europe to provide information for displaced people considering settlement in Canada.[71]

Despite these exchanges, the government remained wary of associating itself too publicly with the Canadian Scene for fear of how common knowledge of this relationship might affect the agency's ability to influence publications. This concern was present from the earliest days of Canadian Scene's operation, when, in response to requests for government funding, government officials expressed concerns "that they would lose some of their independence in the eyes of their opponents."[72] The combination of anti-communism and the appearance of editorial autonomy were particularly important given the prominent role that editors and publishers who fled from the Soviet bloc played in the democratic press of the 1950s and 1960s. In this sense, the commitment to anti-communism espoused by Canadian Scene was not simply a position imposed on subscribers; rather, it supported the views of many of the editors who had come to newspaper editing after having lived under totalitarianism in Eastern Europe. This general anti-Soviet sentiment encouraged Canadian Scene to become even more outspoken in its criticism.

Over time, the government worried that the ideological zeal of Canadian Scene and some of its members could be a problem, inflaming readers already opposed to communist governments. Upon the naming of Margaret Zieman as Canadian Scene's editor-in-chief, it was noted that, at the risk of increasing discontent among immigrants, the service was taking a more partisan perspective on global events. Responding to an article critical of Kruschev's 1959 visit to the United States, government representatives felt that "to feed this to the ethnic press can only encourage demonstrations."[73] Concerns that the organization's ideological commitments might go beyond simply informing the public to soliciting discontent was repeated in a report prepared for the government in 1965 by Robert Adie. In this report Adie cautioned that Canadian Scene's "position is stated often enough and sufficiently dogmatically to suggest that it could easily become a little hysterical on the subject of communism on certain occasions."[74] The report goes on to question if, in the long run, circulating such material might even undermine Canadian Scene's credibility as the dogmatic anti-communism found in it "[gave] its entire material a faint whitewashing, if not brainwashing, aura."[75] Despite these concerns, during the 1960s the organization was frequently featured in discussions of the ethnic press in mainstream newspapers and, upon the publication of commemorative volumes marking significant anniversaries for the Canada Press Club, the Ethnic Press Association of Ontario, and the Canada Ethnic Press Federation, Canadian Scene was given a prominent place in recollections of these groups' activities.[76]

NEW CANADIAN ADVERTISING

The circulation of editorial material through Canadian Scene was, however, a relatively weak means for government to assert control over the ethnic press given that the decision to publish material was ultimately left up to the individual editors. Some papers, such as the Polish-language *Zwiazkowiec*, published general interest articles about taxes or social benefits throughout the 1960s. Others, like *El Popular*, primarily made use of the shorter informational articles about contemporary events through the 1970s. There is little evidence that Canadian Scene had a consistent effect on the editorial policies of its subscribers let alone its readers. A more direct means of ensuring compliance from the editors involved the ability of government representatives to control and influence the purchase of advertising space. The ethnic press was not unique in its dependence on government support through advertising: most Canadian newspapers relied upon this form of indirect subsidy. Jonathan W. Rose has documented the significant role government advertising played in the development of both the Canadian advertising industry and the nation's newspapers.[77] He observes that the Canadian government has remained among the highest-spending advertisers in the nation through a number of significant changes in the structure of the relationship between the political establishment and the newspaper industry.[78]

It would, however, be a mistake to see the ethnic press as simply an echo of the mainstream English- or French-language newspapers as the industry's development has followed different trends. For mainstream papers, the major industrial trend during the first part of the twentieth century was the emergence of national newspaper chains, which provided a way for companies to save money by sharing the costs of news gathering and some kinds of administration.[79] After the war, the industry went through a period of decline resulting in cost cutting and closures while it absorbed the impact of television's rise as a medium for the distribution of news and information.[80] A very different situation unfolded among minority newspapers. The ownership and operation of newspapers in most languages was not centralized until much later, and television did not become a significant source of competition for print until the 1980s. Of greater importance to the health of a publication was the amount of time that a particular community had been in Canada, along with the level of continuing migration over the years. This was because language retention was the key determinant of readership (an issue about which the press associations made frequent inquiries and appeals to government officials).[81]

Editors faced many difficulties operating a newspaper published in a minority language, despite the rhetoric that, by citing the millions of Canadians who spoke a language other than English or French so as to indicate potential readership, was used to persuade politicians and businesses to support the ethnic press. While such figures highlighted the importance of recognizing the influence of the ethnic press on Canadian society, they gave a poor picture of the financial situation faced by individual editors and publishers. The more or less fixed number of potential readers meant that it was difficult to sustain multiple publications serving a single linguistic or cultural group in the same market unless these publications were rooted in stark religious or political divisions. Indeed, it was only the very largest of communities (Chinese, Italian, Ukrainian, Italian, German, and Jewish) that were able to support more than a single publication for an extended period of time in a single market. As a result of these limitations on the growth of the ethnic press, each publication remained relatively small in size. Aside from a handful of papers with circulations above ten thousand copies, most newspapers printed between one and four thousand copies of each issue.[82]

In order to make ends meet, most of the newspapers were operated as one of many activities in which their owners were engaged. Indeed, most of the long-surviving publications were able to navigate times of financial hardship because of the diverse activities in which publishers and editors were engaged. For example, Montreal's Alfredo Gagliardi was the editor of the *Corriere Italiano* and, later, host of the weekly television program *Teledomenica*. However, he supported his media activities through his ownership of the travel agency Italian Express as well as by offering accounting services (free with a subscription to the newspaper during tax season).[83] Some companies diversified across languages producing papers that might serve a number of different audiences. Such was the case of Winnipeg's National Publishers, which was, under the leadership of Frank Dojacek, responsible for *Der Nordwesten*, Ukrainian-language *Canadian Farmer*, and the Polish-language *Czas*.[84] However, this was not a common arrangement as the strong ties between community organizations and newspapers made it difficult for outsiders to establish a sustainable business.

With regard to the concentration of ownership, the trend towards national newspaper chains did not take root among newspapers published in languages other than English or French due to the cultural and linguistic obstacles to such expansion. A few companies produced multiple publications, but these were often different kinds of newspapers that would not be in direct competition with each other. For example, both the *Jewish Daily Eagle* and the *Canadian Jewish Chronicle* were owned by the Wolofsky family, but the *Eagle* was published in Yiddish and the *Chronicle* in English.[85] Others expanded their operations to include other titles (literary magazines, almanacs, books), and, over time, some of these would include other media, such as cinemas and television programs. Dan Iannuzzi, editor of the *Corriere Canadese*, is perhaps the most notable example of this later trend. Through Daisons Publishing, Iannuzzi published three titles serving Toronto's large Italian community and was also an investor in an Italian-language movie theatre. He later expanded into television through Daisons Multilingual Television, which produced programming in a number of different languages for Toronto's CityTV, before he became the first president of CFMT. For the most part, though, the ethnic press was made up of small publications operating in regional markets. They had small staffs and were able to survive due to loyal readerships, yet, due to the process of cultural and linguistic integration, these readerships were often in the process of disappearing.

Given these circumstances, it is not surprising that finances were a frequent problem for all but the largest titles. It was this omnipresent reality of running out of money between issues that spurred the newspapers, at first individually and later collectively, to seek out a stable source of revenue. Recognizing the opportunity that this situation presented, Z.S. (Stan) Mokrzycki's New Canadian Press (which was soon renamed New Canadian Publications) was founded in 1951 with the goal of acting as an intermediary between newspapers, governments, and major national advertisers. He was instrumental in encouraging the Ethnic Press Association of Ontario to develop stronger ties with the provincial government, which included presenting a brief to cabinet entitled "Public Relations of the Province of Ontario with New Canadians" in 1956.[86] A memo produced for the minister of citizenship and immigration in 1958 expressed concern that he was transforming the press associations into "business clubs" rather than into more civic-minded groups. He was described as follows: "Newcomer, Polish, very opportunist, has tried to use both Liberals and Conservatives. Shrewd, can be very charming."[87]

Mokrzycki took the position that the problem of establishing reliable support from government and national advertisers was one of translation rather than of market forces. In putting forward this argument, he was (perhaps unknowingly) repeating a claim made by editors of minority and foreign language papers going back decades. During the First World War, the publisher of *Der Nordwesten* lamented that advertisers avoided the newspaper out of concern that it would link them unfavourably with German culture and that the paper's editorial position and history of patriotic loyalty could do nothing to change their opinions.[88] In Mokrzycki's presentation to the first national conference of the Canada Ethnic Press Federation in 1958, he updated these sentiments for the Cold War by suggesting that the difficulties were in part due to national advertisers' concerns about supporting communist publications.[89]

Mokrzycki pursued two lines of argument in his attempt to convince advertisers to patronize the ethnic press: the first focused on major national advertisers, while the second focused on government agencies. Throughout the 1950s, Mokrzycki frequently appeared at professional meetings of the advertising industry (as well as featuring in newspaper articles about the ethnic press) to speak to the opportunity that most advertisers were missing. In 1953, he appeared at the annual meeting of the Women's Advertising Club of Toronto, where he talked about the economic power of new immigrants as well as the difficulties they faced.[90] The following year he addressed the Association of Canadian Advertisers, at which time he signalled the dangers of the foreign-funded communist press while extolling the potential of newcomers as consumers and citizens.[91]

In 1956–57, New Canadian Publications published ads in the business sections of the *Globe and Mail* and the *Toronto Star* to bring attention to its services (figure 2.3). Mokryzcki appeared in a profile of the ethnic press published in 1962, in which he again outlined the economic significance that was often being overlooked. He recalled: "At first, it was difficult to sell Canadian businessmen on the value of ethnic advertising ... They believed that most of the foreign-language newspapers, if not all of them were subversive because some of them were branded Communist ... now this problem is largely overcome."[92] In 1968, he is quoted in an article about the potential of the ethnic press saying, "All these newcomers are buying refrigerators, stoves, food, clothing, cars."[93]

Despite being neither an editor nor a publisher, Mokrzycki was one of the most prominent members of the Canada Ethnic Press Federation in its first decade. Through to the 1960s, he would insist on participating in every delegation that the national federation sent to Ottawa. There are few records regarding New Canadian Publications operations in its earliest days, but government memos from the time note that, despite the high cost of his services, Mokrzycki had secured a near monopoly on the placement of advertisements purchased by the provincial government.[94] His arrangement with the papers granted him as much as a 33 percent commission on the ads placed in those that had signed an exclusive contract with the service.[95] Over the course of the 1960s, Mokryzcki developed strong ties with the federal Liberal Party, sensing its growing interest in cultivating relationships with the ethnic press. Central to this was his relationship with Andrew Thompson, who served as

Memo to Advertising Executives

"VRAAGT DADELIJK OM VOLLEDIGE GEGEVENS"
Can you read this line?

125,000 Canadians can. They are the citizens of Dutch birth who have immigrated to this country since 1945 and who—like 1,256,000 Canadians—turn naturally to their own language in preference to English.

A recent survey by Gruneau Research showed that 8 out of 10 newcomers read no other publications but those of their own language. One in 15 Canadians is now a "New Canadian". In Toronto the figure is one in six!

Can you afford to pass by this vigorous, free-spending market?

Only New Canadian Publications can offer you full translation, placing and checking service for your advertising in 55 democratic publications, in 23 languages with an aggregate sworn circulation of 311,388.

GET THE FACTS AND FIGURES NOW!

Specialists in Foreign Language Advertising

NEW CANADIAN PUBLICATIONS
137 Wellington Street West, Toronto 1, Ont.
Telephone EM. 3-5386

Figure 2.3 An advertisement published in April 1957 in the *Globe and Mail* for Stan Mokrzycki's New Canadian Publications, offering "full translation, placing and checking service for your advertising in 55 democratic publications, in 23 languages with an aggregate sworn circulation of 311,388."

the party's liaison with ethnic communities in Toronto. In the lead up to elections in 1963 and 1965, Thompson made a case to the Liberal Party that an investment in advertising with the ethnic press could bring a significant number of voters, given the party's support for immigration.[96]

By 1961, New Canadian Publications had placed advertisements for the following companies: Air France, Bank of Montreal, Bank of Nova Scotia, Bulova Watches, Canadian Imperial Bank of Commerce, Consumers Gas, Dodds Medicine, Elias Rogers Co., Fleischmann's Yeast, Gillett's Lye, Holland America Line, Imperial Tobacco, INCO, KLM, Libby's Sauerkraut, Magic Baking Powder, Molson's Brewery, Northam Warren (maker of Cutex cosmetics), Ogilvie Flour Mills, Ontario Hydro, Penmans, the Royal Bank of Commerce, 7 Up, Seven Seas (Europe-Canada), Toronto-Dominion Bank, Volkswagen, Whitehall Labs, and MacDonald Tobacco. The company also managed advertisements for the province of Ontario's Treasury, Department of Agriculture, and Department of Commerce.[97] Mokrzycki's success in placing himself as the intermediary for this sponsorship further encouraged the shifting of power from Winnipeg to Toronto as differences between the laws regarding newspaper advertisements in the two provinces, particularly pertaining to promotions for alcohol, gave the Toronto papers greater access to lucrative advertisers than was available to their western competitors.[98]

Mokrzycki's pursuit of government advertising was markedly different from his attempts to convince national advertisers of the hidden value to be found in the newspapers serving immigrant communities. The approach to government that Mokrzycki took both in his capacity as president of New Canadian Publications and as a leading member of the Ethnic Press Association of Ontario was based upon the idea that the government owed the ethnic press a share of its annual advertising budget that was commensurate with its size and influence in the nation. In contrast to the ongoing relationship between the newspapers and the political parties, where influence over opinion was traded for revenue, the discussions with the government were articulated in the language of entitlement. To help him achieve his goal of increased advertising, Mokrzycki, until the mid-1960s, played a central role in how the Canada Ethnic Press Federation (CEPF) prepared and presented materials to government officials.[99] In each of these presentations, the fair share of advertising was clearly articulated among the demands the editors brought to the government.

Mokrzycki was not alone in articulating this argument to increase the amount of government advertising allocated to the ethnic press. A 1958 letter from CEPF secretary Karl Julius Baier to John Diefenbaker succinctly explains the situation: "I feel that the language press, the non-communist group, and I re-emphasize that, is doing a great and valuable service to Canada and also for the preservation of the democratic way of life. Believing that, I feel that every consideration should be given not only by the Department of National Defence, but by other departments of the government to preserving this press in the work it is doing, not by hand-outs or by assistance but simply by the allocation of a reasonable and fair share of national advertising."[100] The government, however, remained the largest sponsor and was essential for the survival of the ethnic press. An increase in the government's advertising budget was seen as the only way to absorb a 1968 increase in postal tariffs for bulk mail, a decision that had a much greater impact on the ethnic press than on mainstream newspapers, given the former's geographically dispersed readership and reliance on Canada Post for distribution.[101] The editors argued that the amount of advertising they received was unfair given that it did not accurately reflect their circulation in comparison with that of the major English and French newspapers.

Mokrzycki's two main competitors were both formed in early 1961. They were able to establish a foothold in the industry as a number of editors had become increasingly tired of Mokrzycki's monopoly over the allocation of advertising. Multilingual Counselling Associates was owned by R. Despotovich, who was a former employee at New Canadian Publications, and Lingua Ad Service was owned by Frank J. Kowalski, who was also its president and editor of the French-language Toronto paper *Courier-Sud*.[102] Despotovich's company was only able to survive a short while, but Lingua Ads Services continued to operate into the 1970s. This was likely due to Kowalski's success in developing close ties with Ontario's governing Progressive Conservatives, much as Mokrzycki made use of his close connection with the Liberal Party in Ottawa. Kowalski cemented this good relationship with the provincial government by assuming the position of "ethnic media consultant" in 1967.[103]

Mokrzycki and Kowalski operated for the next decade as the most powerful, yet least known, figures working in ethnic media. Their near invisibility in the public life of the country was confirmed by the scandal that surrounded public discussion of their role, which was brought to light by NDP members of the Ontario House of Commons. After an editor sympathetic to the NDP came forward to complain he was being excluded from contracts for government advertisements, the MPs denounced what they saw as an arrangement that allowed for significant amounts of provincial monies to be skimmed from transactions between the province and newspapers.[104] Kowalski in particular attracted attention given that his role in representing both the provincial government and private business interests raised concerns about conflicts of interest. Nonetheless, both men attempted to downplay their significance. "I am nobody, I am a tool," Kowalski is quoted as saying to the *Globe and Mail*. This did not mean that he missed the opportunity to express his political views, stating that he was opposed to papers that supported the New Democratic Party or the Communist Party "in a free-enterprise country."[105]

While partisan politics were never far from the agenda, another issue of long-standing concern that continued to haunt the government's engagement with the ethnic press was the threat of foreign influence. Beyond the quest to garner influence and retain power in Ottawa, the over-arching purpose of organizing and managing the ethnic press during these years was to ensure the development of foreign language newspapers as "Canadian," both culturally and economically. Strong ties with international sponsors increased the dangers of influence from international parties. This situation came to a head in the context of the two world wars, when many enemy nations were found to have had influence over the media serving immigrant populations in Canada. Italy, for example, invested in programs providing materials that would help Italians living abroad to maintain their language and identity, programs that were taken over by the fascist government and operated out of the Italian Ministry of Popular Culture.[106]

While this was rarely mentioned at the meetings of the Canada Ethnic Press Federation, it was an issue that, from time to time, was remarked upon by members of the government, who noted that, in some cases, international parties were supplying publications with both material for publication (although often carefully selected to remain apolitical) and direct subsidies. The government's insistence on supporting the ethnic press was an attempt to counteract any foreign influence by making it unpalatable both ideologically and financially. The adoption of multiculturalism as official policy would bring a great deal more money into the relationship between the government and the newspapers. The program introducing multiculturalism to the nation purchased $230,000 in advertisements (totalling approximately four full pages in most publications) during 1972–73.[107] Official multiculturalism cemented the relationship between the ethnic press, provincial and federal governments, and members of the dominant political parties.

THE MEANINGS OF "ETHNIC PRESS"

In tracing the history of the organizations that supported and served the ethnic press, it is important to recognize the role played by these groups in defining the concept of "the ethnic press" itself. At the beginning of this chapter, I note that the founding charter of the Canada Press Club explicitly excluded fascist, communist, and socialist publications from membership. This was a decision that was carried over to provincial foreign press groups. However, the framing of the Canada Press Club in relation to a specific range of political ideologies was not the only way that the meaning of the phrase "the ethnic press" as used by these provincial groups affected the kinds of inclusion that they practised. Of particular significance is how the emergence of "the ethnic press" as a term in Canadian public discourse reflected the implicit understanding of the role played by race in the reformulation of national culture in light of the emergence of multiculturalism.

This recalls comments already noted about the preference among the members of the Ethnic Press Association of Ontario for the term "ethnic" over "foreign" as a way of describing the minority press in Canada.[108] The interactions between the government and the press during these years involved a process of engagement that cannot be separated from ongoing surveillance.[109] A symptom of the intersecting practice of engagement and surveillance was the ongoing practice of list-making undertaken by representatives of the Citizenship Branch. Far from a neutral activity, the making of these lists was intimately involved in the organization of the ethnic press, not just on the page but as an institutional field in which the government might intervene. As Liam Young writes, "listing is a technique by which orientations to the world congeal as practices, systems and institutions ... [T]hey materialize assumptions and enable categorizations that follow ... [L]ists are constitutive, creating categories and subject positions for people and things, the easier to be calculated and circulated."[110] This is why it is significant that the repeated listing of newspapers according to language and nationality was supplemented by other forms of categorization that indicated membership in trade organizations (such as the CEPF), religious or political affiliation, and frequency of publication.

A list compiled in 1958 divides the press into "Non-communist Ethnic Daily, Semi-weekly and Weekly Newspapers," "Non-communist Monthly and semi-monthly publications," and "Ethnic Publications in which the Department does not advertise." A handbook prepared by the Foreign Language Press Review Service notes that it is "arranged in alphabetical order by language and names of paper," with "an appendix listing and describing the Communist ethnic press, organizational, religious, business, sports and other specialized publications."[111] Each of these taxonomies of the press highlights the way that ideology and language intersect as ways of organizing the press in advance of interaction. The effect of these practices of organizing the press was to clearly identify the field in which government advertising could be expected to have its intended effect. Language became the operative criterion for inclusion.

The importance of language as the marker for inclusion in the ethnic press was reiterated in private communications in which discussions regarding the allocation of advertising funds raised the question of how to deal with "ethnic" publications that were published in English. As part of the preparations for a reception to be held in conjunction with the annual meeting of the Canada Ethnic Press Federation in 1961, a background report discouraged inviting English-language ethnic publications. Speaking of the *Chinatown News* and the *Jewish News Bulletin*, the author explained: "To invite them would be to give them a recognition tantamount to a moral claim on departmental advertising ... If we should invite the representatives of these four papers we would be in a delicate position to refuse them advertising. And if we should ever consider opening up advertising to publications published exclusively in English, we would have to squarely face the legitimate and oft expressed claims of weekly and daily newspapers of non-ethnic origin in English and French."[112]

While not the explicit intention of this policy, the use of language served to produce a particular form of racialization that seemed to be in keeping with the "ethnic press" concept. The use of language and migration as the two key criteria for inclusion effectively excluded most publications produced by the African Canadian community. At the same time, Indigenous peoples were excluded from these debates shaping the adoption of multiculturalism as a pillar of Canadian public policy. In this way, the replacement of "foreign" with "ethnic" in discussions of the press produced a form of inclusion that aligned cultural, economic, and racial difference with popular and governmental anxieties rooted in the geopolitics of the Cold War while effacing the legacies of colonialism. The black press in Canada existed within the orbit of the ethnic press, as defined by these organizations, overlapping in many ways but kept distinct. For example, Alfred Hamilton – who would later edit *Contrast Magazine* – started his career selling advertisements for Dan Iannuzzi at the *Corriere Canadese*. Despite these connections, the long history of newspapers for African Canadians and the postwar expansion of newspapers for recently arrived migrants from the Caribbean and Africa (beginning in the late 1960s) were both overlooked because published in English or French. While the African Canadian community in Canada is heterogeneous in its origins, cultures, and languages, it remained a marginal presence within the press federations. These publications were also absent from the mailing list of Canadian Scene. For example, a list prepared in 1951 cites twenty-four "Publications in English of Foreign Racial Groups" but only mentions "Yugoslav, Ukrainian, German, Danish Icelandic and Jewish" publications.

If language became a criterion for defining the ethnic press during these years, it is also important to recognize that the development of these organizations took place alongside the emergence of Indigenous print media. Louis St Laurent merged the Indian Affairs Branch with the Nationalities Branch following the introduction of the Canadian Citizenship Act, 1947, to create the Department of Citizenship and Immigration. St Laurent justified this as an attempt "to make Canadian citizens of those who come here as immigrants and to make Canadian citizens of as many as possible of the descendants of the original inhabitants of this country."[113] Bohaker and Iacovetta have documented that, along with these educational initiatives, the department was also engaged in wide-ranging communication and information initiatives.[114] The centre of these initiatives was the publication of the *Indian News*, a monthly magazine that first appeared in August 1954 and that would continue to be published until 1982.

The kinds of materials that appeared in the *Indian News* were similar in many ways to the kinds of articles that were being circulated by Canadian Scene. The focus on citizenship training and a broader ideology that praised individualized forms of achievement are clear indications of the common ideological ground shared by discourses of citizenship targeting both Indigenous and Immigrant communities at the time. It is, however, important to recognize the fundamentally different organizational structure that supported the *Indian News*. Unlike the ethnic press, which drew its legitimacy in part from the claim that it was the product of private initiative, the *Indian News* was under the direct control of the state.

Taken together, the exclusion of Indigenous and African Canadian publications is integral to the process by which the ethnic press was defined. Structuring the ethnic press as an industry, but also as an object of public policy, contributed to the complex interaction of race, identity, and culture that grounded the emergence of multiculturalism in Canada. In this regard, it is helpful to draw on Haque's assessment of the Royal Commission on Bilingualism and Biculturalism, for whom "the need to re-articulate the formulation for nation-building and national belonging meant a decisive shift onto the terrain of language and culture for organizing and maintaining white-settler hegemony while also disavowing racial and ethnic exclusions."[115]

MULTICULTURAL FUTURISM

The definition of the ethnic press put in place did not explicitly invoke logics of racial inclusion; rather, it produced exclusion through the historical narrative it invoked when accounting for its origins. By emphasizing the importance of postwar migration, it foreclosed debates and discussion of the constitution of Canadian citizenship and national identity that would have considered their emergence in the context of colonialism. The values of liberty and freedom of expression were not universal but, rather, were framed by the fight against communism. The result of this was not just a forgetting of parts of Canadian history: it effectively allowed emergent discourses of multiculturalism to erase the legacies of colonial violence and oppression. In this way, the ideological alignment of the ethnic press during the Cold War involved a broad temporal and spatial alignment with the hegemonic forms of national culture in Canada that not only did not look back but also looked to the future.

The most visible evidence of the deployment of the ideological alignment of the ethnic press with the hegemonic temporalities of the nation is found in the participation of these organizations in public forums discussing the future of culture in Canada. The ethnic press was not alone. Across the country, there was a significant opening up of government to organizations that represented minority communities. By way of illustration, in 1951, minority communities, aside from the Jewish and Ukrainian communities, were entirely absent from the proceedings of the Massey Commission. In contrast, dozens of briefs on behalf of groups representing minority communities and immigrant support groups were submitted to the hearings of the Royal Commission on Bilingualism and Biculturalism.[116] It is no exaggeration to say that the adoption of multiculturalism was the result of these interventions, not the cause.

The importance of this involvement in government proceedings for the press associations is apparent in the commemorative volumes published by the Canada Press Club (1974), the Ethnic Press Association of Ontario (1971), and the CEPF (1985). These volumes are primarily made up of testimonies from past presidents as well as significant documents pertaining to the history of each organization. Throughout, careful attention is given to briefs and submissions made on the part of the associations to government. Nearly one hundred pages of briefs and correspondence with members of government form the final section of the CEPF's twenty-fifth anniversary publication. The rhetorical effect of this should not be overlooked as it is clearly an effort on the part of the authors to assert the legitimacy of their organizations as advocates to government on behalf of minority newspapers. Yet the significance of the submissions from the ethnic press organizations is only partly due to their symbolic importance to them. The briefs themselves provide an opportunity to consider the means by which the associations were able to advocate for their interests.

It is obvious from the outset that the relationship between the state and the ethnic press is not a meeting of equals. The state's control, albeit not always coordinated, over the postal system, advertising budgets, and even censorship meant that it retained a dominant position. The ethnic press stood as a well-established and trusted means of information distribution among new Canadians, but it had a little else with which to leverage its position in discussions about government support. On the contrary, suspicions about the loyalty and professionalism of the press undermined its legitimacy and the value of it work. In response to the inequality of this situation, the press associations sought to make use of rhetorical strategies capable of building on the undeniable demographic shifts taking place in the country. In this way, the government's recognition that increased levels of immigration following the Second World War would have a profound effect on the culture of Canada could be directed so as to recognize both the importance of the role played by the ethnic press and the value of supporting their activities.

At the heart of the appeals made by the press associations over the course of the 1960s was a discourse that could be called "multicultural futurism." This discourse built upon the implicit temporality already present in the government's approach to migration. There were effectively two timelines at play. The first of these allowed for the focus to be fixed on immigration since the end of the Second World War, effectively closing off discussion of how the history of migration was implicated in the emergence of settler colonialism and its relationship to the transatlantic slave trade. The second timeline mapped the progression from migration through education (both civic and linguistic) onto integration. There were few attempts on the part of the organizations discussed here to disrupt the logics of settler colonialism. The arc following the immigrant from arrival to settlement was appropriated by the press associations, which turned away from the assimilationist endpoint preferred by the government and towards the preservation and cultivation of cultural diversity as a new goal of Canadian society. However, this did not challenge the nation's broader involvement in racialization.

In its embrace of multicultural futurism, the language of the press associations can be situated in relation to the broader interest in future-oriented modes of social and cultural analysis taking place during the period, such as the rise of future studies, or futurology. The rise of future studies is deeply rooted in the Cold War period, drawing on global anxieties about nuclear war and increasingly rapid advances in technology.[117] Multicultural futurism adds the cultural and economic effects of global migration into this mix. The temporality of multicultural futurism turned the established understanding of the relationship between heritage, identity, and migration on its head. Rather than being something that should be left in the past, multicultural futurism argued for the importance of bringing one's identity into the future as a contribution to a newly imagined national community. While the activities of the organizations remained focused on more prosaic matters related to political influence, the daily challenges of running a publication, and the need for stable financing, the public statements made throughout the 1960s draw upon the trope of the multicultural future as a means of both justifying and engaging the Canadian political and business establishment. The origins of this seem to lie with the distinction made by members of the group, most prominently Stan Mokrzycki, between "old" and "new" migrants as a way of distinguishing the wave of immigrants who entered the country following the Second World War. This was the theme of many of the presentations he made throughout the 1950s, including in a brief to the government of Ontario. However, Mokrzycki's vision of the future was limited to its commercial aspects, as made clear in the copy of an advertisement for New Canadian Publications from 1957: "You must sell them NOW, while their buying habits are forming."[118]

A broader vision came to be articulated by the press associations in their presentations before various public hearings over the course of the 1960s, specifically to the Royal Commission on Publications in 1961, the Royal Commission on Bilingualism and Biculturalism in 1965, and the Senate Committee on Mass Media in 1970. Walter Lindal, the founding president of the Canada Press Club, was the leading figure when it came to encouraging the press groups to appear at government hearings, and he served as the spokesperson for the group on these matters. Lindal's visibility in this process is not surprising given his history with the Manitoba Liberal Party and his continued connections to the federal Liberal Party. Blanding argues that Lindal was an important voice in the development of a language supporting multiculturalism in Canada, through his public work with various organizations, his speaking engagements, and his private correspondence with like-minded individuals such as Senator Paul Yuzyk.[119]

However, the presentations he made to royal commissions in the 1960s do not so much provide a clear picture of his commitment to multiculturalism as insight into the complex context the ethnic press faced during these years. This is indicative of both the emergence of a need to open up the nation's public life to greater diversity and the precarious support for multiculturalism in a period that continued to be defined by the anti-communist anxieties of the Cold War. Yet, returning to the briefs and the appearance of the associations at these hearings, one can see the futurist orientation of multiculturalism taking shape. The common agenda across these interventions was a future-oriented perspective that enabled people to move beyond concerns about the patriotism and loyalty of the ethnic press in order to more forcefully advocate for greater recognition of the nation's multicultural make-up within a bilingual framework.

In his initial remarks before the Royal Commission on Publications, Lindal began by outlining the role of the ethnic press as "an agency of value in citizenship building" while asking for "recognition" and "enlightenment."[120] By "recognition," Lindal meant "recognition of the value of the service being rendered by the ethnic press."[121] In terms of "enlightenment," he asked the commission to encourage "the dissemination of information on the ethnic press."[122] It is a measured attempt to put forward a view that, while recognizing the role the ethnic press plays in the integration of newcomers, holds that it deserves broader acknowledgment of how it contributes to Canada in ways that go beyond its instrumental purpose. This is most clearly summed up in the final paragraph of Lindal's remarks: "It is good for Canada that it is bilingual. It is also good for Canada that during the decades, when the Canadian identity is being developed, an ethnic press exists which broadens the outlook, softens tendencies towards exclusiveness, helps create a unity in variety. Perhaps it will help the Canadian nation to fit into its destined place in the multilingual one world of today."[123] In its final flourish, this turn towards the future marks a break from the notion that the ethnic press should exist as a bridge to the dominant cultures, suggesting that cultural and linguistic variety should be encouraged to persist as a permanent feature of the nation.

The import of Lindal's presentation was, however, muted by its context. Followed by a presentation from Charles Dojack, who spoke in his capacity as owner of National Publications, the focus of the discussion returned to the difficulties of running "language papers" and the need for greater support from the government.[124] Dojack's requests, however, were quickly reframed according to anxieties about patriotism. Drawing attention to the use of prefabricated material produced by foreign-based publishers, he called for a stop to a practice that he believed allowed for unfair competition with Canadian publications.[125] Lindal's address, while praised as being "a very splendid and eloquent presentation," was overlooked in the questions asked by the commissioners, who were particularly interested in the economic and political implications of newspapers printing material produced outside of Canada.[126] Drawing the commissioners' attention to an issue of *Der Zeit*, Dojack highlighted an advertisement for Germany's military service that he saw as particularly worrisome.[127] The presentation from National Publishers had clearly made an impact as, during the presentation of the Ethnic Press Association of Ontario to the commission a few weeks later, one of the commissioners followed up by asking about material coming from the "East German Republic."[128] The commissioner's question transposed the material Dojack cited, which actually originated in West Germany, into something that implied communist influence.

Lindal's appearance before the Royal Commission on Bilingualism and Biculturalism a few years later returned to similar themes. Concerned about the possible outcomes of the commission for members of the nation's cultural and linguistic minorities, Lindal wrote to his successor at the CEPF, Bruno Tenhunen. He urged Tenhunen to encourage the CEPF to participate in the hearings as he was worried that a decision to codify the nation's bilingual and bicultural status in too rigid a fashion "would relegate all other languages to a very secondary position."[129] Lindal very quickly sent along a resolution to be adopted by the CEPF, which passed at the next general meeting in Toronto, that stated: "Canada is multicultural, a unity in variety, which will enrich our distinctive Canadian identity."[130] Similar themes would form the main contribution of the Canada Ethnic Press Federation's presentation. "Unity with diversity must be accepted as a basic principle of Canada ... It is not difficult for anyone to agree that in Canada there must be 'unity with diversity,' but it is more difficult to give meaning to those words. Here it seems necessary to add or insert another word. The diversity must be constructive not divisive; it must not mar the essential overall unity."[131] Importantly, Lindal follows up his defence of diversity by charging the nation's cultural minorities with the task of bringing this new national compact into existence. He writes: "It is not open to either of the parties of the original pact to make unilateral change. Through immigration the original terms have been modified but the purpose of that variant is to add strength and provide additional hue and color to a tripartite national entity."[132] Lindal once more concludes, invoking the potential of Canada's diverse future: "If out of this heterogeneous mass of opposites, clashes, seeming impossibilities, there emerges a united democracy, an example will be set for the world, an example which, in the present state of international tension, it greatly needs."[133]

In her history of the Royal Commission on Bilingualism and Biculturalism's attempt to find a path towards multiculturalism within a bilingual framework, Haque emphasizes that the CEPF, as "one of the largest representatives of other ethnic groups," was a significant voice in favour of multiculturalism.[134] However, the representations made on behalf of the ethnic press reveal a more complex set of interests than such a description suggests. The Canada Ethnic Press Federation brief submitted to the commission outlined many of the points regarding the central importance of Canada's bilingual history and national unity alongside strong support for "unity in diversity," which Lindal had already presented to the Commission on Publications four years earlier. However, it was not as explicit in its embrace of multiculturalism and the necessary importance of maintaining the nation's diversity as was the earlier brief. Though central, this softening of the emphasis on cultural diversity may have been in part because the brief was co-signed by the Manitoba branch of the Royal Commonwealth Society, a group more committed to the "spiritual values" of the commonwealth than to the broader linguistic and cultural diversity of the ethnic press.[135]

Interestingly, the national federation's presentation was accompanied by a shorter presentation from the Canada Press Club, which presented itself as the local branch of the national organization. Where Lindal's presentation highlighted the constitutional and cultural importance of supporting "unity in variety," the Press Club's presentation emphasized the importance of recognizing the ways in which minorities across the nation also experienced discrimination. The background papers prepared by the commission staff stated that the difference between the two groups was that the national federation had become more "political," while the Winnipeg branch "purport[ed] its main concern to be the service of the ethnic communication, especially those 'Canadian-born.'"[136] It is unclear where this distinction comes from or how accurate it is, but the difference between the two groups highlights a difference in views regarding the need to advocate for multiculturalism before the Royal Commission on Bilingualism and Biculturalism.

By the late 1960s, multicultural futurism became part of the broader generational shift taking place in the Liberal Party, personified by the rise to power (and popularity) of Pierre Elliott Trudeau. Indeed, Trudeau's campaign offered a heavy dose of future-oriented rhetoric, positioning him as the "man of tomorrow."[137] In the words of a biography from this time: "Trudeau exerts a strong symbolic appeal as a forerunner of what the true Canadian of the future may be – completely bilingual and bicultural, combining Gallic verve and charm with English hard-headedness, and espousing multi-nationalism unconcerned with petty nationalist emotions."[138] Trudeau himself would occasionally adopt the voice of multiculturalism, albeit transposing its speculative appeals into the actualization of his own government. This is perhaps most clearly expressed in his pronouncement that, "by an historic accident, Canada has found itself approximately seventy-five years ahead of the rest of the world in the formation of a multinational state and I happen to believe that the hope of mankind lies in multinationalism."[139]

CONCLUSION: POWER AND CONTROL OF THE ETHNIC PRESS IN THE AGE OF MULTICULTURALISM

The literature on the ethnic press often positions it as a bridge between the customs and culture of an immigrant's country of origin and the customs and culture of his or her new home. Much of this research views the ethnic press as contributing to the public sphere, although more recent work has challenged the notion of a unified space for public debate in favour of a more fragmented view of "sphericules" or a "multi-ethnic public sphere."[140] To cite one frequently mentioned definition that has also been used by researchers regarding their work on ethnocultural media, the public sphere "is the space between Government and society in which private individuals exercise formal and informal control over the state: formal control through the election of governments and informal control through the pressure of public opinion."[141] Such an approach to ethnocultural media emphasizes their location within civil society and their capacity to amplify the voices of local community members otherwise excluded from the institutions of mainstream media.

The efforts to organize, represent, and influence the ethnic press after the Second World War bring to light the role of the government in the evolution of the ethnic press during the decades leading up to the adoption of official multiculturalism. This history complicates analyses of the ethnocultural press and the public sphere by highlighting the role played by the state (and para-state) agencies in its activities. This is not to discredit the efforts and activities of the many members of the ethnic press who struggled to serve their communities in the decades following the war; rather, it is to highlight the fact that the construction of the postwar public sphere rested, in part, upon the establishment and activities of organizations such as those discussed in this chapter, many of which bridge the divide between the state and community media. In this sense, the organizations discussed in this chapter served as an essential part of the cultural infrastructure of state multiculturalism in the years leading up to its adoption as an official goal of Canadian public policy in 1971. The efforts to organize and influence the ethnic press after the Second World War were an extension of the involvement of liberal democratic states in cultural production as part of a broader program of ideological governance linked to the geopolitics of the Cold War. Yet, as is noted in this chapter, the Cold War engagement with the ethnic press cannot be separated from the longer history of anxieties concerning the patriotism of minorities in North America – a history in which censorship was the most frequent mode of intervention, even though less restrictive modes were also available.

This chapter shows that it would be a mistake to view the evolving relationship between the ethnic press and the state as instrumental, as one in which control over the activities of the press were appropriated by the state itself. Yet it would also be a mistake to view the role played by the ethnic press during these years as being the result of the machinations of an invisible hand structuring the marketplace of ideas. Rather, it was a product of the modes of direct and indirect institutional intervention that defined the interaction between the state and civil society during the period now seen as defined by the "welfare state." From the vantage point of several decades later, it is possible to see how this particular arrangement served to promote an agenda in support of the establishment of state multiculturalism. However, it is also possible to see how this arrangement gave rise to a number of critiques regarding the limitations on the expression and visibility of diversity in Canada.

Self-regulation played a key role in shaping the actions and agenda of both the government and the press. It is perhaps not surprising that, given the legal and economic threats that government agencies were able to wield, editors and publishers policed their behaviours in order to ensure that they did not break with the expectations of the state. However, it is essential to recognize that the government's power was limited and that it had to act within limits. It was not able to assert direct control, being bounded by the constitutional and political limitations that protected freedom of expression in the Cold War context. The radical press could be silenced, but it was more difficult to intervene directly in the operation of more mainstream papers. This ideological project transformed the press itself, but it did not transform it into a loudspeaker for the government's message; rather, control came to be replaced with engagement as both sides espoused an emergent state multiculturalism.[142]

3

Format: Inventing Multilingual Radio in Canada

CHIN-AM, only the second radio station to be licensed with "new Canadians" as its primary audience, moved its transmission towers from their original site at the western edge of Toronto to the northern suburb of Willowdale in the summer of 1967. Residents in the area started to complain almost immediately that the station's signal interfered with radio and television reception in their homes. When it disrupted the local CBC television station during the Stanley Cup playoffs, an article in the *Toronto Star* later that year noted that "CHIN is still trying to live down the impression its bouncing Greek music and Italian commercials made upon hockey fans then."[1] The neighbourhood newspaper, the *Willowdale Enterprise*, covered the story over the following months and encouraged readers who encountered any problems with their reception to contact the station directly for service.[2] Following another public incident involving crossed signals, the *Enterprise* published a cartoon showing a parson at the local United Church being drowned out by a sound system taken over by an advertisement for pasta, a sly reference to CHIN president Johnny Lombardi's grocery and food importing business.[3]

Media coverage of CHIN's technical problems with its transmitters – soon remedied thanks to actions by the broadcaster and the Department of Transportation – is symptomatic of the broader cultural impact of multilingual radio's growth in Canada at the time. Although it would later switch to third-language programming, CHIN broadcast almost exclusively in English at this time. The emphasis on "bouncing Greek music and Italian commercials" disrupting the Stanley Cup playoffs and a church service suggests that the mix-up with the transformer was registered practically for a small number of listeners and symbolically for a much larger audience. The other-ness of the music and the advertisements noted in the article (which, again, would likely have been in English) suggests that the discontent with the station inscribes a broader concern and anxiety about the changes taking place in Canada (or at least Toronto) during these years. The interruption of the Stanley Cup playoffs serves as a metonym for the public debate taking shape around identity and culture in the nation.

The anecdote echoes the way in which Canadian broadcasting is often discussed in terms of how it was mobilized in support of national culture. Calling this broader project "Canadianization," Ryan Edwardson describes these debates as belonging to "a paradigm in which nation-builders tried to use culture to imprint a sense of nationhood."[4] The push to include a greater diversity of cultures and languages on Canadian radio, which is the focus of this chapter, takes place in the context of this process of Canadianization but differs significantly from the more frequently discussed concerns about cultural imports from the United States. As the number of immigrants arriving in Canada increased following the Second World War, discussions took place about the need and feasibility of establishing new broadcast services that would reach a wider range of ethnocultural communities. Yet there remained concerns that these new services would impede the ability of recent arrivals to integrate into Canadian society or that they might even displace the cultural practices embraced by the English and French mainstream. In other words, the debate circled around the question of how, and in some cases whether, both CHIN and the Stanley Cup playoffs could coexist on Canadian airwaves.

Linguistic diversity on Canadian radio was not a new phenomenon: there are records going back to the 1930s of listeners in many parts of the country who tuned into programs in languages other than English or French. It was not uncommon for people to listen to broadcasts in languages they did not speak not knowing the origin of the transmission.[5] Many of these programs were produced by stations based in the United States, while others were found on the shortwave band from around the world.[6] As for programs broadcast from Canada, there are indications that some stations north of the border would rebroadcast programs in other languages from the US.[7] There were also a few programs produced locally. For example, the "Jewish Radio Hour," produced by newspaper publisher and travel agent Dorothy Dworkin, was broadcast across southern Ontario in Yiddish beginning in 1936.[8] Following the introduction of the Defence of Canada Regulations in 1939, a blanket ban on broadcasts in foreign languages was implemented, and it continued until after the Second World War.[9] Many of the US-based programs also disappeared during the war as concerns grew about the use of international radio as a propaganda tool.[10]

Although restrictions were loosened after the war, no explicit framework governing programing in languages other than English or French was introduced.[11] This created the peculiar situation in which "foreign language" programs, or simply "language" programs as they were sometimes called, were produced and broadcast by Canadian stations even though it remained unclear whether or not they were permitted. It was not until 1963 that such broadcasts were explicitly mentioned in the Broadcast Act (and a systematic framework governing third-language broadcasting was not adopted until 1985).[12] The cultural and linguistic opening up of radio broadcasting did not take place through policy reform; rather it took place in a piecemeal fashion thanks to the initiative of broadcasters and individual producers, and it was supported by means of ad hoc adjustments that, over decades, regulators made on a case-by-case by basis.

As with the newspapers discussed in the previous chapter, the federal and provincial governments encouraged the use of radio to support the education and integration of new Canadians. However, beginning in the 1950s, the development of multilingual radio involved a fundamentally different set of government concerns than did the development of the ethnic press. There is little evidence of official interest in examining whether monthly, bi-weekly, or daily media were best suited to spreading information to immigrants, let alone in determining which genres common to mid-century journalism were most effective for communicating messages designed to support the government's program of "Canadianism." By contrast, the evolution of "foreign language" radio in Canada involved extensive discussions about the forms and genres that were appropriate for informing, educating, and entertaining recent immigrants as well as long-time Canadians who spoke languages other than English or French.

The level of detail found in these deliberations was due, in part, to the differences between how the press was regulated and how broadcasting was regulated. The public forums discussing the operation of broadcasters did not exist for print media. However, it would be a mistake to believe that the development of radio in Canada wholly conformed to the interests of the government or the needs of the state. The state's political and cultural agenda competed with the interests of private broadcasters, whose primary concerns remained attracting audiences and advertisers even when couched in the language of community service and public responsibility. Because of this, many of the forms of autonomy that were produced in the relationship between newspapers and the state can also be observed in the relationship between radio broadcasters and the state, albeit with significant qualifications.

Because broadcasters were oriented towards the commercial market, the government's attempts to shape radio offerings in languages other than English or French were tempered and transformed by the reorganization of the radio industry taking place at the time. Among the most significant elements of this reorganization was the move towards "formats," which involved broadcasters adopting clearly defined genres of music and programs.[13] Formats were appealing not only because of the economic and operational advantages arising from the standardization of a station's operation but because they improved the efficiency with which audiences navigated the radio dial when searching for a station that suited their tastes.[14] The formatting of the radio industry was more pronounced in the United States than in Canada, where the prominence of general interest programming on the CBC, the most widely available broadcaster in the country, counter-balanced the transition to clearly defined formats among private broadcasters. Nonetheless, Canadian radio – particularly in highly populated regions served by multiple stations – followed a similar path to its US counterparts in that it tended towards market differentiation.

During the time period under consideration, the most significant development both culturally and organizationally for multicultural radio is the transition from individual programs broadcast by English or French language radio stations, many of which leased time ("brokered programming," in industry parlance), to the licensing of dedicated multicultural and multilingual stations. I follow the creation of multilingual and multicultural radio stations, showing how this process involved the formatting of cultural diversity for Canadian broadcasting. Given the range of interests involved in shaping minority media, it is not surprising that there were significant disagreements about what this radio would sound like. Which languages should be spoken on air and in what proportion? How much music and from which genres? A number of competing views were presented in the attempt to answer these questions, ranging from those who advocated for broadcasts entirely in languages other than English or French to those who were concerned that the use of any language other than the country's two official languages would impede the process of integration and assimilation.

By the end of the 1960s, most of these questions had been resolved either in practical terms through the decisions of station managers or through policies. What emerged was a format for ethnocultural radio in Canada that was privately owned, commercial, and explicitly multilingual rather than multicultural. Tracing the emergence of this format effectively traces the generic infrastructure through which the growing cultural and linguistic diversity of the Canadian population was integrated into the broadcasting system. This format was neither natural nor necessary in its constitution; rather, it was the result of a series of specific decisions and actions. It could be described as an industrial rationalization of identity that took place through the development of the multilingual and multicultural format in radio. I argue that the development of this format as the primary means by which multicultural and multilingual broadcasts were made available to Canadian audiences had significant outcomes. The first of these is that the format ensured that ethnocultural programming was designed in a way that would appeal to advertisers. The second is that it allowed for the distinction between ownership and self-expression, putting forward the idea that radio represented but was not owned by members of a particular cultural or linguistic community. This later outcome is particularly significant as it established an arrangement that allowed for the centralization of the ownership of ethnocultural media that, in the 1990s and 2000s, covered all media even as it allowed for a greater diversity of languages and cultures to be seen and heard.

In order to make sense of the context within which the formatting of ethnocultural radio emerged, I first document the emergence of radio that was created for listeners who spoke languages other than English or French following the loosening of wartime controls on "foreign" programming. This situates broadcasts in non-official languages within the context of the government's wartime broadcast efforts, specifically the *Canadians All* series and the later "Continental" radio format. *Canadians All,* broadcast by the

CBC, and "Continental" programs, broadcast in English by private broadcasters but targeting minority listeners, were both attempts to respond to the desire for radio programs that would speak to ethnocultural communities while assuaging concerns about too much time being given over to "other" languages and cultures.

In the second part of the chapter I focus on the licensing of the first generation of multilingual radio broadcasters beginning in the 1960s. I follow the licensing of the first two multicultural stations in Canada: CFMB in Montreal and CHIN radio in Toronto. The creation of these stations brings into focus the transition from the partial, semi-official opening of the airwaves to third-language programming towards the establishment of broadcasters that were expressly created to serve cultural and linguistic minorities. If individual programs raised the question of how much time should be given over to non-official languages, the obstacles encountered in the process of the licensing of these broadcasters made it clear that the Canadian airwaves were – at least according to the law – strictly bilingual. The official licensing of broadcasters oriented towards serving ethnocultural minorities, a process that started in 1957, led to the establishment of a new class of broadcaster that, strictly speaking, was neither English nor French but multilingual. The creation and development of this class of broadcasters marked the formal integration of broadcasting that served cultural and linguistic minorities with Canadian cultural nationalism, which coincided with Trudeau's adoption of multiculturalism.

In the third section of the chapter, which echoes my earlier discussion of New Canadian Publications and its efforts to rationalize and develop the ethnic press as a market for major national advertisers, I look into the problem of representing the multilingual audience as consumers. The formatting of the radio industry coincided with the growing importance of audience ratings. If debates about language were the major concern of government officials, the primary concern of broadcasters was commercial viability. Both formats and ratings were involved in the task of establishing standards that would streamline how radio could be used by advertisers to reach consumers. However, third-language broadcasters were outspoken critics of the status quo. Johnny Lombardi, president of CHIN, repeatedly denounced the prominence of audience ratings in the industry as biased against broadcasters that served minority audiences. However, it is not just his critique of audience metrics that is worthy of attention but the ways in which he went about countering their hegemony in the industry. Turning from statistics to street fairs and picnics, Lombardi pioneered the use of community events as a tool for promoting minority media to advertisers. The use of such events became an important technique through which, in the attempt to commodify the audience, community organizing came to serve as an effective alternative to audience surveys.

As is apparent throughout this chapter, there were significant similarities between the development of "language radio" and the "ethnic press," particularly given their role in education programs instigated by the state. Yet the regulatory context made discussions about the "feel" of third-language broadcasting significantly different from what happened with regard to the press. Given that broadcasters understood their independence very differently than did editors and publishers, these two groups did not articulate questions of autonomy from the state in the same way. This is not to say that they were not present but, rather, that radio's alignment with entertainment gave rise to a different way of thinking about independence and autonomy. In this context, editorial independence was explicitly expressed in the language of audience appeal and the demands of the market rather than in a more lofty discussion about the value of the liberal public sphere, which is what governed many interactions between the state and publishers.

CANADIANS ALL

As has been shown, the Canadian government's interest in encouraging immigrants to adopt the cultural and political norms of the country's political elite expanded significantly during the Second World War and intensified during the Cold War. The activities of the Canada Press Club and other intermediaries representing or serving the ethnic press were but one aspect of these efforts. It was in the context of the Canadian government's evolving public information initiatives that the Nationalities Branch collaborated with the CBC on the production of the radio series *Canadians All* and commissioned a pamphlet of the same name written by Watson Kirkconnell. Nearly 400,000 copies of this pamphlet were printed.[15] The program and the pamphlet highlighted the themes of national unity through a discussion of the contributions of European immigrants to Canadian society.[16] The project's goals were framed in relation to the danger of a divided population in the face of the Nazi threat. An article in the *Globe and Mail* recounting Prime Minister King's comments broadcast after the final episode of the series makes explicit the program's relationship to the war effort, noting King praised it for how "speakers of different races had disavowed and denounced the evil doctrines of racial hate and racial superiority."[17]

Canadians All was inspired in part by a series that had been produced in the United States with the similar title of *Americans All*, but it was also informed by Kirkconnell's earlier participation in the production of *Ventures in Citizenship*, a series that was intended to educate new arrivals about citizenship and that was broadcast on the eve of the Second World War.[18] Kirkconnell, like Walter J. Lindal, belonged to the group of experts that had been drawn from the ranks of Canada's universities and whom the government had approached to lead outreach efforts in minority communities during the war.[19] Originally a scholar of Milton, Kirkconnell was a member of the English department at Wesley College (later amalgamated into the University of Winnipeg). Having travelled extensively in Eastern Europe before the war, he had made a name for himself as a translator of Eastern European languages through the collections of poetry he had edited in Hungarian, Polish, and Ukrainian.[20] He also compiled the anthology *Canadian Overtones*, which gathered together translations of poems written by Canadians in a number of European languages.[21] Through his travels and publications, Kirkconnell developed a network of contacts among the Polish and Ukrainian communities of Canada, in particular. By the 1940s, the government viewed him as a trusted expert on Eastern Europe and he was called upon to give a number of public statements and radio addresses regarding the effects of the war in that region.[22] Kirkconnell recalls in his memoir that he "was frequently made the voice of Canada's public conscience" during these years and that he "averaged one hundred public addresses a year, most of them on political issues and in defence of the European-Canadian communities in Canadian life."[23]

Having been involved in meetings with government officials as far back as December 1940 regarding their efforts to involve recent immigrants in Canada's war effort, Kirkconnell was offered the position of director at the Nationalities Branch when its first director, G.W. Sampson, was forced to leave due to illness. He declined the offer because, in his words, "as a civil servant such a director would be completely gagged and could neither speak nor write on public affairs. I foresaw that I could probably guard the rights and welfare of New Canadians much better as a free agent."[24] Throughout this period, though, Kirkconnell was among the more prominent members of the emergent bureaucratic intelligentsia whose responsibilities involved what Caccia describes as "managing the mosaic."[25]

Kirkconnell's *Canadians All* can be seen as a contribution to early experiments in how to acknowledge and represent cultural diversity through Canadian media – experiments that took shape beginning in the late 1930s. An extension of Kirkconnell's ardent anti-communism, his proto-multiculturalist ideas were based upon a belief that the strongly individualistic values he saw as essential to Canadian public life would always moderate the dangers of excessive communalism that might result from an allegiance to one's heritage.[26] Religious affiliation was to be encouraged – Kirkconnell himself was deeply involved in the Baptist Church of Canada – as long as these affiliations did not overwhelm the individual's ability to think and choose freely according to his or her own personal moral code.[27] Despite Kirkconnell's commitment to individualism, the goal of *Canadians All* was integration and assimilation or, in the words of the pamphlet he penned, the "permanent unification of all our groups in one, strong resolute nation."[28] This unification did not require abandoning one's culture and traditions – as long as they did not prevent one from contributing to the social and economic well-being of the nation. Like Walter Lindal's desire to ensure that the ethnic press remained committed to values of liberal democracy, Kirkconnell's elaboration of multiculturalism was deeply embedded in the context of the war against fascism on the homefront and, later, the Cold War.

Canadians All spoke with the voice of the nation's institutions. It was commissioned by the Secretary of State in collaboration with the CBC and the National Film Board. Its relationship to the Canadian political and cultural establishment is even evident in the program's format. While recognizing the contribution of the nation's largest cultural and linguistic minorities, the program was entirely scripted in English. Interviews with prominent Canadians of various backgrounds who had made contributions to politics, culture, or industry were also conducted in English.[29] The approach adopted in *Canadians All* was informed by the politics of immigration that was prevalent in Canada during the Second World War. Even as the number of new arrivals dropped to historically low levels, anxieties about prewar immigrants – particularly Germans and Italians – increased dramatically.[30] The result was a program *about* new Canadians more than a program *for* new Canadians. The extent to which *Canadians All* was successful in reaching individuals who did not speak English as a first language is unknown. And, unlike newspapers, where success and failure could be measured (at least indirectly) through circulation numbers or the waxing and waning of advertising revenue, there is little information about the program's audience since the CBC did not collect audience data until after the war. Circumstantially, occasional references in English-language papers suggest that the series was more successful in reaching individuals who already identified with English Canadian culture than in improving how new arrivals viewed Canada.

The broadcast of *Canadians All* came to an end in the Spring of 1941, although there is evidence that the ideas behind the series continued to have influence into the postwar period. A profile of "language programs" on Canadian radio makes mention of a series on "Canadian Citizenship" produced by the Imperial Order Daughters of the Empire, an initiative that belongs to the efforts by organizations made up primarily of English Canadian elites seeking to help new arrivals (like Canadian Scene, discussed in the previous chapter).[31] The article also mentions a series called *Citizens All* that was produced by CJSP in Leamington and that was designed to attract new Canadian listeners and educate them about life in Canada.[32] An article from 1958 outlining the efforts made to reach new Canadians by Toronto's CFRB explains that CFRB did not carry foreign language programming. "We have one rigid policy," said the promotion manager of CFRB in Toronto, "and that is we do not broadcast in a foreign language. We feel that no matter what the original nationality of the listener, one of his prime interests is to learn English, and not to hear his mother tongue. Also, we feel that an English-speaking listener almost reflexively reaches for the dial when he hears a foreign language being spoken." Like *Canadians All,* these programs consisted primarily (if not exclusively) of English-language material and presented themselves as helping new arrivals to improve their language skills while learning about Canadian laws and culture.

Yet even before the war had ended there was growing interest in loosening the restrictions on broadcasting in languages other than English or French, especially if the programs could be used to bolster patriotic sentiment and reduce the risk of alienation among communities that had been targets of wartime xenophobia.[33] However, there was less agreement over the kind of programming that could best accomplish this goal. A survey of "language programs" published in *Canadian Broadcaster and Telescreen Magazine* in August 1955 provides an overview of the various formats that were developing and the motivations behind them (Figure 3.1).[34] Claiming that "policy rather than pocket-book decides whether stations will produce any foreign language shows at all," the article explains that it was the beliefs of owners and station managers regarding how best to reach and encourage the integration of new Canadians that determined the type of programming that would be put on air. The article goes on to explain the range of policies put in place regarding the broadcasting of languages other than English or French. These cover a number of formats and styles, from the policy adopted by CKFH in Toronto that all programs serving minorities include at least 60 percent English-language material to CHML in Hamilton, Ontario, and CJOY in Guelph, Ontario, where the amount of foreign language is limited to no more than one minute at a time (and, in the case of CHML, to no more than five minutes per hour).[35] Other stations, such as CHUM in Toronto, where the top and tail of each "ethnic" hour was dedicated to English-language material, developed other formulas.

The explosion of program formats that took place during the 1950s coincided with a significant increase in the volume of programming in other languages. In 1955, as part of its submission to the Royal Commission on Broadcasting led by Robert Fowler, the Canadian Association of Radio and Television Broadcasters (CARTB) compiled a report on the activities of its members. Among the information presented in the report was a survey documenting the number of hours broadcast in languages other than English or French. Of the forty-five members who responded to the survey, twenty-eight said that they programmed some kind of "language" broadcast, although this included stations that offered English-language programs in predominantly francophone parts of the country outside of Quebec and French-language programs in predominantly anglophone communities.[36] Three years later, CARTB organized another survey of its membership. The rate of response was much higher this time, with 101 of 147 members responding, of which fifty-four responded in the affirmative when asked whether or not they broadcast programs in languages other than English or French.[37]

Figure 3.1 Cover of *Canadian Broadcaster and Telescreen Magazine*, 17 August 1955, showing a meeting between Bill Hall, supervisor of specialized programming at CHML in Hamilton, Ontario, with the producers responsible for the station's Dutch, Italian, Polish, Ukrainian, and Continental programs.

A report in *Sponsor* magazine published in August 1958 described the significant increase in the amount of programming in various languages: "On the basis of this survey, the CARTB found a total of 44 hours weekly of Italian programming, almost double the amount in 1955; 36 hours of German programming, almost triple the amount in 1955; 15 hours of Ukrainian programming compared to 11 in 1955; 10 hours of Polish programming, a slight increase over three years ago; eight hours of Hungarian shows, compared to only one hour in 1955; seven hours of Dutch shows, an increase of four hours over 1955."[38] The overview concludes by noting that this marks an increase of eighty-two hours in the three years since the previous survey was conducted, with the majority of this growth taking place in Ontario and Quebec (with fifty-seven more hours than the previous survey) and a smaller amount of growth in western Canada (an increase of twenty hours). The number of hours broadcast in other languages would continue to grow over the next decade. By 1966, there were nearly 210 hours of programming broadcast with more than half of these hours broadcast in Ontario and a quarter of the total broadcast in Quebec.[39] The distribution across languages remained roughly constant during this period, with Italian-language programming making up by far the largest number of program hours at nearly eighty-eight hours a week (again, mostly concentrated in Ontario and Quebec) followed by German at thirty-three hours. Ukrainian (twenty-six hours) and Greek (twenty-three hours) made up the next largest blocks.[40]

However, "language" programs were not the only attempts to make listeners of recent immigrants. The 1955 *Canadian Broadcaster* article goes on to note the emergence of a new format, known colloquially as "Continental," in which "the announcer speaks English only, but in a heavy though perceptible foreign accent."[41] The Continental format is one of the more interesting, if mostly forgotten, experiments in multicultural broadcasting to have taken place on Canadian radio. These programs were primarily music-oriented, although they did include local news and some commentary. The music itself consisted primarily of light instrumental and popular classical music that could be identified with various European countries. Continental programs were common, for example, at CFRB in Toronto. While foreign language programming was absent from the station, a half-hour program entitled *Continental Concert* and hosted by Walter Kanitz was broadcast six nights a week (Sunday to Friday) beginning in 1953.[42] The program is described as playing "the very latest versions of European selections," which Kanitz purchased himself "direct from Europe."[43] Kanitz was described as "the true continental; been everywhere, done everything; an author and writer, even a Foreign Legionnaire at one time."[44] The station's program manager explained his appeal: "He seems to cut through international borders and maintain an interest among a variety of nationalities."[45] Kanitz also collaborated with the Toronto-based advertising firm S.W. Caldwell on the production of "Continental Echoes" – a thirty-minute program described as originating "from a mythical European concert hall" – and "Continental Magazine," featuring five-minute vignettes selected by Kanitz, which were designed for national syndication.[46]

CFRB was not unique in embracing the Continental style. In Edmonton during the mid-1950s, CHED broadcast a program called *Continental Bandstand* for which both the recordings and program notes were supplied by "a small European shop" and sponsored by "a local organization."[47] There was an Italian-language program called "La Continentale" on CJMS in Montreal beginning in the mid-1950s.[48] By the mid-1960s, Southern Manitoba Broadcasting, operating both CFAM in Steinbach and CHMS in Altona, adopted a format that included fourteen and a half hours of "ethnic ... or cosmopolitan programming" that included Continental music (including a program called *Continental Melodies*).[49] Canada was not unique in its experiments with Continental radio and music. In the United States, bandleader Percy Faith's first full-length album was titled *Percy Faith Plays Continental Music*. Released in 1953, it featured a selection of pop classical selections such as "Under the Bridges of Paris" and "April in Portugal." The Australian popular music historian John Whiteoak documents the circulation of Continental music in Australia prior to the embrace of multiculturalist discourse in the 1970s, where it served as a way of describing a mixture of genres, including Samba, Italian popular music, and Latin American jazz.[50] The "Continental style" of music drew upon the connotations of Old World prestige and glamour, markedly different from the discourse of cultural and economic integration that surrounded the activities of groups like the Imperial Order of Daughters of the Empire. It presented popular forms of music that were already legitimized, effacing the experience of working-class migrants in favour of misty memories of Europe's major landmarks

Figure 3.2 *Percy Faith Plays Continental Music*, Columbia (1953).

and an air of Old-World sophistication. The background of *Percy Faith Plays Continental Music* is emblematic in this regard, with tiny icons of major European landmarks circling a woman wearing diamond earrings and fur stole (figure 3.2).

CANADA'S FIRST MULTILINGUAL BROADCASTER

That such a variety of formats for radio programs speaking to (or on behalf of) new Canadians developed in the late 1940s and early 1950s is due to the absence of a clear policy on the part of the Board of Broadcast Governors, the regulatory body in charge of broadcasting prior to the creation of the CRTC in 1968. However, by the end of the 1950s, popular and political momentum was building for the creation of a dedicated multilingual broadcaster. The earliest gestures in this direction took place in a less than official manner in the form of a private letter from the Department of Transport dated 26 November 1957 and addressed to Casimir Stanczykowski. The letter encouraged him to explore the possibility of proposing a multilingual station in Montreal to replace CHLP, which had closed only nine days earlier.[51] However, it was not until 1962 that a public announcement was made on the topic of foreign language broadcasts.[52] That same year, the Broadcasting Act was amended to allow all radio and television broadcasters to dedicate 15 percent of their schedules to "Foreign Language Broadcasts" and to make provision for stations to exceed that limit with special permission.[53]

However, of perhaps greater significance than the evolution of broadcasting policy was the CBC's decision not to produce programming in languages other than English, French, or Indigenous languages (with this latter group of languages primarily on the CBC's Northern Service).[54] This decision by the CBC shaped the entire subsequent development of third-language broadcasting in Canada by making it the responsibility of private rather than of public broadcasters. In documenting this decision, it is important to note that this policy was developed at the CBC independently and not a result of the wording of the Broadcasting Act.[55] As there was no mention of broadcasting in languages other than English or French in existing legislation, the CBC had the same latitude with regard to interpreting the law's silence on the issue as did private broadcasters after the end of the Second World War. However, unlike private broadcasters, the CBC developed a different approach to the issue, stating that productions in other languages were not possible both because of economic constraints and because it contradicted the broadcaster's mandate. "It is natural," read the CBC's statement on the topic, "that some of these groups should want broadcasts in their own language, but the Corporation is not in a position to meet their demands ... The CBC is a federal agency, the statutory creation of parliament ... Parliament recognizes only two languages."[56] It would broadcast programming, like *Canadians All*, that featured Canadians of diverse backgrounds, but it did not take up the task of producing programming that would extend its public service mandate to the nation's cultural and linguistic minorities.[57]

Despite its role in encouraging the proposal, the uncertain response of the Board of Broadcast Governors (BBG) to Stanczykowski's initial application upon its submission in January 1959 threw into stark relief the problems that multilingual radio raised for the existing broadcast system. As already noted, there was no existing framework within which multilingual radio as such could be licensed. Stations could be English- or French-language broadcasters, but there was no third option.[58] Thus, the issue of how to license a multilingual station was a new one, despite the dozens of hours of programming already being produced across the country in more than a dozen languages. In the eyes of the BBG, the existing programs were no different from shows in English or French as they regulated the language of the broadcaster, not that of individual programs.

In his application and during his first appearance before the BBG Stanczykowski made a strong case that the existing arrangement was far from ideal for either producers or their audiences. Indirectly referring to the letter he had received, he explained that the motivation for his application was the recent unexpected reduction in airtime available to producers of programs in languages other than English or French. Prior to 1957, radio listeners in Montreal were able to enjoy approximately sixty hours of programming in various languages per week, an amount that he likened to the total weekly broadcast schedule of a daytime-only radio station. However, many local producers were left without access to airtime when CHLP closed on 15 November 1957 shortly after its acquisition by *La Presse* newspaper (which already owned the station CKAC) as part of its takeover of rival daily *La Patrie*.[59] The situation was made more difficult when the other major home for minority radio in the city, CJMS, similarly reduced its multilingual offerings as it was able to make greater profits by broadcasting in French thanks, in part, to an influx advertisers who had previously purchased time on CHLP.[60]

Stanczykowski's presentation details the precarious status of third-language radio in Canada during the 1950s. Across the country, programs were produced by independent producers who either leased time from the broadcasters at a fixed rate or agreed to produce the program for a percentage of advertising revenue that the producer itself was responsible for selling.[61] Since programs were only as viable as their ability to attract advertisers, many of them were dominated by advertisements and music and had little time for community news or information. In other cases, the producer was also the program's primary sponsor. This was the case with Toronto's Johnny Lombardi – later president of CHIN radio – who used his radio program to advertise the grocery store and food importing company he owned as well as to promote concerts featuring Continental music. While this arrangement was able to support numerous programs, it risked the near total integration of many so-called "community" media productions with the interests of advertisers.

Arguing that it was important to ensure that community (not just commercial) interests were also represented, Stanczykowski stated in his presentation that one of his motivations for applying for this licence was to moderate the influence of advertisers in order to provide more time for community news and debate.[62] Beyond the consequences of this arrangement for the sharing of community news, Stanczykowski also lamented the difficulty producers faced when building an audience given the ability of station managers to reschedule programs with short notice in the interest of other programs with more lucrative advertising prospects.[63]

Stanczykowski's familiarity with the shifting ground of Montreal radio came from first-hand experience of the turbulent mosaic of multilingual radio in Montreal beginning in the early 1950s. Originally from Poland, he had come to Canada to pursue studies in sociology at McGill. Having started out with a monthly arts and letters column in a Polish-language daily based in Buffalo, NY, that had a sizeable readership in Montreal and other Canadian cities, Stanczykowski started a program serving the city's Polish and Ukrainian communities on CFLP in 1952.[64] He would later move to CHRS then CFCF while he waited for the final decision on his application for what would become CFMB, or Canada's First Multilingual Broadcaster.

Stanczykowski's application met with strong opposition from many of the stations in Montreal that broadcast programs in non-official languages. This is not surprising as the existing arrangements generated a profit while involving little labour on the part of broadcasters. But perhaps of greater long-term significance than the proposed station's effects on the radio market in Montreal was a series of questions about where multilingual and multicultural broadcasting might fit within the existing categories of Canadian broadcasting. Indeed, Stanczykowski's initial application was met positively yet did not receive a definitive response from the BBG because it was not clear if a station broadcasting in non-official languages could be licensed for broadcasting in Canada at all. This was because, as already noted, there was no policy for such an undertaking.[65] Taking time to reflect on the issue more broadly, the BBG returned the following year to grant Stanczykowski a conditional approval for the application in July 1960, but it asked him to resubmit the application.[66] It was not until 1962 that the licence was finally approved, by which time amendments to the Broadcast Act explicitly permitted foreign language broadcasting for both radio and television.

For this reason, the BBG's public announcement in 1962 regarding broadcasting in other languages should be read as the culmination of ongoing deliberations that had been taking place since 1957 rather than as a catalyst that initiated subsequent changes in the industry. Indeed, the statement outlines a programming philosophy that echoes the justifications for broadcasting in languages other than English or French that Stanczykowski and his competitors had already been using for many years. Emphasizing the role radio might play in integration, the statement reads:

> There is a need particularly in the larger centres of population for broadcasting in languages other than English and French to help in the task of integration. This applies particularly to the housewife who is largely confined to tasks within her home and does not have the same opportunities as husband at work or children at play to become quickly conversant in either English or French.
>
> By mixing some periods of foreign-language broadcasting with English and French over a broadcasting station, the broadcaster can assist in not only making the newcomer feel less lonely in a new land but can help to inculcate instruction in the Canadian way of life – government, customs, tradition, culture – more easily than would otherwise be the case.[67]

In its goals and justifications, the statement echoes themes that were frequently repeated throughout the hearings for Stanczykowski's proposal. On numerous occasions, he is clear that the overarching goal of the station would be to encourage and ensure the adaptation of immigrants to the laws and norms of Canadian society. It is a position that he advocated to the press as well. In an interview with *Variety* in December 1963 (about a year after the launch of CFMB) Stanczykowski comments: "All the hostilities and prejudices which has caused such tragedy in Europe during the past century ... are left at the door of the station. We are interested mainly in good Canadianism while maintaining the ethnic cultures at a high level."[68]

At the centre of Stanczykowki's appeal (and of many other later proposals for multilingual broadcast licences) was the homemaker who was unable to acclimate to Canadian culture because she remained isolated at home.[69] Speaking before the BBG, he noted", "Some ladies, they go out and work, but most of them with children stay home, they have to, and in most of the cases they have no contact with Canadians."[70] While including a significant amount of material intended to educate listeners about life in Canada (such as regular features "Know Canada Better" and "Job Opportunities"), Stanczykowski described the station as taking a less formal approach to citizenship education. "We don't use a class approach," he commented to *Maclean's* magazine in 1966: "Our announcers just chat about subjects which most new immigrants need to know in order to assimilate."[71]

Although a direct comparison risks overlooking the differences between the origins of the two stations, it may be said that, compared to the CFMB's application, CHIN's application in 1966 had a smoother path to approval. Unlike CFMB, the creation of CHIN was as a result of the relationship between the new station's principals and Ted Rogers. Rogers, who had been broadcasting CHFI on the frequency CHIN-AM would later occupy, was required to sell his licence following CHFI's move to 680AM (which was undertaken so it could expand from a daytime-only schedule to a full-time broadcast operation). Lombardi's ambitions were already known as he had submitted an unsuccessful application for a Toronto-based multilingual broadcaster in 1962, around the time that the licence was finally granted to CFMB. This time, however, the transaction was technically a share transfer rather than the licensing of a new service on a new frequency, even though Lombardi and his associates submitted a complete application to the BBG and the Department of Transport.[72] The arrangement did not come out of the blue, although, in his statement to the BBG, Lombardi made much of his independence from Rogers. The two had known each other professionally for at least three years by the time the application had been filed; Lombardi sat on the Board of Directors for Rogers' company and also owned shares in Rogers Broadcasting.[73]

Lombardi's relationship with Rogers was only a small part of his considerable public reputation, which contributed both to support

Figure 3.3 This image, published in the *Toronto Star* with the caption "Who's Minding the Store?," shows Johnny Lombardi wearing a coverall from his grocery store while playing music on the radio (1966).

for and opposition to his application. Since opening a grocery store in Toronto's Little Italy following his return from serving in the Canadian Army, he had become widely known through his activities as a broadcaster and promoter of cultural events, bringing well known Italian performers to the city.[74] He was identified in newspapers and magazines as the "unofficial mayor of Little Italy" and, beginning in the early 1960s, was called upon to comment on many issues affecting Italians in Toronto.[75] He was also involved in early attempts to launch an Italian-language daily in Toronto in partnership with Arturo Scotti (who would serve as the first editor-in-chief of the *Corriere Canadese* when he partnered with Dan Iannuzzi, who later became the first president of CFMT).[76]

Continuity between all of Lombardi's activities and businesses was central to his public persona, as is evident in a magazine profile in which the blending of his grocery store and radio station at his headquarters on College Street is described in vivid detail. "It's a remarkable, cozy place," the article reads, "you enter the station from a narrow stairway on College St. Where a neon sign will soon blink out CHIN's call letters beneath Lombardi's name. As you walk down the corridor of what were once store rooms, the exotic smells of Italian meats and cheese caress the nostrils. Downstairs there is a symphony of Italian marketplace voices."[77] A series of photographs taken for a profile of Lombardi in the *Toronto Star* makes visual this aspect of his persona (figure 3.3), showing him wearing a butcher's white coat with his name embroidered on the lapel. The caption for the photo reads: "Who's Minding the Store?" In the mainstream media, Lombardi's status as a trusted representative is in no small part due to the view that his continued engagement with his community through his commercial activities kept him in contact with everyday people even as his media interests expanded.

This public persona, carefully cultivated by Lombardi, presented him as a figure who was able to articulate the interests of the rapidly growing Italian community in ways that did not threaten the city's Anglo establishment. His image was carefree, his business acumen passed off as nearly accidental. "Some say he's top noodle in the macaroni business," wrote one profile of Lombardi that was published in 1959.[78] Another profile described his growing business interests as the product of casual interest and good timing: "This war vet liked to eat so he opened a grocery. To advertise it he broadcast Italian music. That was such a hit he hired a hall for Italian singers and imported Italian movies. In Toronto they call his many-sided business Johnny Lombardi's kingdom of music and macaroni."[79] This was an approach that carried some risks as there were certain issues upon which it was not possible to speak on behalf of the city's

Italians without upsetting the political establishment. This was most clearly in evidence in Lombardi's statements regarding the treatment of Italian workers in Toronto, for which other community leaders chastised him because he appeared to be trying to downplay the problems encountered by recently immigrated workers.[80] Despite such problems, Lombardi was able hold such a position by presenting himself as a cheerful, and at times clownish, intermediary.

Lombardi built upon his position as a friendly representative and intermediary for the city's Italian community in his application for CHIN. In presenting the new direction of the station, Lombardi took up the ideas about cultural and linguistic diversity that informed the rise of Continental radio in proposing a new multicultural (but not multilingual) station for Toronto. Its format was described both to advertisers and government regulators as "cosmopolitan," a term that occupied much the same territory as "continental" (indeed, Lombardi used these terms interchangeably). This was in keeping with the profile of Lombardi's own radio program, which he had hosted on CHUM and other stations in the Toronto area since 1947. Although the program was broadcast exclusively in English (Lombardi did not speak Italian fluently), the advertisements for it described it as offering "music, mirth and melody from sunny Italy."[81] An industry columnist described the format in more detail: "Italian music has reached a new high on this show. All this music is interspersed with social announcements, a post of advertising plus interviews of well-known Italian singers."[82]

The CHIN application effectively expanded the format of Lombardi's radio show across the entire day and beyond his focus on the Italian community. The kind of programming he proposed throughout his appearance before the BBG on 24 March 1965 fits squarely within the "Continental" format. He describes the new station as follows: "With over three-quarters or a million people living in Toronto of non-Anglo-Saxon origin, I feel these people should be catered to in the English language but with cosmopolitan music. If I am successful in this application, I will program Monday to Friday in the English language from sun-up to sun-down with cosmopolitan music, news, sports and special features. I am not asking for an ethnic station – I will repeat, I am not asking for an ethnic station, I am not asking for special privileges."[83] Over the course of the hearing before the BBG, on several occasions Lombardi and his associates emphasized their commitment to cosmopolitan music and their desire to create a cosmopolitan radio station. His partner and legal representation, James Service, noted "We believe we present an ideal trio for a cosmopolitan radio station" before going on to note the ethnic and religious backgrounds of the three principals behind the CHIN application (Service, Lombardi, and former mayor of Toronto Philip Givens).[84] Describing his programming philosophy, Lombardi stated: "I call it music with a cosmopolitan flavour. Cosmopolitan in programming and in outlook, to create a bridge or a link between the various cultures. The cosmopolitans are really the third culture. We have much to offer in the third culture, the whole of Europe with the exception of France and Britain. The potpourri of distinct, unique, colourful, artistic and intelligent minority groups."[85] He concludes: "Toronto is more and more each day cosmopolitan in every way."[86] In newspaper coverage of CHIN's launch, however, the station was described as "continental," with an article from the *Toronto Star* describing it as having a "continental flavor."[87]

The motivation for adopting this way of discussing the intersection of identity, culture, and language on radio was likely an attempt by Lombardi and his partners to navigate the cultural and political complexities of immigration in Canadian culture in the mid-1960s. The difficulties encountered by Stanczykowski in Montreal, which continued with his subsequent application for another multilingual station in Winnipeg, made asking for a "cosmopolitan" station seem like a safer bet than asking for a community-oriented multilingual station. Lombardi's statement – repeated for emphasis – that he was "not asking for an ethnic station" is a clear indication that broadcasting in languages other than English was still considered something outside of the norm in 1966. At one level, these complexities speak to the status of ethnic and third-language radio in relation to cultural policy at the time (e.g., "I am not asking for special privileges"). However, there are also broader cultural anxieties regarding the process of acculturation for new Canadians. In his appearances before the BBG, Stanczykowski is very explicit about the importance of his station in local communities and its educational agenda. Lombardi, squarely focused on the potential of entertainment to serve as a means of cultural integration for new Canadians, justifies his station through a less instrumental understanding of the role that radio could play in the project of integrating recent immigrants into Canadian culture.[88] "Continental" and "cosmopolitan" music both define themselves in relation to an "elsewhere" as well as in relation to a process of cultural improvement and refinement. Speaking of the common musical culture of Europe, Lombardi takes care to note that "there is generally a repudiation of rock and roll," while extolling the quality of his preferred music's arrangements and its "master musicians."[89]

It is telling that the other station identified with Continental music in the Toronto area at the time was CFRB, which had rejected programs broadcasting in any language other than English.[90] Lombardi's appeals identifying his application with the Continental continuum was likely motivated by both the desire to attract audiences from among new immigrants and the desire to have his relationship with these listeners contribute to a process of cultural uplift and education. CHIN's application proposes increasing cultural diversity (but not linguistic diversity) for the Toronto airwaves in the context of the broader generic and generational shift taking place in the industry at the time. Many stations – including Lombardi's erstwhile home CHUM – transitioned to rock and roll in an effort to capture the vibrant youth market that would drive the industry into the next decade.[91] Through this process of triangulation, which sought to connect and manage the tensions between the shifting demographics of Toronto and anxieties about cultural decline associated with both youth and immigrants, the CHIN application was designed to provide an acceptably Canadian version of international radio. Its programs would not alienate or arouse concern among anxious listeners who were not used to hearing languages other than English on the radio, but they were also open enough in their claim to non-anglophone identity to be able to attract an audience among New Canadians.

This transition from programs produced by freelancers to licensed broadcasters unfolds over more or less the same period as did the Royal Commission on Bilingualism and Biculturalism. The licensing of CFMB and CHIN make clear that an ad hoc transition to multiculturalism had been taking place in radio long before the publication of the fourth volume of the commission's report, *The Cultural Contributions of the Other Ethnic Groups*, in 1969. By the end of the 1960s, CHIN had moved away from its attempt to establish a multicultural radio station by means of "cosmopolitan" music and commentary, and applied to increase the proportion of foreign language programming to 40 percent. This brought it into line with the level of foreign language programming already broadcast on CFMB. In 1971, Jan van Bruchem applied for a licence to create a multilingual station in Vancouver. His proposal followed many of the tropes pioneered by Lombardi and Stanczykowski regarding the social role of the station.[92] Shortly after beginning his presentation to the CRTC, Van Bruchem explained: "The purpose of our station is to assist new Canadians in the task of integration and to make them feel at home in Canada; and to install in them a pride of heritage; to maintain and promote the ethnic cultures and to bring peace of mind and happiness to the lonely, the immigrant housewife who is confined to her home, and the elderly."[93] In line with the licences granted CFMB and CHIN at this time, van Bruchem planned for the station to allocate 40 percent of its programming to languages other than English. The application filed by Roger Charest for a multilingual station for Edmonton followed a similar linguistic breakdown of its programming. Yet, despite 40 percent being set as the upper limit for programming in non-official languages, the stations carried on the promises made by Stanczykowski and Lombardi to represent as wide a range of communities as possible.

The establishment of norms (both in terms of licence conditions and everyday operation) involved translating the broad policy goals of multiculturalism into practical multilingualism on Canadian radio. Of equal importance in this history, however, was the early decision that single-language services would not be granted broadcast licences. This decision was a response to the limited number of available frequencies, but it had far-reaching consequences for the political economy of third-language media in Canada. The transition worked out well for new licence holders like Lombardi and Stanczykowski, who traded the precarity of being independent producers for positions that enabled them to become key brokers across numerous ethnic communities. The formatting of multilingual radio in this way also entailed an ongoing process of commodification. This is not to imply that the early days of "language radio" were not driven by market relations – indeed, the opposite is the case. Rather, it is to recognize that the emergence of the format further clarified the social relations related to media production and consumption, which were organized around ethnocultural identity.

ETHNIC CAN'T BE MEASURED

The standardization of commercial radio formats took shape in tandem with the development of audience research as a way of convincing sponsors to purchase advertising time. The development of multilingual radio did not take place outside of these developments, but its relationship to audience research and advertisers was distinct from that of mainstream media. The earliest audience research in Canada was conducted in the 1930s, with the first survey of radio listening being carried out by Ethel Fulford at Canadian Facts in 1932.[94] By the 1940s, the Toronto-based market research company Elliott-Haynes conducted monthly surveys of radio audiences in the country's major metropolitan areas (Montreal, Toronto, Winnipeg, and Vancouver) using telephone surveys. In 1944, the major private broadcasters joined together to create the Bureau of Broadcast Measurement, a non-profit cooperative tasked with conducting surveys of radio audiences across the country. In light of their rhetorical role in selling air time to advertisers, it is not surprising that measuring the number of radio listeners (and later television viewership) developed into more of an art than a science. Methods were tweaked and adjusted to provide believable if not always entirely accurate data in order to satisfy the competing interests of broadcasters and advertisers in the buying and selling of commercial time.[95]

While the system worked well for most broadcasters, there was concern regarding its ability to effectively capture the behaviours of listeners who didn't speak English or French as their first language. The profile of "language radio" published by *Canadian Broadcaster* in 1955 emphasizes the limitations of the existing audience numbers for showing the size and economic power of the audiences listening to these programs.[96] This is not to say that these listeners were entirely ignored. Enterprising public relations experts recognized this as a significant opportunity. One of the key figures in this effort was Wilfred A. Hoellige, an Austrian market researcher who, in the early 1960s, positioned himself as an expert in selling products to recent immigrants. Having immigrated to Canada during the mid-1950s, Hoellige was a member of an upper middle-class Austrian family. His father had been a member of the Austrian Parliament and the editor of a financial newspaper. Hoellige had previously worked in film and television in Europe, and upon his arrival in Canada he made a splash in the industry by claiming that he had purchased the film and television rights to the 1956 Summer Olympic Games taking place in Melbourne, Australia.[97]

Echoing the claims Stan Mokrzycki made in his efforts to market minority newspapers to national advertisers, Hoellige argued that new Canadians were being ignored by Canadian companies. As a result, new arrivals were sticking with the brands they knew from back home rather than shifting to buying Canadian brands. Alongside a number of appearances in both mainstream and trade publications, one of Hoellige's earliest ventures in this area was a partnership with the Toronto-based advertising firm S.W. Caldwell in which they hired local radio announcers who worked in languages other than English to create multilingual ads and the production of ten-minute news programs in a variety of languages (German, Italian, Polish, Dutch, and Ukrainian are mentioned). Hoellige's primary focus was the selling of advertising time on "language" programs broadcast by stations that primarily broadcast in English. Like Mokrzycki, he saw himself as a broker between the independent producer and larger Canadian businesses that were not used to thinking of the cultural differences among their prospective consumers.

Yet it was CHIN's Johnny Lombardi who established himself as the most visible spokesperson for the problems faced by multilingual broadcasters in their attempts to attract advertisers. In his role as the "unofficial mayor of Little Italy," Lombardi had already served as a commentator in the English-language press on the commercial habits of new immigrants to Canada.[98] Soon after CHIN launched, Lombardi established himself as a vocal critic of how industry ratings misrepresented his audience. Barbara Frum notes that Lombardi had contacted her to contest the ratings for the station, which she had quoted in a previous column. She wrote jokingly: "Lombardi says he knows for a fact that there are at least 200 devoted listeners. That's how many relatives he has, and apparently every last one of them wouldn't dare listen to anything else."[99]

Less than a year later, Lombardi's attitude towards audience ratings had become even more strident. Speaking to Frum again, he said: "Those are the Anglo-Saxon ratings. Ethnic can't be measured. We're going to show advertisers we can do a job without ratings. We raised $38,000 in five days after the earthquake in Sicily. And a mall promotion for an Italian soft drink pulled in 52,000 cards. Somebody must be listening to us."[100] In 1969 he participated in a forum on the "future of ratings services" (published in *Canadian Broadcaster*), lamenting that ratings were incapable of accurately reflecting the size of the audience the station was attracting. Despite a representative from the Bureau of Broadcast Measurement stating that "ethnic populations and audiences of certain radio and television stations do not warrant special treatment," Lombardi declared that "the rating situation is so outdated and unattractive to a newcomer to broadcasting and this country."[101]

Lombardi's response to his unfavourable showing in audience surveys was to create an annual picnic that was sponsored by CHIN and that was to serve as a way of showing the station's reach. While linked to Lombardi's radio (and later television) station, the event very quickly came to be seen as symbolic of the demographic and cultural transformations taking place in the city following the arrival of thousands of immigrants. Variously known as "Italian Day," "National Spaghetti Day," and, later, the "International Picnic," the event took place in early July – and later the July first weekend – initially on Toronto's Centre Island and later on the grounds of the Canadian National Exhibition.[102] Nicholas Harney highlights the picnic as an example of how the city's Italian community created temporary communal spaces – an argument that parallels some of my discussion about cinemas as spaces of semi-public community. Yet Harney's argument that the picnic was "more collective than corporate" underplays the important commercial and political uses to which Lombardi put the event.[103]

First held in 1967 with funds designated to support the country's centennial celebrations, the picnic was sponsored by Lombardi in collaboration with Dan Iannuzzi, editor of the *Corriere Canadese*. Iannuzzi described the event to the *Toronto Star* as "the biggest picnic the country has ever had."[104] It attracted politicians from all levels of government and representatives from the Italian government. The attractions included a number of contests with vaguely Italian themes, such as pizza-throwing and spaghetti-eating. The annual bikini contest was the source of the event's most widely circulated images, with papers publishing dozens of pictures of Lombardi beside young women in bikinis. The event also included a number of draws with prizes that included trips to Hawaii and Italy as well as cars and home appliances. While glossed over in coverage of the picnic's more spectacular successes, the draws highlight Lombardi's ability to integrate sponsorship with his community event.

This was a trend that would become even more pronounced the following year when the event was co-sponsored by future Toronto mayor Mel "Bad Boy" Lastman's furniture stores (figure 3.4). While the picnic would retain its carnivalesque atmosphere, it came to be described in press coverage as a celebration of multiculturalism. This can be taken as an indication of the event's growing political

BAD BOY BREAKS ALL RECORDS IN HIS 2nd ANNUAL SPAGHETTI DIG-IN

by Al Terry

TORONTO (BB) A record-breaking crowd of 40,000 turned out to enjoy the BAD BOY's and Johnny Lombardi's second annual "Great Spaghetti-Dig-In" on Centre Island. NATIONAL SPAGHETTI DAY won't be forgotten for a long time in the Italian community.

It was the biggest crowd ever to be on the Island — plus, 7,000 people were turned away in the 82-degree heat because the ferry was so overloaded.

The "Dig-In" started out with balloons and suckers being passed out to the children. The first contest was a 'Baby Crawling' event; the first baby to reach its mother received a John Inglis washing machine. Teen-agers competed in a 'Go-Go Dancing Contest' with the winners receiving transistor radios and record albums from Columbia. The 'Children's Spaghetti-Dig-In Eating Contest' winners received toys from the Reliable Toy Company. Crowds overran the ropes to get a closer look at the beauties as they paraded down the ramp. Judges, which included the BAD BOY himself, had a tough time choosing one, but finally, lovely Miss Adele Hayes, a 16-year old student from Etobicoke won the title of "Miss Mini-Bikini 1968."

POLICE ON HORSEBACK were called in to control the crowd as the popular 'Adult Spaghetti-Dig-In' was announced. After 1½ hours of eating and 4½ bowls of spaghetti, a tie was finally declared between Johny Piruzza and Peter Dinardo to be the grand winners of the General Electric Colour TV.

I asked the BAD BOY if he learned any Italian from all of this, and he replied, "I'm learning to speak Italian from my comparee Johnny Lombardi, but right now, after the terrific day we had on Sunday, all I can say is that I'm looking forward to next year to double the attendance,... and Chow! Chow!!".

Figure 3.4 Article-style advertisement of the events of the second annual "Great Spaghetti-Dig-In" held on Centre Island on National Spaghetti Day. *Globe and Mail*, 18 July 1968.

significance as it became an important venue in which politicians could pose for photos with leaders from different ethnocultural communities. However, the picnic remained tied to the promotional economy in which CHIN radio served as the conduit connecting advertisers to audiences. Thus, the event came to function in three different ways: (1) it provided a venue in which many minority communities could gather in public; (2) it provided Lombardi with a venue through which to develop his connections with politicians; and (3) it served as a tool for convincing sponsors of CHIN's ability to reach audiences across many different communities, a fact of particular importance to national advertisers who were less directly connected with ethnic consumers.

OTHER VOICES

When the policy concerning third-language and minority broadcasting was finally outlined in 1985, it made explicit that "a basic tenet of the CRTC's approach has been that the scarcity of broadcast frequencies will not permit the licensing of a single language service to each ethnic group in a given market."[105] However, alongside these multilingual broadcast services there emerged a number of other services that took advantage of the absence of regulation for audio programs distributed by means of cable and telephone systems. It is unfortunate that there is no comprehensive history of non-broadcast audio services in Canada during these years. Beginning in the mid-1970s, these services expanded significantly when the cable industry and radio broadcasters saw a mutually beneficial opportunity in the possibility of distributing FM radio stations through cable networks. Cable distribution extended the broadcast range of stations without diminishing the quality of the signal.[106]

For the most part, audio-only signals distributed by cable rebroadcast existing over-the-air stations. However, alongside these conventional broadcasters, a number of specialty services were introduced, including a number of third-language channels.[107] In Montreal, three such services operated beginning in the early 1970s: CHCR (Canadian Hellenic Cable Radio) was incorporated in 1974, Radio Italia (CICR) has operated since at least 1970, and Radio Portugal Montreal launched in 1976.[108] In Toronto, CHTO, also known as Canadian-Hellenic Toronto Radio Limited (which also went by Greek Canadian Radio Limited), was a Greek-language only service that operated under the direction Peter Maniatakos and that was launched in 1965.[109] This would later be recognized as the starting point for the team that launched the Greek-language television station Odyssey in 1996. Also operating in Toronto, the Canadian Portuguese Radio Club (CPRC) broadcast via cable throughout the 1970s, and a number of key participants in the CPRC went on to establish the multilingual music station CIRV-FM in 1986.[110] Some of these stations were initially distributed through the phone, but they soon recognized that the structure of the phone system limited the growth of their audience.[111]

Given that they attracted thousands of subscribers, it is surprising that there are few traces of the existence of these stations beyond advertisements published in community newspapers. Their schedules were not mentioned in weekly newspaper listings, and, with the introduction of more stringent regulations, many of them struggled to survive.[112] Unlike their broadcast counterparts, these services operated in a single language and were able to survive with much smaller audiences. This key distinction is important as it serves to highlight the complex ecosystems of local services that emerged to serve the ethnocultural market even as interest grew in making space for national multilingual services.

Another outlier in the history of multilingual radio in Canada is Montreal's Radio Centre-Ville. Despite Stanczykowski's expressed intent to serve community interests and inform recent immigrants, CFMB was an explicitly commercial station whose programming decisions were a product of advertiser and audience preferences. Radio Centre-Ville, emerging from the cooperative media movement that emerged in the late 1960s and early 1970s, followed the general format for multilingual radio with its call letters CINQ being a reference to the five languages in which it broadcast (English, French, Spanish, Portuguese, and Greek).[113] If Stanczykowski traced his roots in the industry back to freelance radio programs on commercial stations, the group that formed Radio Centre-Ville saw itself as coming from a very different place than did the "straight radio scene."[114] Daniel Lavoie, one of the key members of the group that founded the station, explains: "It wasn't community radio in the real sense of the term, meaning a station managed by a board of directors elected by a certain community. It was more an 'alternative' or 'counterculture' radio, defending citizens' rights. A radio station which wasn't out to make money or do business, but to broadcast popular information, unlike the whole mainstream information machine."[115] Radio Centre-Ville's political orientation and programming philosophy distinguished it from other stations providing programming in languages other than English or French. However, it followed a similar path through the margins of Canadian media, where there was greater latitude to deviate from the formats and program genres that dominated mainstream media.

Originally launched as a cable-only station, Radio Centre-ville transitioned to over-the-air broadcast in 1975 when it was granted an experimental licence by the CRTC at the same time as was Vancouver Co-operative Radio (CFRO-FM), where a number of individuals who would later play a role in ethnocultural television on the west coast, including Justine Bizocchi, started their careers.[116] While Stanczykowski described CFMB as an important instrument for the distribution of information about public institutions and government policies, Brian Fautaux explained that CINQ-FM saw its mandate differently: "The station was able to do what neither a national public broadcaster, nor a locally-oriented private broadcaster could do, which was to provide information relevant to a particular segment of the city without promoting nationalist ideology from the federal government, or be bound by the demands of corporate advertisers, as were many stations in the private sector (although some sponsorship from the local community and non-profits was permitted on CINQ-FM)."[117]

These alternative radio services not only differed with regard to the kinds of programs they produced but also attempted to develop a different understanding of the relationship between community, identity, and broadcasting. Claims regarding the ability of broadcasters to understand the interests and desires of their listeners were an important part of all of the stations that were operating in Canada in the early 1970s. Implicitly informing the statements of key individuals working in multilingual media like Johnny Lombardi was the fact that they were able to speak *for* their listeners, not just *to* their listeners. Claims of representing the community were weakened given the multilingual format that Canadian regulators came to prefer. While such stations often employed a multilingual staff of producers, writers, and hosts, the stations themselves were owned by a small group of individuals and were later integrated into much larger media corporations rather than into the community. Looking at cable radio offerings and Radio Centre-Ville both bring into focus how the multilingual format itself was central to how diversity of ownership was undercut in the name of spectrum scarcity. This is not to say that these alternative services did not encounter problems when it came to community outreach; rather, it is to say that they were founded on a much different relationship between the identity of the broadcaster and the identities of audience members.

CONCLUSION: MOBILE FORMATS

This chapter shows how the emergence and evolution of multicultural and multilingual radio involved the establishment of a format that would distribute programs in languages other than English or French. While the language of broadcast was the most immediately apparent aspect of this format, there were a number of other features. The most important of these was a commitment to the goal of integration with Canadian society and Canadian culture as well as the peculiar temporal structure of these stations, which built on the brokered-time model of the 1950s. This gave stations adopting the multilingual format a particular political orientation while, at the same time, allowing broadcasters to participate in multiple ethnic economies. This enables us to recognize the infrastructural role played by the multilingual format, which established a set of social relations and coordinated a series of exchanges that were both symbolic and commercial.

The emergence of "formats" as a keyword in recent research in media studies builds upon an attempt to better understand the mobility of culture. Albert Moran, who studies the development of formats in the television industry, compares the format to a recipe. He emphasizes that their function in media industries is to allow successful media properties to move across cultural and linguistic borders in ways that permit them to adapt to local surroundings. I have made some reference to similar developments in other national contexts, specifically the circulation of the word "continental" to describe a variety of forms of cultural difference in the United States and Australia. A similar history could be traced in relation to the multilingual format that would encompass both stations broadcasting in multiple languages in the United States beginning in the 1930s and the creation of the Special Broadcast Service in Australia, which was launched only a few years after the events detailed here.

The purpose of this chapter, however, is not to determine either precedence or provenance; rather, it is to consider the function of the multilingual format in the Canadian context. The emergence of a relatively standardized multilingual radio format by the middle of the 1970s took place in response to the limited success of alternative formats, from Continental stations to cable radio, in achieving the political, cultural, and economic goals of multiculturalism. Echoing the development of the organizations and associations discussed in the previous chapter, the long-term significance of the development of multilingual radio broadcasting was its ability to manage the tensions and discontinuities between multiculturalism as a political project, linguistic diversity as a marker of identity and belonging, and commerce. This is an important reminder that, as much as they are globally mobile, formats are grounded in the particularities of their local context. Most important, it set into place a particular balance between the local context and the global movement of peoples and cultural goods in which the nation could be seen as a necessary, and mostly benevolent, arbiter. However, this balance was temporary, a product of the political, cultural, and technical context within which it emerged. In the next chapter I show how the subsequent push towards national and, later, international services in the context of the expanding media universe reopened a number of questions and concerns that, due to both political agreement and technical limitations, had been closed with regard to radio.

4

Scale: Remaking the Spatial Logics of Third-Language Television

In January 1966, Casimir Stanczykowski filed an application with the Board of Broadcast Governors to establish a multilingual radio station in Winnipeg.[1] Coming a few months after Johnny Lombardi had successfully launched CHIN-AM in Toronto, the application would have created the country's third "ethnic" radio station. The proposed station would adopt the same format as Stanczykowski's other radio station, CFMB in Montreal, only adapted to reflect the cultural and linguistic make-up of Winnipeg (more German and Ukrainian programs, fewer Italian). Despite joining with locally based partners (including Charles Dojack of National Publishers, soon-to-be elected president of the Canada Ethnic Press Federation), the application was rejected over concerns regarding the Montrealer's lack of history in the city. Stanczykowski persisted and applied three more times – a second time in 1966 and again in 1967, leading to a hearing before the CRTC in 1968, and a fourth time in late 1968, although this application was never granted a hearing and was not acknowledged until 1972 – before he was awarded the licence in 1974 for what would become CKJS.[2]

At the very beginning of his presentation to the CRTC on the occasion of his fifth application, Stanczykowski made a point of noting that "a Torontonian" had been allowed to launch a multilingual station in Vancouver only two years previously.[3] The reference to Jan van Bruchem, who was president of Vancouver's CJVB and who was living in Toronto when he filed his application in 1971, was clearly meant to highlight what Stanczykowski saw as selective adherence to the principle that multilingual radio stations should be owned locally. Stanczykowski went on to note the absence of competing applications from interested local parties in the face of the CRTC's preference for an owner who had a longer relationship with Winnipeg. Recalling the history of his multiple applications, he pointedly observed that "if there was anyone else interested in filing an application, they had a lot of time to do so."[4]

The nearly decade-long back-and-forth between Stanczykowski and regulatory agencies speaks to the contested place of localism in the licensing of third-language and minority media in Canada. Localism plays a complicated role in Canadian broadcasting generally. The desire to ensure the viability of a national media industry in Canada has contributed to highly concentrated ownership and has undermined stated commitments to locally owned media.[5] The history of third-language broadcasting complicates these tendencies for a number of reasons. Any competitive advantage resulting from economies of scale is limited by the smaller audiences for many third-language services, which has encouraged even "national" services to operate locally. At the same time, the integration of minority broadcasting into the Canadian media system is troubled by the perceived contradictions between the local, national, and transnational networks and communities to which third-language and minority broadcasters belong. In many ways, these issues run parallel to the concerns arising from the prominence of US-produced media content on Canadian broadcasters. However, they constitute a different history in which there is a constant struggle to manage the cultural, economic, and political tensions of being both too local to generate significant interest from audiences or national advertisers and too global due to relationships with international distribution networks that are viewed as challenging the nationalist orientation of Canadian media policy.

Symptomatic of these complications are ongoing concerns about the control and influence of Canadian media on the part of non-Canadian governments, companies, or individuals. There exists an ongoing back-and-forth between praising diversity as an essential characteristic of Canadian society and anxiety about the transnational implications of the community politics of ethnic groups. Managing the tension between these two tendencies, it has been argued that Canada's cosmopolitan nationalism, of which multiculturalism is but one manifestation, has allowed the country to avoid both virulent xenophobia and vacuous cultural relativism while managing the flow of ideas and people across national borders.[6] However, such an explanation is far too simplistic and self-congratulatory in its analysis of the simultaneous processes of recognition, integration, policing, and marginalization that have defined the history of minority media in Canada.

My purpose in this chapter is not to provide a catalogue of the degree or kind of "foreign influence" on ethnocultural broadcasting in Canada and the responses (just or unjust) to these moments of transnational encounter and exchange; rather, it is to explore the processes through which the distinction between what is "foreign" and what is "domestic" has been produced in the history of minority and third-language television broadcasting in Canada. To examine the shifting grounds upon which media services are categorized "foreign" or "Canadian" is to analyze the politics and pragmatics of scale. Scale is not simply a descriptive method of measure, it is a normative process.[7] The production of scale is a political, even strategic, activity through which the complexities of identity, belonging, and collective action are categorized and managed.

This chapter shows how the development of third-language television has involved the continuous unworking (and reworking) of stable distinctions between the local, national, and international that have guided the operation and regulation of mainstream media. At the centre of this is a shift in how "the local" is defined, moving from a definition determined by technical limitations (i.e., the limited range of broadcast signals) to one that is shaped by political and cultural criteria. Casimir Stanczykowski's repeated attempts to establish a multilingual radio station in Winnipeg is telling in this regard since it overlays the limited range of radio broadcasts with regulators' concerns about an outsider's ability to understand the local culture of the city. In the case of CKJS, an emphasis on preserving local culture was used as protection against undue "foreign" influence from a Montreal-based media entrepreneur. While the prehistory of CKJS involved radio, this chapter traces the development of this dynamic in relation to television. The transition from a localism based on technical limitations to one defined by legal and cultural criteria is perhaps even more evident with regard to TV than with regard to radio because the global integration made possible by satellite and (later) digital distribution has repeatedly disrupted the protectionism that defines Canadian media policy.

This chapter may seem to depart from this book's focus on the manifestations of media infrastructure through industrial practice.

The previous chapters have all focused on some aspect of how media industries operated from places of business to professional associations to broadcast formats. Scale differs from these forms of infrastructure, yet I argue that it is better understood as infrastructural than as descriptive. As infrastructure, it is the product of norms and practices intended to organize and order individual and collective action.[8] Questions of scale proliferate across the history of multiculturalism; this is to read the "within" in the phrase "multiculturalism within a bilingual framework" as not simply indicating relations of legal precedence according to Canadian law and history but also of implicating claims about cultural recognition within a spatial order.

I first revisit the early history of third-language and minority television, highlighting the central role played by forms of "local" media, ranging from closed-circuit television to programs on community and cable-access channels. The development of third-language television occurred in the context of the expansion of the number of services available to Canadian viewers made possible with the licensing of Ultra High Frequency (UHF) broadcasting and cable distribution a few years later. Perhaps the most well-known example of televisual localism from this period is Toronto's City-TV, Canada's first private UHF broadcaster. City's programming mandate was centred on its commitment to serve the city in which it was located, not the geographically abstract audience imagined by national network executives.

One of the ways that City-TV made an early name for itself was to include a significant amount of third-language programming reflecting Toronto's multi-ethnic residents. I conclude this section by considering the initial steps towards licensing the first dedicated multilingual television in Canada, CFMT, in 1979. I situate the creation of CFMT in the context of the broader debates organized by the CRTC during these years concerning the topic of multilingual television and its role in fulfilling local demand for television programming. I argue that the emergence of these "local" services broadcasting multilingual programming in the 1970s entailed the integration of a variety of transnational media genres and practices into Canadian media culture in ways that did not disrupt the hegemony of the nationalist orientation of Canadian cultural policy. In other words, localism was a strategy of simultaneous engagement and containment for a variety of forms of media production and consumption that existed outside the regulation of Canadian culture.

The following section explores the subsequent creation of national third-language services beginning in 1984 – Telelatino (originally named Latinovision) and Chinavision (which is now known as Fairchild) – as part of the hearings pertaining to the licensing of subscription-based specialty services for distribution via cable. At the hearings in 1984 for the first group of specialty services to be licensed, these channels were described as national networks, and there was an implied scalar progression from local to national in the comments of all the applicants and commissioners involved. Tremendous energy went into the distinction between "national" and "local" services, but these efforts were counter-balanced by the pragmatics of daily operations in which broadcasters recognized that their audiences and advertisers were concentrated in a handful of "local" markets across the country. I document the elaboration of these new national services as representative of a failure of imagination on the part of the CRTC, which attempted to established new third-language channels without disrupting the status quo in Canadian broadcasting.

The final section of this chapter focuses on the introduction of the digital distribution of television in Canada in the early 2000s and its impact on third-language broadcasters, specifically, the conflicts between international and national services. If the preceding two sections put forward a vision of television broadcasting that used the local, and later the national, to moderate the influence of international media in Canada, the licensing of digital cable networks disrupted the arrangement that had first taken shape in the 1950s. Two cases – the introduction of Italian public broadcaster's global service, RAI International, and Qatar-based news service Al-Jazeera – highlighted the emergent political economy of third-language media in Canada. The last part of this chapter puts forward an argument that serves as the starting point for the book's conclusion – namely, that framing Canadian multiculturalism as a national project advocated by government officials and public regulatory bodies has come under increasing strain as Canada's media have become integrated with global markets. I argue that the fragmenting of the arrangement between Canadian broadcasters and regulatory agencies that organized minority and multilingual media in Canada since the 1950s speaks to the emergence of a new scalar logic that is underwritten by digital media networks.

The argument made in this chapter implicitly revisits and reflects on the materials presented in earlier chapters. The constitution of multi-ethnic urban space discussed in relation to film exhibition and theatrical spaces as well as the formation of regional and national associations representing ethnic and minority newspapers both contributed to, and were informed by, the hegemonic scalar logic through which multiculturalism developed in Canada. Yet the opening of Canadian television to a wider variety of languages and cultures since the 1960s revealed a number of tensions regarding the relationship between the local, national, and international scales at which media operate in a more acute manner than was the case with other media. This is due in part to the uneasy relationship between television's role in the promotion of cultural nationalism in Canada and its simultaneous identification with internationalism and globalization.[9]

INTERSTITIAL TELEVISION

Even as more multilingual radio broadcasters went on the air across the country, the scarcity of available frequencies for Canadian television channels meant that there was little consideration given to the establishment of a dedicated multilingual television service until well into the 1970s. Yet even before regulators entertained the possibility of creating a dedicated third-language television station there were a number of ways that third-language and ethnocultural media made its way onto screens. Following quite closely the path of third-language radio, a number of programs produced by freelancers were broadcast on "brokered time." By the end of the 1960s there were dozens of programs across the country, usually aired on Saturday or Sunday mornings, that explicitly defined themselves as speaking to ethnocultural minorities. Many of the pioneers of third-language television had established reputations in other media, whether print or radio. In Montreal, Alfredo Gagliardi –publisher of the *Corriere Italiano*, host of an Italian-language radio program on CHLP since 1955, and a prominent businessman in the Italian community – was the host of *Teledomenica*, which was broadcast on CFCF every Sunday beginning in 1965.[10] In Southern Ontario, Emilio Mascia took over *Italian Journal* on CFTO (later moving to CHCH), on air since 1963. Mascia had already established himself as the voice of Italian-language radio in Hamilton and was part-owner of Italian-language cinemas in Toronto and Hamilton.[11] Daniel Iannuzzi, who had started as the publisher of *Corriere Canadese*, established himself as the largest producer of third-language television programming in Canada through his company Daisons Multilingual Television. This was in the years before he became president of CFMT, the first multilingual television broadcaster in the country.[12]

The growth of community television in the late 1960s and early 1970s provided another means through which a younger generation of producers was able to develop the skills and experience necessary to make the transition to television. Cable distributors, the effective gate-keepers of Canadian television, were less than willing supporters of community access initiatives.[13] Yet, as community access channels came to be established thanks to pressure from the CRTC, these new channels provided important outlets for programs that might otherwise have been ignored over concerns about the size of their audience.[14] A range of programming, from community information to cooking programs, was produced by local cable broadcasters during this period (see figure 4.1). The long-term significance of these programs is both economic (as it provided evidence of the growing demand for ethnocultural programming) and cultural (as it provided opportunities to acquire the necessary skill to enter the television industry). Madeline Ziniak, who would subsequently move to CFMT and become a key figure in the national development of Rogers ethnocultural operations, started her career as a producer at the cable access channel operated by Keeble Cable in the northwest corner of Toronto (located only a block from the headquarters of Iannuzzi's Daisons Multilingual Television studios).[15] In Vancouver, Bernard T.C. Liu was the host of the local Chinese-language program before he became the president of World View television, a multilingual cable channel that operated between 1982 and 1986.[16]

Francis Cheung collaborated with Toronto's Rogers Cable (and Madeline Ziniak in particular) in the early 1980s to produce what he called the "Cable 10 Experiment" in advance of his application for Chinavision in 1984.[17] In its early days, ethnocultural television brought together these two very different ways of approaching broadcasting. On the one hand, there were many producers who saw television as an extension of their existing business interests; on the other hand, there were a number of groups and individuals with stronger ties to the emergent tradition of community and public access television. Both groups used the language of "community service" to describe their activities, but their economic and political commitments varied widely.

Figure 4.1 Pasqualino Carpino on the set of his cooking show, a production of Rogers MCTV (1975).

Yet it is important not to limit the history of television to these locally produced programs. Alongside these independent programs must be placed the emergent forms of transnational television whose history has been less frequently documented. These include closed-circuit television featuring sporting events that catered to diasporic audiences. As mentioned in chapter 1, these telecasts were one of the ways that film exhibitors tried to keep pace with the challenges and new possibilities resulting from the development of new technologies associated with television. Thus, despite their location in cinemas, they were technically and generically closer to television than to film.[18] Finally, an important adjunct to these activities taking place in Canada were broadcasts originating from US-based stations.[19] A number of programs oriented towards African Americans on WKBW, based in Buffalo, New York, such as "A Matter of Pride," were widely viewed across Metropolitan Toronto and elsewhere in southwestern Ontario.[20]

One way of making sense of both the diversity and the continuity of these televisual forms of media is through the concept of interstitial media. Approaching the forms and genres of televisual culture that were oriented towards cultural and linguistic minorities as interstitial media provides a way of making sense of two key aspects of these diverse phenomena. First, it highlights the way that the dominant forms of television were connected to the maintenance of cultural and legal norms designed to demarcate and protect national boundaries. Many of the most important forms of minority media during the 1970s existed outside of the institutions of Canadian television proper. From this perspective, the emergence of third-language television in Canada developed in the grey spaces of the cultural and political apparatus. However, the concept of interstitial media is also helpful for describing an important approach taken by producers and broadcasters, who often framed programming from other parts of the world by means of short "local" productions that would situate the program in its Canadian context. The subsequent development of third-language and minority television, documented in the following section, can be seen as an attempt to integrate into the Canadian media system the transnational circuits of distribution and translation that defined early third-language television.

MAKING ETHNIC TELEVISION LOCAL

Third-language television came to be more enthusiastically supported by the CRTC following Prime Minister Trudeau's 1971 statement announcing the adoption of multiculturalism as official policy. The declarations of support that marked the beginning of official multiculturalism in Canada coincided with the launch of a number of new television services. This was due to the introduction of new distribution platforms, cable, and UHF, which allowed "third" channels to appear in the larger markets across the country.[21] Between 1970 and 1980, a number of new channels were established in the country's largest markets, where the CBC and CTV, along with a number of US-based network affiliates broadcasting from across the border, were available. Particularly important in this regard was the country's first privately owned UHF station, City-TV (Channel Seventy-Nine), which went on the air in September 1972.[22] Guided by its owners (Phyllis Switzer, Moses Znaimer, Leon Weinstein, and Jim West), the channel's programming philosophy, unlike the two national networks, emphasized local needs.[23] An important component of this local mandate was a block of third-language programming that was to be broadcast in the late evenings and on weekends. While the station's owners touted its commitment to original productions, City did not produce its third-language programming itself; rather, an agreement was reached with Daisons Multilingual Television for the production of four hours of programming a week at its studios in the north end of Toronto when the station launched. By 1978, this amount had been increased to thirty-six hours a week.[24]

The success of City's "multicultural" programming showed that there existed an audience for even more hours of third-language programming in southern Ontario than were available as part of the slate of third-language programs on CHCH, which was based in Hamilton and that had started in the 1960s. Global Television introduced a few hours of third-language programs on Sundays soon after its launch in January 1974. Some of these programs were produced by the team at CHIN Radio and included "Festival Italiano" hosted by Johnny Lombardi, which television listings show starting in 1970 on Barrie's CKVR. Looking to exploit the profitable Toronto market, Rogers Cable gave over its second community channel (Channel 20) in Toronto to multilingual programs in the evening beginning in 1974; this led Rogers to rechristen the channel as "Multicultural Television," although its call letters (MCTV) actually stood for "Metro Channel." By the mid-1970s, Rogers formalized an arrangement with City-TV and Daisons Multilingual Television to rebroadcast the third-language programs originally produced for City on MCTV, effectively increasing the number of hours of third-language programming while keeping production costs low.[25]

Recognizing the financial limitations of his current position in the multilingual television market, Daniel Iannuzzi filed an application for a multilingual station with the CRTC in September 1976.[26] The commission acknowledged that there was indeed sufficient demand for such a service but felt that the issue needed to be more fully explored before such a channel could be launched. Taking place in the ballroom of a Holiday Inn in downtown Toronto from 20 to 23 September 1977, the initial hearings that would lead to the establishment of CFMT were peculiar in that the CRTC both heard applications for a multilingual television station serving the Toronto area and hosted a broader debate about whether or not such a channel should exist at all. The general debate, entitled "The Function of Multilingual Broadcasting in Canada," preceded the hearing of the applications for the new channel.[27] Presentations were heard from existing broadcasters, notably from Stanczykowski on behalf of CFMB and CKJS, Jan Van Bruchem on behalf of Great Pacific Broadcasting (CJVB), and Bill Evanov on behalf of CHIN, along with community groups representing the Italian, Finnish, Jewish, and Ukrainian communities. Forty-three other groups and individuals submitted material to the commission but did not appear at the hearing. The topics addressed during the hearing included a consideration of the "need" and "demand" for such a service, its economic viability, and its potential impact on existing broadcasters as well as the linguistic breakdown of programming on the new channel and whether or not Canadian content quotas should be applied.

The main players in the hearing were the three applicants, each of which had histories producing multilingual media. Johnny Lombardi put forward an application under the name Heritage Broadcasters, which would translate and extend his current operations at CHIN onto television. He argued that, given the small local market it would serve, a multilingual television station would only be economically viable if it could draw upon the pooled resources of an existing broadcaster.[28] Daniel Iannuzzi, who was already the largest producer of third-language television in the country thanks to his agreement with City-TV, applied to establish Multilingual Television Network (initially shortened to MTV and, later, to MTN to avoid confusion with US-based Music Television). The MTN team argued that going national was the inevitable next step for Daisons. In the words of Bev Oda, who was to be director of programming and community affairs on the new station, "it is inevitable in our logic as much as yours that we should expand, leave the womb of City-TV and start the creative process anew with the establishment of an independent third language television station."[29] Iannuzzi's team included noted architect Raymond Moriyama as well as Stan Mokrzycki, now going by the name Stan Martyn, whose work in advertising was discussed in chapter 2. The third application was led by Leon Kossar, originally a columnist at the *Toronto Telegram* where he established himself as a prominent advocate for cultural diversity in Toronto.[30] While less experienced in broadcasting than his competition, Kossar was well known as a promoter of Toronto as a multicultural city and, in 1967, was the founder of Toronto's Caravan Festival with his wife Zena.[31] To bolster his team, he brought along Emilio Mascia, drawing on his experience in film, radio, and television.

It was a fraught hearing in which all of the participants claimed to speak without prejudice on the topic, even as they prepared to be heard about the formal applications soon after. Critical voices – many coming from the radio industry – were asked not to take sides in the television licensing process, even as their interventions made clear they believed the creation of a new station would threaten the viability of third-language radio.[32] The CRTC rejected all three of the applications and revised the terms of the call in a public statement issued on 13 January 1978.[33] The statement requested that the applicants submit revised proposals in light of the clarifications resulting from the hearing. Key among the revisions was a more explicit definition of multilingual broadcasting, which notably increased the percentage of third-language programming to 60 percent during daytime and primetime hours. The applications were then submitted for a second set of hearings, which took place later in 1978.[34]

While an important part of the clarifications issued by the CRTC in January 1978 involved defining what constituted a third-language television broadcaster, other important elements related to how broadcast regulations and licence conditions for the new stations would be enforced.[35] The practical problem of how to monitor and police broadcasters operating in languages that were not spoken by the commission was at the forefront of these concerns. Many of these programs occupied a similar status to "foreign language" radio programs during the 1950s, when, prior to the licensing of CFMB, broadcasts in languages other than English or French were a visible but not official part of Canadian radio. Iannuzzi was already established as the largest producer of third-language television in the country, but he did not hold a broadcast licence himself and, as such, was not required to answer directly to the CRTC or any other public body. The other programs produced by independent producers or community groups similarly fell outside the direct regulatory powers of the CRTC.

Similar to the anxieties about the power of newspapers to foment discontent within Canada by importing conflicts from elsewhere, there was an increasing anxiety among regulators and politicians alike that radio and TV needed to be monitored and managed to avoid the risk of their causing damage to the Canadian social order. As is noted in chapter 1, concern was frequently expressed about gatherings of minority groups, something that was evident in the media coverage of public viewings of World Cup soccer. While this concern was implicit throughout the licensing of third-language radio stations in the 1960s, the issue came to a head in January 1970 when CHIN's Serbian-language program broadcast a short radio play dramatizing the assassination of a representative of the Yugoslavian government. The program aroused the concern of both the Yugoslavian government, which saw it as an indication of hostilities from the local Serbian community, and the Canadian government, which was worried that Toronto's Serbian community was being infiltrated by foreign-born agitators.[36]

The controversy that followed the broadcast brought CHIN before the CRTC the following month during its routine licence renewal to face questions about its role in stirring up unrest in the city. The hearing focused on the responsibility of the station to support the integration of its audience into Canadian society and flagged the lack of oversight on the part of the station managers. The licence was renewed, albeit for a reduced period of time, with CHIN introducing a new policy regarding content and establishing a board of directors made up of community members.[37] The scandal surrounding the Serbian broadcast confirmed many of the anxieties about third-language broadcasting – namely, that such programs risked fragmenting the social cohesion among Canadian residents.

After the incident on CHIN that angered the Yugoslavian government, Jan Van Bruchem felt the need to explicitly outline both a framework for community involvement and that framework's role in editorial oversight on the part of the station's management. For Van Bruchem, this meant shifting the implied role of the licensee from being a representative of audience members, with producers playing the role of intermediaries, towards being part of a more explicitly defined structure for community input.[38] The CJVB "advisory council" involved a number of members – teachers, religious leaders, and social workers – who were involved in "immigrant service" in the Vancouver area. This was less a form of community representation (although it was described as such) than it was a means to further ensure the CRTC that the station would fulfill its broader educational mandate and encourage the social integration of immigrants in the Vancouver area.

The creation of boards designed to ensure community oversight was supplemented by the growing emphasis on direct control over the programming of multilingual broadcasters. By the time the CRTC entertained applications for a third-language television broadcaster in 1977, all of the applicants, and many of those who intervened on behalf of broadcasters, were asked about their attitudes regarding brokered programming. The commission made it clear that it was not interested in having the brokered model dominate third-language television, even though it had been common across the radio industry for decades. The preference for structures that made licence holders responsible for content can also be seen in the expectation that applicants would file detailed plans for monitoring and managing programs across multiple languages. It was a direction that was later formalized in the statement issued by the commission in January 1978 in response to hearings that had been held the previous September, which declared that brokered programming was "undesirable, as it reduce[d] the licensee's control over program content which is his specific responsibility under the Broadcast Act."[39]

Reconciling these seemingly contradictory processes of centralized oversight and the incorporation of increased community input must be seen in relation to the development of a particular enactment of the "local" as the proper scale at which cultural identity should be lived in a multicultural society. That the "local" would be a defining parameter of the hearings was set in advance, given that the licence awarded would be for an over-the-air, UHF frequency that would serve only Toronto and surrounding areas. Yet the local was manifest in a variety of different ways, from the social to the economic to the political. For the radio broadcasters, this was a practical issue: How would the new service affect the economic viability of their operations? Most of the applicants responded to this economic argument, claiming that a television service would not affect the viability of radio even though both services would rely upon revenue from local businesses primarily in the retail sector. Implicit in these arguments was the presumption that third-language services could not be anything but local in nature, thanks in part to their difficulties in attracting national advertisers (a problem they shared with third-language newspapers).

Daniel Iannuzzi's successful application was unique in that he structured his presentation to the commissioners around an explicit discussion of the relationship between scale, programming, and its effects on audiences. "We believe," he explained in his prepared remarks, "that the Commission should carefully examine the difference between local, regional and national programme values, each of which is crafted to have a different impact on audiences. The mandate for regional or national audiences tends to fragment existing television services since such programmes in essence must have a mass audience appeal. We believe that the bulk of multilingual television services should be locally crafted for local audiences to serve local contours."[40] To be able to provide third-language television was to operate as a local service since the audiences such programs would attract were local, not national. Iannuzzi elaborated a vision of interconnected, but distinct, services serving different local audiences but, given the lack of overlap in the issues facing each community, unable to share programs. Iannuzzi's ideas about the differences between local, regional, and national television parallel the views implicitly expressed in the commission's resistance to the applications for a multilingual radio station in Winnipeg filed by Casimir Stanczykowski throughout the 1960s. The BBG (and later the CRTC) saw the aim of the policies encouraging multilingual broadcasting as ensuring that local communities be given a voice on the airwaves, but not the creation of a national or international alternative public sphere such as might be supported by a national or international third-language network.[41]

This is not a universal, or even a fully elaborated, definition of the local but, rather, a recognition of how the strategic deployment of localism might serve as a framework for governing the economic, cultural, and political tensions surrounding the creation of third-language television. These tensions were not entirely or permanently resolved through this strategic invocation of localism. On the contrary, there emerged a pattern of intermittent crisis and scandal through which anxieties about identity were expressed in terms of the competing scales at which Canadians of different backgrounds experienced community.

NATIONAL POLICY AND LOCAL NETWORKS

When the first round of subscription-based specialty television services was approved in 1982, among the six new channels to be launched was a regional multilingual service known as World View Television under the direction of Bernard T.C. Liu.[42] World View would be available only in British Columbia, serving a number of different communities but with an emphasis on Chinese-language and South Asian programming. Liu was well known among Vancouver's Chinese community thanks to the program he hosted on a local cable channel and was described as "a flamboyant figure who would often dress in cape, top hat and carry an ivory-tipped cane."[43] The channel was operated by Liu with investments from the BC Development Corporation and prominent members in the Chinese business community.[44] As a regional service, World View followed the cultural and economic logics that led to the creation of CFMT in Toronto three years previously. It was effectively a local channel, only available in southern BC, with a primary focus on Vancouver. Despite the tendency towards the establishment of services covering multiple provinces among the first generation of subscription-based television offerings, World View existed as an outlier in its focus on a much smaller geographic region and even more narrowly defined audience.[45] Ultimately, the primary difference between World View and CFMT was its revenue model, not the scale at which it understood its audience or developed relations with advertisers.

By the time hearings for cable specialty services were held in February 1984, it was already apparent that World View Television was a failure. The channel struggled to break even, requiring regular infusions of capital from its investors. Even though it had moderately strong subscription rates among Chinese-speaking viewers, the channel struggled to attract other viewers. For some, such as Italians, it was claimed that potential subscribers were not offered a sufficient number of hours of programming to merit the monthly subscription fee. In the case of Vancouver's South Asian community, representatives of the channel claimed that the growing popularity of the VCR significantly limited the number of subscribers.[46] Soon after the call for new specialty channels was made, World View started to develop a plan for taking the channel national in the hope that this would resolve these issues.[47]

World View was not the only licensed broadcaster to put forward an application. Daniel Iannuzzi brought together a team that included a number of his long-term freelance producers at CFMT, including Shan Chandrasekar (who would later become president of ATN) and Marie Griffiths (who had been working in local third-language programming in Montreal for more than a decade.) Iannuzzi proposed taking CFMT national under the name Multilingual Television (MTV) with a schedule that would broadcast 76 percent of its schedule in "the root language of 19 of Canada's ethnocultural groups ... including native peoples."[48] The proposal was attentive to how the service would adapt by scaling up to the national scale, with the team's legal representation Milton Winston explaining the relationship between CFMT and MTN: "We have come a long way. This application for the MTN multilingual network with its provision of access and assistance for locally produced and supported programming will allow us, for the first time, to become an integral part of the Canadian television scene as a bona fide regional producer with an opportunity to produce for the national network as well as local."[49] The approach to be taken would involve the development of local programs across the country, which would then be broadcast nationally. Although a national network, it would remain local in its production.

There were three other applications under consideration. These had varying degrees of broadcast experience but did not currently hold broadcast licences. Wah Shing Television, led by John Leung, was one of two applications for a Chinese-language-only station. Leung did not have extensive experience in broadcasting but was a partner in the Leung Brothers Travel Agency. He had also made a name for himself in Toronto's Chinese community, having been one of the organizers of a national Chinese Canadian conference that took place in 1975.[50] His more recent media-related activities involved the informal distribution of "radio tapes" to elderly members of the Chinese Canadian community in southern Ontario, but the content (and legality) of these activities is not clear.[51] The name of the company was taken from a video store owned and operated by another partner, Gilbert Waung. Waung was one of the few members of the team with experience in television, having worked for broadcasters in Hong Kong prior to his immigration to Canada.[52] Leung hired James West, a founding partner at CityTV, and Bev Oda, who had been responsible for the block of ethnic programming produced by Daisons for CityTV, as consultants on the proposal. Another application was filed by Francis Cheung for a Chinese-language network to be called Chinavision. Prior to his application, Cheung had worked extensively in film and television production in Hong Kong as president of Cheung Film Production, founded in 1961.[53] Through a variety of connections with Canadian investors and lawyers, Cheung was encouraged to apply for the third-language licence even though he had relatively little familiarity with the Canadian context up that point (and was not a Canadian citizen at the time his application was initially filed).[54] As mentioned above, his only involvement with Chinese-Canadian media was the production of a weekly cable program, which had been supported by Rogers Cable.

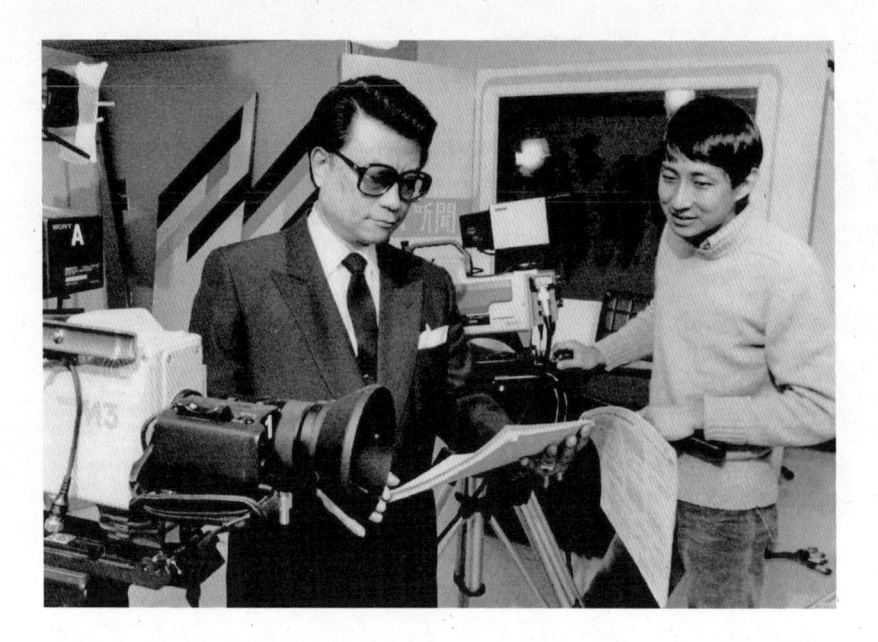

Figure 4.2 Francis Cheung on set at Chinavision in 1986, when the station was already experiencing financial difficulties.

The final applicant was Latinovision, led by Emilio Mascia and investors he had met during his time hosting the weekly Italian-language program *Italian Journal* at CHCH in Hamilton. Mascia had a long career in Italian-language media in southern Ontario, having been involved in radio, film, and television since the 1950s. However, Latinovision would not be an exclusively Italian service but would also broadcast programs in Spanish – a decision based on the repeated claim that the two languages were sufficiently similar to allow for crossover viewing rather than any perception of the size of the prospective audience.[55]

The framing of the hearings was one in which the stakes of taking multilingual television national were a frequent topic of discussion. Specifically, the question was how it would be possible to balance the expectation of serving community interests that had been central to the creation of the previously licensed broadcasters with the demands of covering a greater geographical area. Considerations of the relationship between national services and service to local communities were tempered by the recognition of the financial difficulties encountered by existing multilingual services. In their programming strategies, it was apparent that the licensing process was primarily a competition over access to the largest and wealthiest ethnocultural communities: Italian Canadians and Chinese Canadians. Iannuzzi's MTV and Liu's World View were both multilingual stations, but even they specified significant amounts of programming in Italian and Chinese.

All of the applications specified how they would avoid direct competition between existing local broadcasters and the new national services. The result was the structuring of licences in ways that would clearly differentiate between national and local services in terms of formats, distribution, and revenue. The licence for Latinovision laid out the breakdown of languages (52 percent in Italian and 46 percent in Spanish) and the genres of programming that the station would broadcast.[56] Films, drama, sports, and variety programs would make up the bulk of programming, but there would be no news or information programming as this would remain part of the Italian-language block broadcast on CFMT in Toronto, which was expected to be the main market for any service with significant Italian-language programming. Given that World View was already in operation as a predominantly Chinese-language service, the licence conditions for Chinavision barred the service from being distributed in the province of British Columbia.[57] There was also an explicit reference to the new station's commitment to helping both World View and CFMT develop their respective Chinese-language services. Yet, unlike Latinovision, Chinavision argued that the absence of adequate news programming on existing services in major markets required it to dedicate 25 percent of its schedule to information programs by its third year in operation.[58] While the specifics of the two licences differed, the effect in both cases was to limit direct competition between the local and the new national services.

Despite these expectations from the CRTC (and the promises from applicants to meet them) the subsequent roll-out of these broadcasters came to rely on the same local markets as did CFMT and World View. The new services encountered difficulties in signing affiliation agreements with local cable systems.[59] Cable distributors were interested in expanding the number of channels they offered to subscribers but preferred to introduce English-language American channels before the new Canadian third-language services. Attempting to encourage cable companies to distribute the third-language services, a policy outlining the distribution of the new specialty services was introduced specifying that the commission "would not ... allow the carriage, at this time, of non-Canadian specialty programming services which, in the Commission's opinion, could be considered either totally or partially competitive with Canadian discretionary services."[60] This effectively served as the counterpart to the distinction between local services and national services by further distinguishing national from international services.

Both Chinavision and Telelatino (as Latinovision was renamed shortly after its licensing) complained to the CRTC when they encountered difficulties achieving a sufficient number of subscribers to make the channels sustainable. In response, both channels proposed expanding their advertising. In the case of Chinavision, it asked for permission to program "local" advertising, claiming that it was already serving local markets across the country (rather than a single national market).[61] In 1986, Telelatino requested permission to supplement subscription revenue with advertising but clarified that the sponsors would be of "national interest."[62]

In the years that followed, there emerged two different processes through which these national services localized. After merging with Cathay International Television (the new name given to World View upon its relaunching in 1986), Chinavision was available in Toronto, Calgary, Edmonton, and Vancouver. By the late 1980s, the network operated four different services in which tapes were "bicycled" across the country following three different feeds calibrated to different time zones.[63] Less successful at establishing itself in markets outside of southern Ontario, Telelatino effectively operated as a local station. This regional orientation was supported by a series of marketing techniques, including most prominently the distribution of a program guide that was only available in southern Ontario and Montreal.[64] By 1990, Telelatino requested an increase in the amount of advertising it was allowed to carry (from three to eight minutes per hour) and the inclusion of local and regional advertisers in this time.[65] The CRTC recognized the stress this would put on local third-language programs, but it still allowed the station to allocate three minutes per hour to local advertising. In both cases, it became apparent that "going national" for third-language services was more accurately described as going multi-local.

The difficulties encountered by the new specialty channels was the result of the disjunction between policies designed to encourage

Figure 4.3 The cover of the Telelatino programming guide, September 1985, an example of the station's approach to promotion in the early years. With three stories in Italian and one in Spanish, it highlights how the economics of advertising shaped the balance between the station's two languages.

national third-language services and the economics of ethnic media in Canada. For this reason, an important parallel to the development of the cable-only specialty services is the expansion of CFMT across Ontario. As early as 1984, Dan Iannuzzi had spoken of the possibility of distributing the channel nationally via satellite.[66] In 1988, MTN (the parent company of CFMT, now owned by Rogers Broadcasting) offered to purchase a majority share in Telelatino, which was struggling to break even at the time. The proposal was rejected by the CRTC due to concerns about the proposal to eliminate Spanish-language programming entirely.[67] Following this, Rogers started to explore other ways of expanding the station. In September 1993, CFMT opened offices in London and Ottawa.[68] These two stations mostly rebroadcast the Toronto signal, but freelancers were hired to cover community events in both locations (and "national" events in the case of the Ottawa bureau). Yet, even here, the regional and the local remained the dominant framing of how programming decisions were made across the country. While the Toronto station would remain the flagship station (and, for many years, the only broadcaster wholly owned by Rogers), the growth of the regional services was described as creating local services similar to those at the Toronto station. The development of these regional stations, which would later extend into Alberta and British Columbia, laid the foundation for the rebranding of Rogers' multilingual and multicultural network as OMNI in 2011. However, these stations, which operated in major cities across the country, followed a strategy that is more accurately described as multi-local than national in its programming philosophy.

Yet perhaps the most significant development here was Rogers' purchase of CFMT, which highlights the most successful aspect of the attempt to "scale up" third-language television: the separation of on-air diversity from ownership. While third-language media would develop and diversify in line with changing patterns of immigration to Canada, there was no expectation that there would be a similar economic or executive diversification. Returning to the story of Stanczykowski, the emergence of multilingual and multicultural broadcasting depended on particular kinds of minority ownership that were realized through a particular understanding of localism. However, this interpretation of economic localism faded with the passing of time. It is worth noting that the neither 1985's *Broadcasting Policy Reflecting Canada's Linguistic and Cultural*

Diversity nor its revision in the *Ethnic Broadcasting Policy* in 1999 raised the question of ownership. Accordingly, the following years would witness the integration of minority media into major media companies. Rogers' takeover of CFMT in 1986 was the first instance of this trend, but Shaw's purchase of Telelatino was further evidence of a long-term decline in the diversity of ownership that would continue for decades. The 1992 takeover of Chinavision and Cathay International by Fairchild Communication, a partnership between Hong Kong-based TVB and Happy Valley Investments, a holding company for a variety of properties of Thomas Fung, integrated the broadcast operations within a larger, transnational business that included property development and commercial real estate. The justification for these developments was rooted in the difficulty of operating an economically sustainable independent broadcaster in Canada, but the effect was to shift expectations for third-language broadcasting from involving ownership to being focused on the diversity of programming. These expectations regarding ownership would be further undermined with the introduction of a framework for the distribution of foreign-owned services through digital cable, which was introduced in 2000.

FROM LOCAL NETWORKS TO INTERNATIONAL SERVICES

At the margins of the development of the new arrangement between local and "national" ethnocultural services were concerns about the relationship between the new services and non-Canadian parties. The most explicit formulation of these question came in the form of discussions about the amount of Canadian content the stations would carry. However, there were also concerns about attempts on the part of foreign governments to surreptitiously influence the services. In 1989, there were inquiries made regarding Chinavision's coverage of protests in Tiananmen Square, with allegations that the station had taken financing directly from the Chinese government.[69] No conclusions were reached regarding these investigations, although presentations on the topic were made to the CRTC. After the sale of the network to Thomas Fung in the early 1990s, and its renaming as Fairchild Television, the new management team said that it would be impossible to determine what had taken place in the past.[70] The coverage the story garnered in the press makes clear that the kinds of international relationships that may be involved in third-language television raised different kinds of issues than did the concern about undue American influence on Canadian culture.

However, these concerns did not result in further restrictions on international content. Like most Canadian networks, much of the content on Fairchild and Telelatino already came from international sources. Fairchild was transformed into the Canadian franchise of Hong Kong-based TVB (short for Television Broadcasts Limited), who also held a minority ownership position in the broadcaster.[71] Much of Telelatino's Italian content was taken from the international services of the Italian public broadcaster *Radiotelevisione Italiana* (RAI). Some of this was taken from the seven hundred annual hours that were provided free to broadcasters around the globe, amounting to roughly two hours a day, as part of the public service mandate of the Italian broadcaster. An additional agreement was later signed that allowed the Canadian broadcaster to supplement these hours with more programming at a fixed cost that included sports programming in particular.[72]

However, the introduction of digital cable distribution in the late 1990s allowed for the separation of international services from their Canadian partners. In anticipation of the introduction of digital cable across the country, the CRTC outlined a process that made the addition of international services to digital programming packages easier.[73] Unlike with the previous approaches to the licensing of ethnic television in Canada, these new services could be made available with minimal or no requirements to produce local or national programming.

If issues relating to the relationship between national and local services constituted the defining debate during the previous period in the development of third-language television in Canada, this debate shifted with the rise of these new channels, which speaks to the new scale at which cultural and linguistic diversity was to be regulated. These services were increasingly seen as one of the ways in which the Canadian media market was connected to the international television industry. No longer an issue internal to the nation, these new television offerings were now seen as straddling the increasingly porous and volatile borders of the nation itself.

The new scale of third-language media in Canada became most apparent in the debates that surrounded the introduction of the Italian-language RAI International and the Arabic-language news service Al-Jazeera. The details of the conflict between RAI International and Telelatino have been outlined in greater detail elsewhere; here, it is sufficient to draw out only a few aspects of this conflict.[74] Most important among these is that RAI's application included among its justifications the importance the service would have for the electoral rights of Italian citizens residing in Canada. The debates that followed involved not just the broadcasters involved, the CRTC, and interested stakeholders; it also involved the Department of Foreign Affairs and Trade, the cabinet, and representatives of the Italian government. It was a debate in which older, nationally framed understandings of multiculturalism and assimilation came into conflict with an understanding of cultural diversity shaped by the introduction of digital distribution and expanded global mobility.

If the case of RAI International brought into focus the stresses on the existing arrangement in which Canadian channels were given preference over non-Canadian services, the case of Al-Jazeera highlights the extent to which the shifting economic and technological consensus continued to be shaped by geopolitical tensions.[75] Having been established in Qatar in 1996, there were concerns regarding the content of the station. Earlier I noted that the government and advertisers were both wary of the ethnic press because of potential links to communism and socialism. By 2002, when applications were made to include Al-Jazeera Arabic among the approved services for digital distribution in Canada, the anxieties of the Cold War had been replaced by those of the global war on terror. Concerns about anti-Semitism and sympathies for Islamic terrorism contributed to the CRTC's imposing regulations that required cable distributors to accept liability for any violation of Canadian laws.[76]

The decision to license RAI International and the conditions placed on Al-Jazeera's licence resolved debates about the status of international broadcasters operating in Canada in ways that ostensibly maintained the integrity of the nation's broadcasting system and its culture, but in neither case were the stations refused access to Canada. This turn suggested that there was a new understanding of the role international services might play in Canadian media. This was followed with new criteria for licensing non-Canadian ethnic services developed between 2004 and 2006.[77] As a result, it became significantly easier for new third-language services, now referred to as international channels by cable companies, to enter the Canadian market. What followed was a rapid increase in the number of third-language television channels available to cable subscribers in Canada. Some of these new channels were the product of arrangements between international broadcasters and Canada-based distributors. Eventually, the complexity of navigating the borders of television distribution in Canada supported the growth of intermediaries who broker the relationship between broadcasters and distributors. The largest of these is Ethnic Channels Group, founded in Richmond Hill in 2004 by Slava Levin. It holds the licences for more than sixty international channels currently available in Canada and has filed applications for dozens more that have yet to be launched.[78] While the Ethnic Channels Group does have production facilities, the bulk of its business comes from consulting and supporting the applications of international channels seeking to enter the Canadian market.

The existing third-language channels have responded to these developments by expanding into multi-channel services that allow for a greater number of program hours. Spread across two channels (Fairchild TV and Talentvision), Fairchild launched a third channel in 2013 known as Fairchild 2.[79] This development is certainly also a product of the population growth and maturation of Chinese Canadian communities into sizable, wealthy audiences in many parts of the country, but it is also a response to the growing number of Chinese-language services available, but not based, in Canada. Telelatino has followed a similar trajectory, although its development has responded to the declining number of Italian speakers in Canada. This has involved repeatedly asking permission to broadcast more English-language programming as well as broadcasting American content with Italian themes (such as *The Sopranos*) translated into Italian and Spanish.[80] At the same time, the station has developed the profitability of its Spanish-language programming primarily through the creation of a new digital service known as TLN en Español in 2007, which was later rebranded as Univision Canada in 2014, reflecting an agreement with the US-based Spanish-language network.

At the level of regulation, however, the introduction of digital distribution raised many issues about how the national television industry regulates the dynamics of international media. These were issues that, while of significance in the earliest days of media, had mostly been put to rest as the distinctions between national, local, and international services were relatively stable. The CRTC's increasingly light-handed approach to regulating competition brought with it new complexities related to the shifting scales of ethnocultural television in Canada. The older "national" services have struggled to survive the arrival of large numbers of international services. The CRTC initially attempted to mitigate the effects of direct competition by requiring cable providers interested in launching services that would broadcast more than 40 percent of their content in one of the languages already covered by an existing service to offer the older service to its viewers as well. This was called a "buy-through," and it was an attempt to ensure that cable companies did not abandon the national ethnic networks for the new services, many of which they had sponsored for entry into the country.[81] Taken together, these changes speak to the emergent scale of media policy, a development that involves audiences that are both increasingly fragmented and focused in their consumption as well as increasingly connected to other similar audiences around the world. The result is an attenuated understanding of the local in which the primary relationship involves the interaction between international media companies and individual consumers, with Canadian media serving primarily as a means for distribution. It is a far cry from the decision to reject Stanczykowski's application on the grounds that he did not live in Winnipeg.

CONCLUSION: MINORITY MEDIA IN THE NARROWCAST ERA

The account provided here is but one of many ways to describe the development and transformation of third-language television. Other accounts might emphasize the expanding diversity of offerings available to television audiences in Canada, connecting it with the transition from terrestrial to cable to digital modes of distribution that made it possible. In this chapter, I attempt to show how the establishment of new scalar logics for broadcasting emerged from the interaction between how media regulators addressed multiculturalism's becoming part of official government discourse and the growth of the Canadian television industry beginning in the late 1970s.

The redefinition of the "local" and the "national" operative between the 1960s and early 2000s relied upon a configuration of the relationship between public institutions, private enterprises, and individual and group identities in ways that were grounded in the continual maintenance of fixed national boundaries for cultural, political, and economic activities. The ongoing discussions, reprimands, and recalibrations through which public regulators structured minority television are evidence of this process. The more recent opening of Canadian television distribution to "international" services abandoned many of the most salient aspects of the policies that created "national" services in the 1980s, including the absolute preference for Canadian services and the avoidance of direct competition between similar services. This transition can be seen as a part of the integration of Canadian media industries into international markets, a common trend globally in recent years.

The CRTC's decision to make the inclusion of Rogers' OMNI Network mandatory in all cable packages in May 2017 is a logical extension of the trends in ethnocultural television outlined in this chapter. Rogers justified the request during its regular licence renewal hearings in economic terms, explaining that, without the fees assessed to every cable subscriber in the country, the service would be forced to close. This decision, and the subsequent hearings regarding the long-term licensing of a mandatory national multilingual service, might be seen as a positive step forward. However, it might also be interpreted as a fitting closing act for the history of multicultural television that started nearly fifty years earlier. This is not because Canada is any less complex culturally or linguistically, but because the fundamental presumptions upon which such a service is based are no longer responsive to the dynamics of the contemporary moment. In the last two decades, the logics of spectrum scarcity and the powers of nationalist media regulation that structured the scalar logic of third-language television, and that of radio before it, have been irrevocably eroded. In contrast to the second half of the twentieth century, the scalar logic that has emerged in recent decades is designed to encourage the movement of media across borders rather than to manage or often slow it down, effectively short-circuiting (literally) the mediating role once played by the institutions charged with the protection of national culture.

CONCLUSION

Post-Digital? Post-Multicultural?

It is a cold, rainy December day in Toronto when I meet Olumide Adewumi in a café near Bay Street not far from the tech start-up where he works. Adewumi emigrated from Nigeria to Canada in 2005 to study information technology at York University.[1] Tired of making physical copies of the music he brought with him from Nigeria for his friends, in 2008 he designed a simple online music player using Flash and posted it online. The player proved successful among his friends at school and quickly gained a larger following as word spread across their network both in Toronto and elsewhere. The site was officially launched soon after as "Gidilounge," a name Adewumi originally intended to use for a news and commentary site for Nigerians in the diaspora. Over the following three years, the site expanded rapidly until it was producing a variety of original programs. In the early years of social media, Adewumi's skills as a software engineer allowed him to develop the digital tools necessary to connect Gidilounge's producers and audiences around the world. At the height its popularity, there were more than fifty thousand regular listeners streaming audio from around the world. Musicians and promoters approached Gidilounge asking to be included on its weekly playlists, recognizing it as one of the more successful digital media companies serving the Nigerian diaspora.

There are a number of similarities between Adewumi's experience at Gidilounge and the individuals and organizations discussed in this book. Like the publications and broadcasts decades before, Gidilounge was an organization that would not have existed if it had not been for the efforts and ingenuity of a small number of dedicated contributors. However, the story of Gidilounge differs significantly from that of radio and television in ways that speak to fundamental shifts in the cultural, political, and technological context that gave rise to the media infrastructures supporting minority media across the twentieth century. Gidilounge struggled to navigate changes in the digital distribution of media beginning in 2012, particularly the centralization of the market for music streaming services around a few key players. Adewumi, a software engineer, describes Gidilounge as a technology company driven by his passion for music. As media industries adapted to the technological capabilities and economic dynamics of platforms, Gidilounge found itself squeezed out of a market dominated by the behemoths of the digital economy – a community media project that was out of place in the age of cloud-based global capitalism.

The ups and down of Gidilounge provide an occasion to reflect on how our contemporary media context, which is increasingly defined by the culture and economy of digital platforms, provides a new perspective on the history of media serving cultural and linguistic minorities in Canada. It brings into sharp focus the insufficiency of the very terms inherited from that history. Multiculturalism in Canada contributes to the context within which Gidilounge developed, but it never provided the cultural or political horizon of its existence. It was always a globally oriented rather than a local or national undertaking. Although Adewumi has lived in Toronto since he launched the company, it is difficult to discern the location of Gidilounge from press accounts or the material circulated by the company itself. In the digital media economy, national borders are of secondary importance to discoverability and the ability to hold the attention of users.

The media infrastructure supporting minority media institutionalized as part of Canadian multiculturalism discussed in the previous chapters is marked by its origins in the second half of the twentieth century. In both its success and its difficulties, Adewumi's story highlights the limitations of this infrastructure in response to the technical and economic logics and scales of digital media. The conclusion of the preceding chapter argues that the CRTC's 2017 decision to establish a national multilingual channel should not be interpreted as an indication of the success of the institutional and cultural dynamics that have developed over the previous fifty years. On the contrary, it is evidence of a significant break with the forms and functions of the media infrastructure of multiculturalism documented here. There are, however, other signs of this transition. For example, the rise of online information sources serving the global diaspora that makes up the ethnocultural sector in media, and the popularity of streaming services distributing media across that diaspora, has transformed the organization and economy of minority print media and third-language radio. Gidilounge's success belongs to the first stages of this transition, which was marked by a radical transformation in how information was able to move across national borders. However, the difficulties it encountered are indicative of the now-dominant organization of digital media in which power and control over digital infrastructure are concentrated in the hands of a much smaller number of transnational companies.[2]

The fragmentation of the cultural, political, and technological arrangements discussed in previous chapters is also apparent in other, perhaps less expected, locations. Expressions calling for a return to narrowly defined forms of nationalism are made manifest through the increasing frequency with which proclamations marking the "death" or "failure" of multiculturalism and the related dismissal of "identity politics" find popular audiences.[3] Some accounts describe this in terms of the ability to express long-held beliefs through social media that run contrary to the long-standing consensus about identity and community, but this overlooks the extent to which reconfiguration of the global cultural landscape in the wake of networked media has fundamentally transformed the terrain upon which the balance between diversity and nationalism that characterized multiculturalism in Canada took shape after the Second World War.

If the problem addressed by the configuration of media infrastructure that developed during the twentieth century was finding a way of supporting and managing diversity within cultural and technological forms that mandated uniformity, we are now confronted with the problem of how to build common spaces within cultural and technological forms that operate by means of individuation. Differentiation is the dominant cultural and economic logic of network media producing forms of identity and community that are more rigorously homogenous.[4] In this way, recent declarations announcing the "death" of multiculturalism can be interpreted as a response to the forms of identification and community that flourish in networked communities.

The individualized modes of address and engagement that characterize contemporary media emphasize particularity, but they often erase its complex interrelation with commonality. If commonality was the de facto ground for political and cultural agency in the twentieth century, there are a myriad of indications that there is no similarly dominant framework for conceptualizing the common in contemporary social and political life. However, a nostalgic recovery of an overly idealized past is not possible or even desirable. Even though the forms of being together across cultural and linguistic diversity that were institutionalized through media infrastructure in the twentieth century might persist, they cannot resolve the tensions and contradictions of our contemporary situation. However, they might serve as a starting point – not as models to follow, but as something that enables us to comprehend how older ways of understanding identity and organizing community now provide the cultural and technical grounds for individual and collective isolation. The task at hand, then, is not the preservation of the forms of media and culture that were only ever partially successful in realizing an ideal of multicultural community but, rather, the development of an approach to this history that contributes to the continuous renewal of the demand for a commonality in and through (rather than against) difference.

Notes

INTRODUCTION

1 Katie Underwood, "Sara Polley: Now Is Not a Time for Women to Keep Quiet," *Maclean's*, 22 September 2017, https://www.macleans.ca/culture/television/sarah-polley-now-is-not-a-time-for-women-to-keep-quiet/.
2 I first noticed the comparison when it was made during the roundtable "Culture Shift: Gender and Diversity in the Film Industry" (23 January 2018, York University, Toronto) by Theresa Tova, president of ACTRA Toronto at the time, who – quoting a third person whose name I did not catch – noted that what she saw on screen did not reflect the people she encountered on the streetcar.
3 Ekwa Ekoko, "How to Teach Racial Acceptance," *ParentsCanada*, 25 March 2015, http://www.parentscanada.com/school/how-to-teach-racial-acceptance.
4 These two ways of thinking about communication have received their well-known development in James W. Carey's essay "A Cultural Approach to Communication," in which he contrasts the "transmission" and the "ritual" view of communication. While the transmission view has traditionally dominated how we talk about communication, the "ritual" view has an equally long history connecting communication to community and ideas about social and spiritual communion across venues as varied as sporting events, religious gatherings, and seances.
5 Fleras, *Racisms*; Bannerji, *Dark Side of the Nation*.
6 Straw, "Circulatory Turn," 23.
7 Ibid.
8 Mayer, Caldwell, and Banks, *Production Studies*.
9 Haque, *Multiculturalism*, 18.

10 Fleras, *Racisms*, 246.
11 Walcott, *Queer Returns*, 94.
12 Taylor, "Politics of Recognition," 34–5. Taylor draws upon a history of interactionist understandings of identity, from Hegel to Fanon to George Herbert Mead.
13 Taylor, *Modern Social Imaginaries*, 83.
14 See the work of Nancy Fraser (esp. "Rethinking the Public Sphere" and "From Redistribution to Recognition") for a particularly detailed and influential critique of the universalizing tendencies of many models of the public sphere.
15 Day, *Multiculturalism and the History of Canadian Diversity*, 221
16 Bouchard and Taylor, *Building the Future*.
17 Ibid., 17.
18 Ibid., 250.
19 Taylor, "Politics of Recognition," 73.
20 Ibid., 73.
21 Coulthard, *Red Skin White Masks*, 25 (emphasis in original).
22 Walcott, *Queer Returns*, 80.
23 For two very different, but foundational, perspectives on infrastructure, see Graham and Marvin, *Splintering Urbanism*; and Bowker and Leigh Starr, *Sorting Things Out*.
24 Bowker and Starr, *Sorting Things Out*, 319.
25 Larkin, "Politics and Poetics of Infrastructure," 329.
26 Peters, *Marvelous Clouds*, 30.
27 Ibid., 32.
28 Larkin, "Politics and Poetics of Infrastructure," 329.
29 Parks, "Technostruggles," 65–6.
30 Parks and Starosielski, *Signal Traffic*, 5 (emphasis in orginal).
31 Peters, *Marvelous Clouds*, 37.
32 See Horkheimer and Adorno, *Dialectic of Enlightenment*, for one of the most influential articulations of this argument.
33 Roth, *Something New in the Air*; and Roth, "Delicate Acts of 'Colour Balancing': Multiculturalism and Canadian television broadcasting policies and practices."
34 See Ahadi and Murray, "Urban Mediascapes and Cultural Flows," 589–94; Murray, "Media Infrastructure for Multicultural Diversity."
35 Murray, "Media Infrastructure for Multicultural Diversity," 63.
36 Husband, "Globalisation, Media Infrastructures and Identities in a Diasporic Community," 31.
37 Murray, "Media Infrastructure for Multicultural Diversity," 63.

38 Ibid., 66.
39 Fujiwara, *Ethnic Elites*.

CHAPTER ONE

1 Miguel J. Tomazo, "Cine Argentino en Toronto", *El Popular*, 9 April 1974, 6.
2 Interview, Wayne Fromm, 27 October 2017.
3 For the history of the Duchess, see Taylor, *Toronto's Local Movie Theatres*, 126–8.
4 Interview, Wayne Fromm, 27 October 2017.
5 "Lights, Camera, cut! Farewell to the Centre", *Toronto Life*, June 1977, 14.
6 Tomazo, "Cine Argentino en Toronto."
7 Information regarding the capacity of the theatre is based on information in "Theatre Regulatory Files," RG 56-9, Archives of Ontario.
8 The earliest advertisement for a screening at the centre published in *El Popular* was 21 March 21 1973 (2) for the Spanish-language version of *Guns for San Sebastian* (Verneuil 1968), starring Anthony Quinn and Charles Bronson. A few weeks later (11 April 1973, 5), advertisements for Spanish films at the Kensington started to run in *El Popular*, but the theatre was already advertising to the Spanish-speaking community (see figure 1.1). The first three films shown were the Spanish-language version of the Portuguese film *Sete Balas Para Selma* (Macedo 1967), *Digan lo que digan* (Camus 1967) from Spain, and *Paula* (Salazar 1969) from Mexico.
9 Cinema Colon established a sister venue of the same name on Boulevard St-Laurent in Montreal that operated for a short period of time during the early 1980s. Ads ran weekly in *El Correo Español* throughout December 1980.
10 Based on a survey of *El Popular* between 1971 and 1980 conducted by Maria Clara Casasfranco.
11 Mata, "Latin American Immigration."
12 There was a significant increase in the number of arrivals to Canada from Argentina beginning in 1973, nearly doubling the number that had entered the country each year during the prior decade.
13 Interview, Wayne Fromm, 27 October 2017.
14 When screenings in languages other than English disappeared from the Centre Theatre in 1975, its importance as a venue for the Spanish-, Italian-, and Portuguese-speaking communities moved to other theatres located along College Street to the north (such as the Kensington Theatre

and later the Royal Theatre) and, in the case of Italian films, to St Clair Avenue, where the St Clair Theatre (St Clair and Dufferin) and the Radio City Theatre (St Clair and Bathurst) were destinations for the Italians who settled along "Corso Italia."

15 For a key early text, see Light, *Ethnic Enterprise in America*. For a more recent approach with an emphasis on space, see Kaplan and Li, *Landscapes of the Ethnic Economy*.
16 Light and Gold, *Ethnic Economies*, 4 (emphasis in original).
17 Gomery, "Who Killed Hollywood?" See also Rutherford, *When Television Was Young*, which provides some insight into the introduction of television to Canada.
18 A notable exception is Longfellow, "Bollywood/Toronto."
19 For all of the similarities between Canada and the United States, the profound differences between the history of immigration in the two countries contributes to a significantly different trajectory for the development of multicultural and multilingual theatres in the 1950s and after. The difference in scale between the two countries makes direct comparisons difficult, but it is nonetheless clear that there are markedly different trends in the volume and sources of immigration. In Canada, the percentage of immigrants rises slowly, but continuously, from the 1950s to the 1980s before increasing even more quickly beginning in the 1990s. In the United States, there is a steady decline in the percentage of the population born in other countries after the end of the Second World War that continues until the 1980s, at which time it begins to increase again. However, even with this increase, foreign-born residents remain at only 15 percent of the nation's inhabitants, which is about 5 percent lower than the figure for Canada for the same period. Of course, aggregate numbers like these hide the disparities in the number of immigrants who settled in different regions, and this is especially important as cities became the most common place for newcomers to settle. New York City would remain an important destination for new arrivals, yet much of the rest of the US experienced a dramatic drop off in the number of immigrants. In Canada, cities were the primary destinations of immigrants, but they arrived in such significant numbers that there was an overall increase in the population. Of equal significance in making sense of the different demographic context in each country are the marked differences in the countries from which migrants were arriving. The rate of migration from Mexico to the United States is significantly higher than from any other country. In the Canadian context, there are certainly countries whose former residents make up a larger portion of migrants, but there is no single country that has the same significance as does Mexico in the United States.

20 Gomery, *Shared Pleasures*, 171–215.
21 Gomery discusses the history of African American exhibition- and movie-going in *Shared Pleasures*, 155–70.
22 Wilinsky, *Sure Seaters*; Balio, *Foreign Film Renaissance*.
23 See Abel, *Americanizing the Movies*; and Allen, "Relocating American Film History" for an account (and critique) of this understanding of early cinema in the United States.
24 For further information about early Ukrainian-Canadian film culture, see Mochoruk, "Orest T Martynowych" and Nebesio, "Zaporozhets za Dunaiem," including a discussion of the first Canadian-produced film in Ukrainian and its exhibition.
25 The publication went through numerous titles, changing to *Canadian Film Weekly* and finally *Canadian Film and TV Weekly*. "Yearbooks" were published annually beginning in 1951 until the 1970s.
26 Taylor, "Our Business," 1956, 20.
27 Ibid., "Our Business," 1958, 23.
28 Ibid., "Our Business," 1960, 23.
29 For a history of this period in film exhibition and the attempt to attract audiences with various "gimmicks," see Heffernan, *Ghouls, Gimmicks and Gold*.
30 Sunday screenings were permitted in Quebec, despite objections from the church, since the introduction of cinema to the province. The sections of the Ontario Theatres Act forbidding "the showing of films or the staging of performances" on Sundays was repealed in February 1961 ("Sunday Movies Gain Approval in Legislature," *Globe and Mail*, 22 February 1961). A number of minority papers supported the decision and published editorials in favour of a change in policy ("New Canadians' Papers Back Sunday Movies," *Globe and Mail*, 26 November 1960). Similar changes were made later in other provinces, including Manitoba (1964), Nova Scotia (1964) and Alberta (1969).
31 Ross, *Burlesque West*, 15.
32 The Cinema Lumiere in Toronto and Mac's Theatre in Winnipeg are two examples of Canadian art house theatres operating during this period.
33 See Arthur Zeldin, "The Curious World of *Real* Foreign Movies," *Toronto Star*, 23 July 1966.
34 Bossin, *Stars of David*.
35 Sebert, *Nabes*.
36 "Theatre Regulatory Files," RG 56-9, Archives of Ontario.
37 At various points, the Pagoda, the Naaz, the Krishna, the Kensington, the Elektra, the Athenian, and the Acropolis are all cited for various problems

with meeting public health and safety standards set for the theatres, concession stands, and washrooms. See "Theatre Regulatory Files," RG 56-9, Archives of Ontario.
38 Saunders, *Arrival Cities*, 20–1.
39 The statements regarding the exhibition of film are based upon an analysis of newspaper reports and advertisements as well as on a quantitative analysis of records related to the licensing of venues and films in British Columbia, Ontario, and Quebec between 1947 and 2000.
40 Described in Cedilot and Noel's *Mafia Inc.* as "a depressing brick structure in an equally depressing industrial no man's land" (101), it garnered notoriety thanks to being the site of a gang-related assassination in 1976 after an Italian-language screening of *Godfather II*. The subsequent coverage highlighted the fact that Puliafito was the sister of a leading figure in the city's organized crime family, Vic "the Egg" Cotroni.
41 Rocco Mastrangelo, interview, 25 January 2015.
42 Longfellow, "Toronto/Bollywood," 89–91.
43 "Vancouver," *Box Office*, 8 March 1976.
44 Greg Klymkiw, "Filmseen," *Manitoban*, 25 October 1979, 5.
45 Advertisement, *El Popular*, 5 February 1974, 8; Advertisement, *El Popular*, 4 April 1974, 5.
46 "Vancouver," *Box Office*, 8 March 1976.
47 "8 Underground Films," *Ubyssey*, 13 September 1967, 14; "Young Swallows Spread Their Wings," *Chinatown News*, 18 September 1964.
48 Cahute, "Bollywood Is Back," *Province*, 26 May 2013.
49 Ibid.
50 Requests were made to the responsible government agencies in Quebec, but searches for older records were "inconclusive."
51 There are a number of absences in these data. Most notably, Hollywood films dubbed into other languages would not be included the data pertaining to film licensing, even though there were a significant portion of films shown in languages other than English. Furthermore, such techniques of cultural analysis do not supplant what might be learned about the experience of film-going from both contemporary accounts published in newspapers and from retrospective discussions such as those being undertaken by Paul Moore at Ryerson University. Nonetheless, they do give a sense of the variety of films that, at the time, may not have been apparent even to industry insiders.
52 The licensing data are themselves an archive of how the globe was mapped at different periods in time. The multiple names used to describe films from the Soviet Union or the use of "Africa" to cover films from a

53 A survey of ads in the *Corriere Italiano* indicates that the Riviera changed films every week, opening only Friday, Saturday, and Sunday. A review of Sing Wah shows a similar turnover at both the Shaw Theatre and the Golden Harvest Theatre beginning in the late 1970s.
54 T'Cha Dunlevy, "Fall in Love with India through Magic of Bollywood," *Montreal Gazette*, 3 May 2013, B4.
55 Beverly Stern. "Movie Industry Pioneer Honored by His Peers," *Canadian Jewish News*, 21 January 1977, 8.
56 For a history of Artkino, see Krukones's ("Unpooling of Artkino") discussion of Soviet efforts at film distribution in North America. Krukones does not mention Clavir in his account, but there are many contemporary accounts of his role in bringing international films to Toronto. Sydney Newman, later known for his role in the creation of *Doctor Who*, recalls in his memoir *Head of Drama* that he worked with Clavir in the early 1940s printing film posters for the "Cosmopolitan Film Company," which appears to have been a forerunner of Artkino Canada. He would later go on to work in television, producing the long-running Canadian quiz show *Going Places* (1973–80.) Clavir was a long-time supporter of the Communist Party of Canada and frequently wrote in support of better Canadian-Soviet relations. He briefly gained international attention in the 1970s when it was claimed he was harbouring Angela Davis (along with his daughter Judith) at his home in Toronto ("Angela Davis Is Sought in Shooting That killed Judge on Coast," *New York Times*, 16 August 1970, 66).
57 The first listing for a film at the Studio is *Il Trovatore* in October 1951 (*Globe and Mail*, 20 October 1951), although there are indications that Italian films were being shown there earlier that year as well.
58 Mary Walpole. "Around the Town," *Globe and Mail*, 14 January 1954.
59 Stern, "Movie Industry Pioneer Honored by His Peers," 8.
60 "Kensington Theatre," Theatre Regulatory Files, RG 56-9, Archives of Ontario.
61 Brunton and Paputts, *Last Pogo Jumps Again*.
62 For a brief overview of the venue's early history, see Taylor, *The Nabes*, 88–90.
63 According to records for the theatre, Thomas Vlahos took over the theatre in 1961 and ran it for a year as the Acropolis before transferring management to William Dundas who operated it as the Dundas, then the Cinema

Ellas Theatre until 1971. At that time James Lai took over the venue and renamed it the China Cinema. These dates are based on the regulatory files at the Ontario Archives (RG 56-9.)

64 Cynthia Brouse. "Indian Summer Little India in Toronto," *Toronto Life*, 2005, http://ezproxy.library.yorku.ca/login?url=https://search.proquest.com/docview/214366469?accountid=15182.

65 My thanks to Pierre Peageau for helping me reconstruct the timeline at this venue.

66 "Vancouver Vaude," *Variety*, 19 February 1958, 51. It's announced in the *Chinatown News* (18 January 1960, 29) that the Gin Wah Shing Musical and Dramatic Society will begin screening weekly Chinese films at the Majestic.

67 Elizabeth Godley, "Eight We've Lost," *Vancouver Sun*, 18 February 1989.

68 Zeldin, "Curious World of *Real* Foreign Movies," *Toronto Star*, 23 July 1966.

69 Frank Jones, "The Good Guy Always Wins in Chinese Films," *Toronto Star*, 26 March 1976.

70 Zeldin, "Curious World of *Real* Foreign Films"

71 Interview, Wayne Fromm.

72 For a discussion of the relationship between sports and ethnicity in Canada, see Fielding, "Ethnicity as an Exercise in Sport."

73 McCarthy, "Like an Earthquake!," 308–9.

74 Jack Marks, "Closed-Circuit TV in Canada May Bring $1-million Fight Gate," *Globe and Mail*, 10 February 1971.

75 Jim Kernaghan, "European Soccer on Closed Circuit," *Toronto Star*, 2 October 1971.

76 Peter Cooney, "Thousands Pay $12.50 to See Cup TV," *Globe and Mail*, 12 June 1978.

77 There is a vast literature on the dynamics of audience behaviour in media studies as well in many adjacent fields in which how people use and interpret mediated communication has been explored. The emphasis of this work, particularly that which has been influenced by British Cultural Studies, has been to make the case for a broadly conceived humanist politics in response to the controlling and constraining dynamics of centralized media industries.

78 Hinther, *Perogies and Politics*, provides a history of the importance of the Labour temple through the twentieth century, and she notes that popular films (e.g., those of Gene Autry and Jean Harlow) were shown on weeknights.

79 Polec, *Hurrah Revolutionaries*, 138.

80 Wilfred List, "Two Laborers' Union Locals Fall Out over Proposed Wage Settlement," *Globe and Mail*, 31 May 1967; "Dismissal Protested by Italian Laborers," *Globe and Mail*, 15 April 1968.
81 See Cunningham and Sinclair, *Floating Lives*, for a discussion of various approaches to thinking about diaspora and the public sphere. Husband elaborates upon what he describes as a "multi-ethnic public sphere."
82 Hu, "Defenders of the Palace."
83 Hansen, *Babel & Babylon*, 62.
84 Hu, "Defenders of the Palace", 138.
85 Although not discussed in detail in the next chapter, the government's definition of the ethnic press often explicitly distinguished between "newspapers" and "Ethnic Religious Papers" (Citizenship Branch, Ethnic Press Brief, 1958).
86 "Barberia Centrale," *Tribuna Portuguesa*, 2 February 1973, 5.
87 "Threats Bring Charges," *Toronto Star*, 15 May 1975; Brennan, Rick, "East Indians Warn They'll Take No More Abuse," *Toronto Star*, 20 May 1980.
88 "Midnight Movie: Pavone Fans Cause Near Riot," *Globe and Mail*, 6 September 1966.
89 Razack, "Introduction," *Race, Space and the Law*, 1.
90 Archives du Quebec, 2000-03-001/2, Bordereau 21697.
91 Rocco Mastrangelo, interview, 23 January 2015.
92 Longfellow, "Bollywood/Toronto," 91.
93 Rocco Mastrangelo, interview.
94 Mascia, CRTC, 2972, 3 February 1983.
95 Ibid., 3007, 3 February 1983.

CHAPTER TWO

1 Park, *Immigrant Press*.
2 Ibid., v.
3 Ibid., 359–468.
4 Park and Burgess, *The City*, 42.
5 Day, *Multiculturalism and the History of Canadian Diversity*, 146–76.
6 Ibid., 158.
7 For the purposes of this chapter, newspapers are defined as publications that appear with a set frequency providing readers with general information about a range of current events. This does not include other types of publications, such as newsletters and bulletins, published by community groups or churches.

8 Reginald Whitaker has argued that Canada's entire immigration policy during this period was centred on ensuring that communists did not enter the country, suggesting that the ideological framing provided by the Cold War aligned business interests, members of immigrant groups, and agencies implementing the government's national security agenda. Complementing this argument, Franca Iacovetta (among others) has shown the ways that Cold War ideology extended beyond the border to transform many aspects of Canadian society, including the creation of a number of programs that served to educate and enforce "Canadianism" among the newcomers throughout the immigrant and settlement process.
9 The primary purpose of conferences of "Ethnic Press Editors of Canada" held in Ottawa was, as articulated with regard to the event in 1961: "Promotion of language classes, citizenship applications and other steps by which newcomers are welcomed into full membership in the family of Canadian citizens" ("Purpose of Conference," Library and Archives Canada [hereafter LAC], RG 26-A-1-a).
10 It is worth noting that the phrase "the ethnic press" was almost unheard of before the Second World War, only beginning to circulate widely at the beginning of the 1960s. That most of the groups discussed in this chapter were formed in the early 1950s suggests that they were well positioned to play a role in defining the phrase as it was understood in the Canadian context.
11 This excludes the prominent role played by churches and gives only limited space to the community groups that sponsored those publications that fall outside the focus of this book.
12 The commemorative volumes for these organizations have provided much of the contextual information about these organizations. See Canada Press Club, Kristjanson, and Bashuk, *Multilingual Press in Manitoba*; Kirschbaum, *Twenty-Five Years of Canada Ethnic Press Federation*; and Kirschbaum, Heydenkorn, and Mauko, *Twenty Years of the Ethnic Press Association of Ontario*.
13 Iacovetta, *Gatekeepers*, chap. 5.
14 Reliable circulation figures for the ethnic press are difficult to locate. The figures here are drawn from a variety of sources, including the *Canadian Almanac and Directory* as well as materials published by the papers and the Press Federation. However, it should be noted that these figures should not be seen as entirely reliable. Most of the papers did not receive audited circulation figures from the Audit Bureau of Circulation and, as was noted by some members of the press, suffered from a tendency to increase their numbers with the aim of artificially inflating advertising rates.

15 Mazepa, "Democracy." Martynowych, "Ukrainian Socialist Movement."
16 Kalbfleisch, *History of the Pioneer German Language Press of Ontario*; Lindal, *Icelanders in Canada*.
17 There are a number of examples of these trends. The Icelandic community in Gimli saw two newspapers and a literary magazine close between 1901 and 1910 only to be replaced by two papers based in Winnipeg that served Icelandic Canadians across the country and in the United States. Similarly, Winnipeg's *Der Nordwesten* and Regina's the *Courier* both saw themselves as regional papers serving the entire Canadian West as well as the province of Ontario following the absence of local German papers between the 1920s and end of the Second World War. There were, of course, exceptions. As noted above, *Der Kanader Yid* (later known as *Der Yiddishe Wort*) was the largest Yiddish-language paper in the west, but other Canadian cities also hosted popular publications serving their local Jewish communities. In Montreal, the *Jewish Daily Eagle*, published in Yiddish, and the English-language *Canadian Jewish Times* both attracted large numbers of readers, while Toronto was home to the Yiddish *Daily Hebrew Journal* and the English-language weeklies the *Jewish Standard* and the *Canadian Jewish News*.
18 Canada Press Club, Kristjanson, and Bashuk, *Multilingual Press in Manitoba*, 15–16.
19 Lindal served as president of the Manitoba Liberal Association in the late 1930s.
20 Lindal, *Two Ways of Life*.
21 Walter Lindal, "Our Democratic Heritage," speech delivered to the Empire Club, 27 April 1939.
22 Canada Press Club, Kristjanson, and Bashuk, *Multilingual Press in Manitoba*, 15.
23 Kirschbaum, *Twenty-Five Years of Canada Ethnic Press Federation*, 14.
24 Canada Press Club, Kristjanson, and Bashuk, *Multilingual Press in Manitoba*, 20.
25 Whitaker and Marcuse, *Cold War Canada*.
26 Pal, *Interests of State*, 70.
27 Ibid.
28 Lindal's account of the formation of the Canada Press Club can be found in Canada Press Club, Kristjanson, and Bashuk, eds., *Multilingual Press in Manitoba*, 19–32.
29 Ibid., 22.
30 There is a considerable literature on the wartime efforts of the Canadian government to monitor and manage minority Canadians. Dreisziger ("Rise

of a Bureaucracy for Multiculturalism") argues that the Nationalities Branch can be seen as one of the earliest steps on the part of the Canadian government towards addressing multiculturalism. Mark Kristmanson (*Plateaus of Freedom*), on the other hand, notes that this overlooks the deep involvement of the Nationalities Branch, and the activities of its director Tracy Philipps, in surveillance and censorship of the ethnic press.

31 For a more detailed discussion of Kaye's activities with the ethnic press, see Iacovetta, *Gatekeepers*, chap. 5.

32 The Dominion Press Censor started surveying the "language press" for signs of radicalism and socialism starting in 1915. Towards the end of the First World War, the government had ordered a blanket ban of publications in "enemy languages," defined as the language of any country or people at war with, or occupied by a country at war with, Great Britain and its allies. This led to the banning of publications in Hungarian, Bulgarian, Turkish, Finnish, Croatian, Ukrainian, German, Russian, and Croatian. In some cases, the war was used to justify the censorship, but in others the motivation for adopting such an expansive definition of enemy languages was driven by domestic events such as strikes in Northern Ontario led by Finnish workers. The result was the suspension of the publication of a number of newspapers, despite their patriotic editorial positions, for a period of six months. The suspension was weathered by many publications but, due to the combined factors of economic hardship and widespread anti-German sentiment, it contributed to the disappearance of the German-language press in Ontario until after the Second World War. It is noteworthy, then, that the government took a different approach to foreign language publications during the Second World War. For discussion of this period, see Thompson, "Ethnic Minorities during Two World Wars."

33 Dreisziger, "Rise of Bureaucracy for Multiculturalism," 22.

34 See Whitaker "Official Repression"

35 Lindal, *Canadian Citizenship*.

36 The *Icelandic Canadian* was launched in 1942 in association with the Icelandic Canadian Club of Winnipeg when it was decided that the future of Icelandic culture in the province would require a publication capable of reaching readers of Icelandic origin who did not speak Icelandic. In 2010, the magazine changed its name to the *Icelandic Connection*.

37 Levendel, *Century of the Canadian Jewish Press*, 178.

38 Canada Press Club, Kristjanson, and Bashuk, *Multilingual Press in Manitoba*, 110.

39 Kirschbaum et al., *Twenty Years of the Ethnic Press Association of Ontario*, 9

40 Canada Press Club, Kristjanson, and Bashuk, *Multilingual Press in Manitoba*, 15.
41 Ibid., 28.
42 Kirschbaum et al., *Twenty Years of the Ethnic Press Association of Ontario*, 12
43 Ibid.
44 Ibid., 28–9.
45 In the earliest days of the press association, Mokrzycki allocated 1 percent of all fees charged to advertisers towards the operation of the press association, an arrangement that was later replaced by the collection of fees directly from member publications. Invoices from the agency are available at Library and Archives Canada as part of the Dojack Papers.
46 Canadian Organizations - Canadian Scene, Central Registry Files of Citizenship Registration Branch, LAC, RG 6-F-4, file CB 9-37.
47 Kirschbaum et al., *Twenty Years of the Ethnic Press Association of Ontario*, 35.
48 For a brief discussion of Davidovich during the war, see Prymak, *Maple Leaf and Trident*, which also notes that Davidovich worked with Vladimir Kaye (Kysilewky) in London at the Ukrainian National Information Service (47).
49 Kirschbaum et al., *Twenty Years of the Ethnic Press Association of Ontario*, 35.
50 Kirschbaum, *Twenty-Five Years of Canada Ethnic Press Federation*.
51 Canada Ethnic Press Fonds, LAC, MG 31-H188, vol. 2, minutes: ethnic editors and publishers meeting, fol. 9, 3 April 1957.
52 Ibid.
53 Canada Ethnic Press Fonds, LAC, MG 31-H188, vol. 2, minutes: conference, Ottawa, 8–9 March 1958, speech from Laval Fortier, deputy minister of immigration and citizenship.
54 Memo to minister, 19 December 1961, review of the Foreign Press in Canada, LAC, RG 26 –A – 1- a, box 76 1-5-11, pt. 3.
55 Memo from Chief Programmes and Material Division to Director Citizenship Branch, 10 February 1961, Canadian Scene Files, LAC, RG 6-F-4, file CB 9-37.
56 "'Newcomers' News Service Established," *Globe and Mail*, 21 April 1951.
57 Annual Reports of Canadian Scene for the year ended 31 December 1951, Canadian Scene Files, LAC, RG 6-F-4, file CB 9-37.
58 Grant filed regular reports about her interactions with Canadian Scene to her superiors at the Bureau of Citizenship and Immigration.
59 West, "Citizens from Afar Thankful," *Globe and Mail*, 20 February 1956.

60 Canadian Scene, Annual Report, 1968, Canadian Scene Files, LAC, RG 6-F-4, file CB 9-37.
61 Ibid., 1951.
62 Ibid.
63 Ibid., 1952.
64 Canadian Scene Newsletter 17, 10 August 1951, Canadian Scene Files, LAC, RG 6-F-4, file CB 9-37.
65 "Articles in Canadian Scene, 1962," Canadian Scene Files, LAC, RG 6-F-4, file CB 9-37.
66 Press release, "Canadian Scene: What It Is – Why It Has Been Organized," 1951, Canadian Scene Files, LAC, RG 6-F-4, file CB 9-37.
67 Adie, Robert. *Supplement: Canadian Scene*, 5.
68 Copies of the complete run of *Ethnic Scene* are available at Library and Archives Canada in Ottawa. A similar publication, *Canadian Ethnic Press Review*, was published between 1972 and 1978. Both were the responsibility of the Citizenship Branch of the Department of Secretary of State.
69 Memo from Pierre Trottier, 2 September 1954, at the Political Coordination section: "I was very relieved to find that Mr. Newton and his staff would welcome our material and would be able to make translations themselves into the dozen or more languages required." Canadian Scene Files, LAC, RG 6-F-4, file CB 9-37.
70 Letter, Osler to Boucher, October 1953, Canadian Scene Files, LAC, RG 6-F-4, file CB 9-37.
71 Letters from Mary Jennings to JW Pickersgill, January 1956, Canadian Scene Files, LAC, RG 6-F-4, file CB 9-37.
72 "Minutes: Ethnic Editors and Publishers Meeting," 3 April 1957, Canada Ethnic Press Fonds, LAC, MG31-H188, vol. 2, fol. 9.
73 Memo, Jean Boucher, 4 September 1959, Canadian Scene Files, LAC, RG 6-F-4, file CB 9-37.
74 Adie, *Other Ethnic Groups and Mass Media*, Canadian Scene supplement, 6.
75 Ibid.
76 Canada Press Club, Kristjanson, and Bashuk, *Multilingual Press in Manitoba*; Kirschbaum et al., *Twenty Years of the Ethnic Press Association of Ontario*.
77 Rose, *Making "Pictures in Our Head,"* 45–78.
78 Ibid., 82.
79 Developments mentioned in both Fetherling, *Rise of the Canadian Newspaper*; and Kesterton, *History of Journalism in Canada*.
80 Fetherling, *Rise of the Canadian Newspaper*; Kesterton, *History of Journalism in Canada*.

81 Although from a slightly later period, data regarding newspaper readership in ethnocultural communities and its change over time were documented by O'Bryan et al., *Non-Official Languages*, 70–2.
82 Circulation figures are taken from the Canadian Almanac and are not entirely reliable, but they give a general sense of how widely some papers circulated.
83 Advertisements for Italian Express Travel Agency published in 1974 in *Corriere Italiano*.
84 After the war, in 1954, National Publishers also launched the *Montrealer Zeitung* with the aim of improving readership in the east. Frank Dojacek's son, Charles Dojack, would later serve as an executive for Winnipeg's multilingual radio station, CKJS.
85 Margolis, "Yiddish Press in Montreal," 14.
86 Kirschbaum, *Twenty-Five Years of Canada Ethnic Press Federation*, 85.
87 "Memo to Minister," 18 November 1958, "Meeting with the Ethnic Press Club of Toronto," review of the Foreign Press in Canada, Department of Citizenship and Immigration Fonds, LAC, RG 26 –A – 1- a, box 75 1-5-11, pt. 2.
88 Letter to J.J. Gibbson from Dojacek, 29 May 1934, Charles Dojack Fonds, LAC, MG31-H188, file 20.
89 Kirschbaum, *Twenty-Five Years of Canada Ethnic Press Federation*.
90 "Advertising Women Hear Immigrant," *Globe and Mail*, 21 January 1953.
91 "Silent War Cited," *Globe and Mail*, 8 May 1954.
92 Graham, Michael, "The Growing Power of the Ethnic Press," *Globe and Mail*, 29 December 1962.
93 Martin O'Malley, "Babel Is a Corner Newsstand," *Globe and Mail*, 12 July 1969.
94 Letter from Jean Boucher to Director of Information regarding lunch with members of Toronto Ethnic Press Club, 29 January 1959, review of the Foreign Press in Canada, Department of Citizenship and Immigration Fonds (1950–66), LAC, RG 26 –A – 1- a, box 75 1-5-11, pt. 2.
95 Memo to Minister, 18 November 1958, "Meeting with the Ethnic Press Club of Toronto," review of the Foreign Press in Canada, Department of Citizenship and Immigration Fonds, LAC, RG 26 –A – 1- a, box 75 1-5-11, pt. 2.
96 Champion, "Courting Our Ethnic Friends," 23–5.
97 Ad Sheets Invoices, 1961, LAC, MG 28 V100, vol. 7, file 38, New Canadian Ad.
98 Memo: Director of Information to Director of Citizenship Branch, 14 December 1960, "Excerpts from report of GA Mendel on his trip to

Winnipeg, October 24–29, 1960," review of the Foreign Press in Canada, Department of Citizenship and Immigration Fonds, LAC, RG 26 –A – 1- a, box 75 1-5-11, pt. 2.
99 LAC, CEPF Fonds.
100 Letter from Office of CEPF Secretary (Karl Julius Baier) to John Diefenbaker, 1 December 1958, LAC, MG 28 V 95, vol. 1, file 5, CEPF.
101 It is interesting to note the increasing scepticism of government officials regarding support for the ethnic press during the late 1960s, even as multiculturalism was coming into focus as a part of Canadian public policy. Not that Trudeau's announcement in 1971 would have a significant effect on the papers as the structure of funds associated with the project were limited to projects of fixed duration rather than to the costs of operating an ongoing publication.
102 Letter to Deputy Minister from Director Citizenship Branch re: Invitations to conference of Foreign Language Editors, 22 November 1961, review of the Foreign Press in Canada, Department of Citizenship and Immigration Fonds, LAC, RG 26 –A – 1- a, box 75 1-5-11, pt. 2.
103 "'I Am Nobody,' But Minister Phones," *Globe and Mail*, 13 May 1976.
104 Peter Moon, "Polish Editor Deplores Profit-Taking on Ads," *Globe and Mail*, 14 May 1974.
105 "'I Am nobody,' But Minister Phones," *Globe and Mail*, 13 May 1976.
106 Principe, *Darkest Side of Fascism*, 26–62.
107 "Multicultural Ads Called Liberal Propaganda," *Globe and Mail*, 14 April 1973.
108 Kirschbaum et al., *Twenty Years of the Ethnic Press Association of Ontario*, 34–5.
109 Kristmanson, *Plateaus of Freedom*, 231.
110 Young, *List Cultures*, 106–7.
111 Foreign Language Press Review Service, *Handbook*, 1.
112 Memorandum to Deputy Minister, 23 October 1961, review of the Foreign Press in Canada, LAC, RG 26 –A – 1- a, box 75 1-5-11, pt. 2.
113 Bohaker and Iacovetta, "Making Aboriginal People 'Immigrants too,'" 428–9.
114 This account is based on the materials presented in Bohaker and Iacovetta, "'Making Aboriginal People 'Immigrants Too'"
115 Haque, *Multiculturalism*, 5.
116 Ibid., 64–8.
117 Tolon, "Futures studies",46.
118 "Advertising Women Hear Immigrant," *The Globe and Mail*, 21 January 1953, 11.

119 Blanding, "Re-branding Canada", 83
120 Canada Ethnic Press Federation, *Submission to Royal Commission on Publications*, 17.
121 Ibid., 18.
122 Ibid.
123 Ibid., 1960, 19.
124 National Publications, *Submission to Royal Commission on Publications*, 26-41.
125 Ibid., 35–6.
126 Ibid., 21.
127 Ibid., 35–6.
128 Canadian Ethnic Press Club, *Submission to Royal Commission on Publications*, 4.
129 Quoted in Blanding, "Re-branding Canada", 85.
130 Ibid.
131 Canadian Ethnic Press Club, *Submission to Royal Commission on Publications*, 10.
132 Ibid.
133 Ibid.
134 Haque, *Multiculturalism*, 101.
135 "*Background Notes* for Presentation from the Canada Press Club," Robarts Library, University of Toronto. Lindal would appear as part of four delegations before the commission that day; the other two were the Citizenship Council of Manitoba and the Icelandic Canadian Club.
136 "*Background Notes* for Presentation from the Canada Press Club," Robarts Library, University of Toronto.
137 A popular book about Trudeau published in 1968 by Steubing, Marshall and Oakes described him as a "man for tomorrow."
138 Stuebing et al., *Pierre Trudeau*, 5.
139 Ibid., 25.
140 Husband, "Right to Be Understood."
141 Curran, "Rethinking the Media," 2.
142 The alignment between the state and the ethnic press, as mediated by the press associations in particular, would continue into the 1980s with the national federation proposing the establishment of a permanent secretariat to be based in Ottawa with close ties to the ministries overseeing citizenship and immigration. This was not an approach that was unanimously supported. In 1975, Marion Ziniak, editor of the *Byelorussian Voice*, broke away from the ethnic press federation because he felt the group was too focused on attempts by publishers to win influence in Ottawa. The

Ethnic Journalists and Writers Club, founded in association with the Canadian Press Club, emphasized the important contributions to be made by ethnic journalists with regard to documenting Canadian culture.

CHAPTER THREE

1 Ron Haggert, "Help! Whatever I'm Listening to, It Still Comes out CHIN!," *Toronto Star*, 13 November 1967.
2 Ibid.
3 Ibid.
4 Edwardson, *Canadian Content*, 136.
5 Throughout the 1930s, queries were often sent to newspapers asking radio columnists about the source of a radio signal based on its frequency. XEW, based in Mexico City, was the station most frequently inquired about in these years.
6 See Luconi, "Radio Broadcasting," for a discussion of Italian-language radio in the US between the world wars; Kelman, *Station Identification*, documents the history of Yiddish Radio in the US before the Second World War.
7 A 1933 article published in *Variety* mentions stations in Montreal picking up Italian-language programs produced by WOV in New York, but it does not specify which station. See "Foreign Language Broadcasting Building Rapidly for Cross-Country," *Variety*, 15 August 1933, 32.
8 Mandel, *Jewish Hour*.
9 Restrictions on "foreign language broadcasts" were put in place under the Defence of Canada Regulations, which were adopted in September 1939. Bizimana, "Canadian Media Coverage of the War," notes that "censorship was aimed not only at military information or other indiscretions that could be used by the enemy but also at any voices strongly opposed to the war effort" (121).
10 Carnevale, "No Italian Spoken," 10.
11 Amatiello, "CHIN Radio and Its Listeners," 10.
12 Public Notice CRTC 1985-139, "A Broadcasting Policy Reflecting Canada's Linguistic and Cultural Diversity"; Public Notice CRTC 1999-117, "Ethnic Broadcasting Policy."
13 Rothenbuler and McCourt, "Radio Redefines Itself," explores this period of transformation in the US through the example of Austin, Texas.
14 See Berland, "Radio Space and Industrial Time"; Ahlkvist and Faulkner, "Will This Record Work for Us?"

15 Kirkconnell, *Canadians All*, 1941. It is worth noting that Lindal's pamphlet, *Two Ways of Life*, was also published with support from the Public Information Bureau the following year.
16 Kirckconnell, *Slice of Canada*, 303.
17 "Must Maintain World Freedom: Mr King Asks Men of Alien Origin to Enlist," *Globe and Mail*, 22 May 1941.
18 Neary, "Ventures in Citizenship", 109–10; Caccia, *Managing the Canadian Mosaic*, 91. For further discussion of the "Americans All" project, see Savage, *Broadcasting Freedom*.
19 For biographical information on Kirkconnell see Kirkconnell, *Slice of Canada*; and Perkin and Snelson, *Morning in His Heart*, 8–65.
20 *The North American Book of Icelandic Verse*, 1930; *A Golden Treasury of Polish Lyrics*, 1936; *A Little Treasury of Hungarian Verse*, 1947; and *The Ukrainian Poets*, 1963.
21 Kirkconnell, *Canadian Overtones*, 1935.
22 In *A Slice of Canada* Kirkconnel mentions that, on 3 May 1940, he delivered a "national broadcast" in which he discussed Canada's commitment to the restoration of the Polish state in the war (271). He later participated in a number of broadcasts on Hamilton's CHML.
23 Kirkconnell, *Slice of Canada*, 123.
24 Ibid., 276.
25 Caccia, *Managing the Mosaic*.
26 Kirkconnell, *Slice of Canada*, 280–1.
27 A recurrent theme in *Slice of Canada* is the determining power of individual faith in the face of the tyranny of the masses. As Kirkconnell writes: "The power of religion, as distinguished from cold creedal formulations, is that its purpose and meaning lie in the relationship of the individual to God or to a path of liberation and salvation ...When such un-integrated individuals are mobilized by slogans in the mass-state, they and their power-hungry rulers become capable of infinite atrocities" (166.)
28 Kirkconnell, *Canadians All*, 1.
29 Caccia, *Managing the Canadian Mosaic*, 91.
30 Palmer, "Ethnic Relations in Wartime," documents the negative sentiments towards Italians and Germans in Alberta, although he notes that anti-German sentiment was greater during the First World War. The collection *Enemies Within*, edited by Iacovetta, Perin, and Principe, provides a comprehensive survey of anti-Italian sentiment across the country.
31 Stern, "Private Broadcasters," 6.

32 Brian Swarbrick, "Swarbricks and Bouquets," *Canadian Broadcater*, 12 June 1958, 18.
33 Government of Canada, *Debates of the House of Commons*, 12 May 1944, 2,873.
34 Stern, "Private Broadcasters," 6–8
35 Ibid., 6.
36 Ibid.
37 Brian Swarbrick, "A New Market: Radio Opens the Door to a Million New Canadians," *Canadian Broadcaster*, 8 May 1958, 6.
38 "The Canadian Market," *Sponsor*, 30 August 1958, 56–8.
39 Adie, *Other Ethnic Groups*, "Section II: The Broadcast Media," 14. The figures were compiled by the BBG rather than by the broadcaster association. They are likely more comprehensive for this reason, although they do not include programming on FM stations (which was likely minimal during these years).
40 Adie, *Other Ethnic Groups*, "Section II: The Broadcast Media", 14.
41 Stern, "Private Broadcasters," 7.
42 Brian Swarbrick, "Swarbricks and Bouquets," *Canadian Broadcaster*, 12 June 1958, 18.
43 Ibid.
44 Ibid.
45 Ibid.
46 "This Man Makes Friends and *Influences* People", *Canadian Broadcaster*, 12 June 1958, 19.
47 Stern, "Private Broadcasters," 7.
48 Casimir Stanczykowski, "Application for a licence to establish a new AM broadcasting station at Montreal, QC," Canada, Board of Broadcast Governors, Public Hearings, 12–13 May 1959, 131.
49 Walter E. Kroeker, "Application for a licence to establish a new AM broadcasting station at Winnipeg, MB," Canada, Board of Broadcast Governors, 13 September 1966, 108.
50 Whiteoak, "Italo-Hispanic Music," 96–7.
51 Stanczykowski, "Application for a licence," 8 February 1962, 671. The date the letter was sent was an important question in the hearings in 1959 as it allowed Stanczykowski to claim precedence over a competing group led by Italian-Canadian journalist Raphael (Ralph) Pirro, who was a prominent voice in the city's Italian-language Catholic newspaper and would later participate in the creation of Radio Ville-Marie.
52 Board of Broadcast Governors, "Foreign-Language Broadcasting," public announcement, 22 January 1962.

53 Changes were made to the Broadcasting Act in 1964 (see section 17). These were revised again in 1968 following some of the recommendations from the Royal Commission on Bilingualism and Biculturalism.
54 Roth, *Something New in the Air*, 64–9.
55 Adie, CBC *Policy*, 1.
56 Ibid.
57 Relations between the CBC and minority communities were fraught on occasion as the broadcaster's coverage of migration and international events was often greeted with disapproval and accusations of misrepresentation (e.g., "Ciao Maria Insulting, Italians Say," *Globe and Mail*, 6 January 1963). By the 1970s the adoption of official multiculturalism encouraged the CBC to produce a number of programs that attempted to represent some aspect of popular multiculturalism. An example of this is *The King of Kensington*, which was set in a culturally diverse Toronto neighbourhood.
58 Stanczykowski, "Application for a licence," 8 February 1962, 699–700.
59 Ibid., 12–13 May 1959, 131.
60 Ibid., 132.
61 Stern, "Private Broadcasters," 7.
62 Stanczykowski, "Application for a licence," 12–13 May 1959, 132.
63 Ibid.
64 Ibid., 128.
65 "A plus tard, le poste de langue étrangère à Mtl", *Le Devoir*, 22 September 1960.
66 "Radio: Un poste, 7 langues?," *La Presse*, 6 July 1960.
67 Board of Broadcast Governors, "Foreign-Language Broadcasting," public announcement, 22 January 1962.
68 "Montreal CFMB in 18-language Pitch to an Ethnic Community," *Variety*, 3 December 1963, 27.
69 Stanczykowski, "Application for a licence," 12–13 May 1959, 134.
70 Ibid.
71 *Maclean's* reviews, *Maclean's*, 20 August 1966, 41.
72 "For Permission to Change the Name of the Licensee of Station CHFI, Toronto, from Rogers Broadcasting Ltd. to Radio 1540 Ltd." Canada, Board of Broadcast Governors, *Public Hearings*, 19 January 1965, 209–15.
73 John B. Lombardi, "Transfer of All the Issued Common Shares of Capital in Radio 1520 Limited," Canada, Board of Broadcast Governors, 24 March 1965, 549.
74 Richard O'Hagan, "Johnny Lombardi's Kingdom of Music and Macaroni," *Maclean's*, 8 December 1956, 20.

75 Brian Magner, "The Unofficial Mayor of Little Italy," *Globe and Mail*, 10 October 1959.
76 "Arturo Scotti: Urged Compatriots to Become Citizens," *Globe and Mail*, 17 October 1959.
77 "Grocer Lombardi Now Leads with His CHIN," *Toronto Star*, 5 February 1965.
78 Magner, "Unofficial Mayor of Little Italy."
79 O'Hagan, "Johnny Lombardi's Kingdom of Music and Macaroni."
80 His most vocal critics were his competitors in Italian-language media, Daniel Iannuzzi at the *Corriere Canadese* and radio personality Frank Carenza. "Italians Not Exploited MPP Wrong – Lombardi," *Toronto Star*, 29 March 1960; "Some of Our People Are Exploiting – Italian," *Toronto Star*, 4 April 1960.
81 "It's June in January!," *Toronto Star*, 31 December 1948.
82 Elda Hope, "More Hope Than Charity," *Canadian Broadcaster and Telescreen*, 23 August 1950, 21.
83 Lombardi, "Transfer of All the Issued Common Sares," 512.
84 James D. Services, "Transfer of All the Issued Common Shares of Capital in Radio 1520 Limited," Canada, Board of Broadcast Governors, 24 March 1965, 507.
85 Lombardi, "Transfer of All the Issued Common Shares," 513.
86 Ibid.
87 "Lombardi Station Okayed," *Toronto Star*, 25 June 1965; "Johnny Lombardi's CHIN about to Go on the Air," *Toronto Star*, 22 February 1966.
88 Lombardi's position was perhaps more in line with the programming actually being broadcast. Despite the lip service paid to language education and citizenship training, the majority of programming that was identified as being in languages other than English or French was entertainment-oriented rather than informational in nature. A survey of programming in 1966 shows that, of the 220 hours of programming reviewed during a single week, nearly 150 hours (70 percent) was dedicated to "light music." The next largest categories were "Religious" and "Classical Music," both of which made up less than 15 percent of the time broadcast. News and community programming made up less than 5 percent of programming combined. Claims regarding their importance as tools for communicating essential information, while frequently mentioned in government hearings, appear to have been exaggerated with the goal of winning the approval of broadcast regulators. Generally speaking, the primary orientation of programming was aligned with the goal of attracting listeners.

89 Lombardi, "Transfer of All the Issued Common Shares," 513.
90 Stern, "Private Broadcasters," 7.
91 See the first chapter of Edwardson, *Canuck Rock*, 26–55, for an overview of the rise of rock and roll music in Canada.
92 Van Bruchem had established himself as a visible member of Canada's Dutch community and had worked in broadcasting through the war for the Canadian government's Dutch language broadcasts. After the war, he worked as a representative of the Dutch public broadcaster in Canada, producing programs in both English and Dutch for distribution both across Canada and in Holland.
93 Van Bruchem, presentation to CRTC, 21–25 September 1971, 627.
94 For a history of audience metrics in Canada, see Eaman, *Channels of Influence*.
95 Buzzard, *Chains of Gold*, documents this history in the context of the United States.
96 Stern, "Private Broadcasters," 7.
97 "Rights Claimed for Olympic Film," *Broadcasting Magazine*, 29 August 1955, 54.
98 In 1962, when asked about how the Canadian National Exhibition might be revived, he noted that the annual fair was failing to address the interests of recently immigrated Torontonians.
99 Barbara Frum, "Radio," *Toronto Star*, 18 February 1967.
100 Barbara Frum, "The Shake-Up in CHUM's Go-Go News Department." *Toronto Star*, 27 January 1967.
101 "What Is the Future of Rating Services?" *Canadian Broadcaster*, December 1969, 18.
102 Scholarly accounts of the picnic can be found in Harney, "Politics of Urban Space," 33–5; and Amatiello, "CHIN Radio and Its Listeners," 70–2.
103 Harney, "Politics of Urban Space," 33.
104 "'Biggest Picnic Ever' for 30,000 Italians," *Toronto Star*, 17 July 1967.
105 Public Notice, CRTC 1999-117, "Ethnic Broadcasting Policy."
106 Hanna et al., *Accommodation of Language Diversity in Canadian Broadcasting*, 38.
107 Fauteux, *Music in Range*, documents some of the "alternative" stations that started out on cable.
108 Some of the history of CHCR is laid out in Broadcasting Decision CRTC 2003-194, which also outlines the station's transition to broadcast in 2003. CICR placed regular advertisements in the *Corriere Italiano* as "Radio Italia" throughout the 1970s. Radio Portugal Montreal similarly advertised in Montreal's Portuguese paper *Jornal do emigrante* (it was also

involved in the release of compilations of Portuguese popular music in association with the Discoteca Portuguesa on St Laurent Boulevard).
109 Greek-Canadian Radio Station, "The Function of Multilingual Broadcasting in Canada," Canadian Radio-Television and Telecommunications Commission, 20 September 1977, 331.
110 "Francisco Sestelo (Frank) Alvarez," in Coehlo and Fernandes-Iria, *Small Stories, Great People*, 911.
111 Greek-Canadian Radio Station (Peter Maniatakos), "The Function of Multilingual Broadcasting in Canada," Canadian Radio-Television and Telecommunications Commission, 20 September 1977, 332.
112 CRTC, *Cable Television Regulations*, Ottawa, CRTC, 1976.
113 Foy et al. "Inventing and Experimenting: Radio Centre-ville," 43.
114 Ibid., 40.
115 Ibid., 41.
116 Justine Bizzocchi, interview, Vancouver, 27 March 2018.
117 Fauteux, "Development of Community Radio in Quebec," 142.

CHAPTER FOUR

1 "Application for a licence by Keystone Broadcasting Manitoba Limited to establish and operate a new AM broadcasting station at Winnipeg, Manitoba," Canada, Board of Broadcast Governors, 13 September 1966.
2 Stanczykowski recounts this history as part of his 1974 testimony in "Application for a broadcasting licence to carry on a multilingual language AM radio station at Winnipeg, Manitoba," Canadian Radio-television and Telecommunications Commission, 17 May 1974, 733–5.
3 Stanczykowski, "Application for a broadcasting licence," 735.
4 Ibid., 738.
5 Ali, "Broadcast System in Whose Interest?" 292, outlines the history of localism in Canadian and Australian broadcast systems, noting that Canadian preoccupations with preserving national culture have often undermined the goal of keeping television, particularly private television, local.
6 Kymlicka and Walker's introduction to the volume *Rooted Cosmopolitanism*, 1–30, outlines some of the possibilities and contradictions at the heart of such an understanding of the nation.
7 There is an extensive literature in Geography that unpacks presumptions about the meaning of scale and how it applies to understanding the interaction between space, action, and agency. Marston, Jones, and Woodward, "Human Geography without Scale," provocatively argue that the concept

itself is incoherent despite its intuitive appeal. They show how an overly simplified understanding of scale risks obscuring the complexity of social relations by imposing a hierarchical spatial order where none exists.
8   An analogue of this claim regarding the performativity of scale can be found in the work of Nick Couldry and Andreas Hepp, "What Should Comparative Media Research Be Comparing?" They have critiqued the dominance of "container thinking" (a term they borrow from sociologist Ulrich Beck) in media and communication research. They use the concept of "cultural thickenings" as an alternative model to traditional understandings of scale as made of up discrete spatial levels (25).
9   See Parks, *Cultures in Orbit*, 21–46. Her discussion of Marshall McLuhan, a key figure in Canadian intellectual history, in her analysis of ideas of global presence brought about as a result of satellite television is a good index of these tensions in the Canadian content.
10 Francesco Pisani, "É scomparso un pioniere!" *Corriere Italiano*, 13 February 1985, 1.
11 Mascia Biography, Telelatino Files.
12 "Corriere Canadese Founder Dead at 70," *Toronto Star*, 22 November 2004.
13 Goldberg, *Barefoot Channel*, 10.
14 Engelman, *Origins of Public Access Cable Television*, 16–17.
15 Interview, Madelaine Ziniak, Toronto, 20 March 2018.
16 Edward Greenspon, "Broadcasters at Odds in Vancouver," *Globe and Mail*, 8 June 1987.
17 Chinavision Canada Corporation, Canadian Radio-Television and Telecommunications Commission, 2 February 1984, 2522–3.
18 McCarthy, "Like an Earthquake," has discussed some of the ways that Theatre Television, particularly its broadcast of boxing, contributed to the formation of black public sphere in the United States through the 1960s. It is also worth noting that many of the recent immigrants to Canadian cities were similarly interested in gaining access to sports events and that these provided important meeting spaces.
19 This was not new with television but was also an important aspect of radio. In his application for CJVB in Vancouver, Jan Van Bruchem noted that the majority of third-language radio in the Vancouver area was being produced and broadcast by American radio stations just south of the border. Van Bruchem claimed that CJVB would make it possible to bring these programs (and their sponsors) to Canada.
20 This is evident from a survey of BBM TV ratings through the 1970s.
21 Raboy, *Missed Opportunities*, 235.

22 Blaik Kirby, "Love and Exhaustion (and a Hunt for Bugs) at the Birth of 79," *Globe and Mail*, 23 September 1972.
23 Ibid., "City: Will a Radical Approach Bring Success to Channel 79?," *Globe and Mail*, 13 May 1972.
24 "Multilingual Television (Toronto) Ltd.," Canadian Radio-television and Telecommunications Commission, 20 September 1977, 133.
25 Jack Miller, "Major Ethnic Programs Planned," *Toronto Star*, 3 October 1975.
26 "Multilingual Television (Toronto) Ltd.," 20 September 1977, 412.
27 "The Function of Multilingual Broadcasting in Canada," Canadian Radio-television and Telecommunications Commission, 20 September 1977.
28 "Heritage Broadcasters Limited," Canadian Radio-television and Telecommunications Commission, September 1977, 641.
29 Multilingual Television (Toronto) Ltd., 20 September 1977, 395.
30 Kevin Budd, "In Memoriam: Leon Kossar," *Canadian Folk Music Bulletin* 35, 3–4 (2002): 19.
31 Nora McCabe, "Caravan Still 'Their Baby' for Cultural Dynamos," *Toronto Star*, 14 June 1998.
32 Barbara Keddy, "Private Radio Warns Third-Language TV Threatens Survival," *Globe and Mail*, 21 September 1977.
33 CRTC, "Multilingual Television Broadcasting," public announcement, 13 January 1978.
34 Jack Miller, "CRTC Opens Public Hearings on Multilingual TV Station." *Toronto Star*, 18 September 1978.
35 CRTC, "Multilingual Television Broadcasting," public announcement, 13 January 1978.
36 Blair Kirby, "Radio Program Called Incitement to Assassinate," *Globe and Mail*, 12 February 1970.
37 "Lombardi Keeps CHIN Frequency," *Globe and Mail*, 7 November 1970.
38 Application by Great Pacific Broadcasters Ltd. for a licence to carry on a new AM broadcasting undertaking at Vancouver, BC, Canada, Canadian Radio-television and Telecommunications Commission, *Public Hearings*, 20 October 1971, 649.
39 CRTC, "Multilingual Television Broadcasting," public announcement, 13 January 1978.
40 "Multilingual Television (Toronto) Ltd.," 20 September 1977, 138.
41 The Ukrainian Canadian Committee was an outlier in this regard, calling for the creation of a national public network serving cultural and linguistic minorities, explaining: "We are not just looking for a local [solution], satisfying local needs."

42 "Pay Television," Canadian Radio-television and Telecommunications Commission, *Decision* CRTC 82-240, Ottawa, 18 March 1982.
43 Greenspon, "Broadcasters at Odds in Vancouver."
44 Ibid.
45 The other channels licensed as part of these hearings all covered at least several provinces, following a division of the country into east and west markets.
46 Justine Bizzocchi, director of programming at the station in its early years, recalls that there were plans to subtitle programs in English in the hope of making the channel more appealing to the largest possible number of viewers. Along these lines, there were discussions with Australia's SBS, where the same model had been implemented. However, it was very quickly realized that any increase in the number of subscribers resulting from such efforts would be outweighed by the increased costs of dubbing or subtitling.
47 "World View Television Limited," Canadian Radio-television and Telecommunications Commission, *Public Hearings*, 1 February 1984, 4.
48 "MTV," Canadian Radio-television and Telecommunications Commission, *Public Hearings*, 1 February 1984, 4.
49 Ibid., 14.
50 "Wah Shing Television Limited," Canadian Radio-television and Telecommunications Commission, *Public Hearings*, 2 February 1984, 4.
51 Ibid., 19.
52 Ibid.
53 "Chinavision Canada," Canadian Radio-television and Telecommunications Commission, *Public Hearings*, 2 February 1984, 6–7.
54 This was not known publicly at the time of the hearings, and it was used by Wah Shing Television as grounds to appeal the licence. See Jack Miller, "Wrangling in Court Stalls Chinavision Delivery of Pay TV," *Toronto Star*, 9 October 1984.
55 "Latinovision," Canadian Radio-television and Telecommunications Commission, *Public Hearings*, 3 February 1984, 3.
56 CRTC Decision, CRTC 84-444, 24 May 1984.
57 Ibid.
58 Ibid.
59 "Cable Carriage of Specialty Services," Public Notice CRTC 1985-174, 2 August 1985.
60 Ibid.
61 Chinavision Canada Corporation, Decision CRTC 88-775, 27 October 1988.
62 Telelatino Network Inc, Decision CRTC 86-815, 2 September 1986.

63 Chinavision Canada Corporation, Decision CRTC 88-775, 27 October 1988.
64 TLN Guide was issued between 1984 and 1986 on a monthly basis.
65 CRTC Decision CRTC 90-630.
66 Dan Westell, "CFMT to Get Second Cable Outlet," *Globe and Mail*, 7 November 1984.
67 Decision CRTC 89-513
68 Decision CRTC 87-739 (London); Decision CRTC 93-632 (Ottawa).
69 Andrew Mitrovica and Jeff Sallot, "CSIS Warned Ottawa of Beijing Media Plot," *Globe and Mail*, 9 February 2000.
70 Ibid.
71 Robert Williamson, "Media Baron Rides a Human Wave," *Globe and Mail*, 19 February 1994.
72 Hayward, "Ethnic Broadcasting."
73 "Improving the diversity of third-language television services – A revised approach to assessing requests to add non-Canadian third-language television services to the lists of eligible satellite services for distribution on a digital basis," public notice, CRTC 2004-96.
74 Hayward, "Il Caso Canadese," 21–37.
75 A thorough discussion of the Al-Jazeera application is outlined in Odartey-Wellington, "Broadcasting Regulation and Building the Multicultural Canadian Nation," 134–8.
76 Odartey-Wellington, "Broadcasting Regulation and Building the Multicultural Canadian Nation," 136–48.
77 Public notice, CRTC 2004-96.
78 Sheldon Kirschner, "Ethnic TV Entrepreneur Brings the World to Canada," *Canadian Jewish News*, 3 February 2011, 40.
79 Broadcasting Decision, CRTC 2013-87.
80 The amount of English-language programming was increased to 25 percent in Broadcasting Decision, CRTC 2002-388.
81 The "buy-through" provisions were eliminated as part of the *Let's Talk TV* hearings in 2015.

CONCLUSION

1 Olumide Adewumi, Interview. Toronto, 14 December 2018.
2 Srnicek, *Platform Capitalism*, 93–129.
3 Ryan's *Multicultiphobia* is notable for outlining some the key aspects of the populist dismissal of multiculturalism, yet – because he looks only at

newspapers – does not address the changing media context within which such discourses developed.
4 Chun, "Queerying Homophily," provides an incisive discussion of the relation between similarity and difference in the context of contemporary forms of community and identity shaped by the parameters of digital media.

Bibliography

Abel, Richard. *Americanizing the Movies and "Movie-Mad" Audiences, 1910–1914*. Berkeley: University of California Press, 2006.

Adie, Robert F. *The Other Ethnic Groups and the Mass Media*. Working paper prepared for the Royal Commission on Bilingualism and Biculturalism, 1966.

–. *Supplement: Canadian Scene*. Working Paper Prepared for the Royal Commission on Bilingualism and Biculturalism, 1966.

–. *Supplement:* CBC *Policy towards All Languages Other Than French or English*. Working Paper Prepared for the Royal Commission on Bilingualism and Biculturalism, 1966.

Ahadi, Daniel, and Catherine A. Murray. "Urban Mediascapes and Multicultural Flows: Assessing Vancouver's Communication Infrastructure." *Canadian Journal of Communication* 34, 4 (2009): 587.

Ahlkvist, Jarl A., and Robert Faulkner. "'Will This Record Work for Us?': Managing Music Formats in Commercial Radio." *Qualitative Sociology* 25, 2 (2002): 189–215.

Ali, Christopher. "A Broadcast System in Whose Interest? Tracing the Origins of Broadcast Localism in Canadian and Australian Television Policy, 1950–1963." *International Communication Gazette* 74, 3 (2012): 277–97.

Allen, Robert C. "Relocating American Film History: The 'Problem' of the Empirical." *Cultural Studies* 20, 1 (2006): 48–88.

Amatiello, Michael. "CHIN Radio and Its Listeners: A Negotiation in the Post-War Commerce of Ethnicity." *Quaderni d'italianistica* 33, 1 (2012): 63–82.

Balio, Tino. *The Foreign Film Renaissance on American Screens, 1946–1973*. Madison: University of Wisconsin Press, 2010.

Bannerji, Himani. *The Dark Side of the Nation: Essays on Multiculturalism, Nationalism and Gender*. Toronto: Canadian Scholars' Press, 2000.

Berland, Jody. "Radio Space and Industrial Time: The Case of Music Formats." In *Critical Cultural Policy Studies: A Reader*, edited by Justin Lewis and Toby Miller, 230–8. Oxford: Blackwell, 1993.

Bizimana, Aimé-Jules. "Canadian Media Coverage of the War: Conditions and Constraints." In *World War II and the Media*, 119–36. Chester, UK: University of Chester, 2014.

Blanding, Lee. "Re-branding Canada: The Origins of Canadian Multiculturalism Policy, 1945–1974." PhD diss., University of Victoria, 2013.

Bohaker, Heidi, and Franca Iacovetta. "Making Aboriginal People 'Immigrants Too': A Comparison of Citizenship Programs for Newcomers and Indigenous Peoples in Postwar Canada, 1940s–1960s." *Canadian Historical Review* 90, 3 (2009): 427–62.

Bossin, Hye. *Stars of David*. Toronto: Canadian Jewish Congress, 1957.

Bouchard, Gérard, and Charles Taylor. *Building the Future. A Time for Reconciliation*. Report of the Consultation Commission on Accommodation Practices Related to Cultural Differences. Quebec: Government of Quebec, 2008.

Bowker, Geoffrey C., and Susan Leigh Star. *Sorting Things Out: Classification and Its Consequences*. Cambridge, MA: MIT Press, 2000.

Brunton, Colin, and Kirk Paputts, dirs. *The Last Pogo Jumps Again*. Screamin' Banshee Productions (Toronto), 2011.

Buzzard, Karen. *Chains of Gold: Marketing the Ratings and Rating the Markets*. Metuchen: Scarecrow Press, 1990.

Caccia, Ivana. *Managing the Canadian Mosaic in Wartime: Shaping Citizenship Policy, 1939–1945*. Montreal and Kingston: McGill-Queen's University Press, 2010.

Canada. Senate Special Committee on Mass Media, and Keith Davey. *The Uncertain Mirror: Report of the Special Senate Committee on Mass Media*. Ottawa: Queen's Printer, 1970.

Canada Ethnic Press Federation. *A Submission to the Royal Commission on Publications*. Toronto: Canada Ethnic Press Federation, 1960.

Canada Press Club, Wilhelm Kristjanson, and Natalia Bashuk. *The Multilingual Press in Manitoba*. Winnipeg: Canada Press Club, 1974.

Carey, James W. "A Cultural Approach to Communication." In *Communication as Culture: Essays on Media and Society*. Rev. ed. New York: Routledge, 2008.

Carnevale, Nancy C. "'No Italian Spoken for the Duration of the War': Language, Italian-American Identity, and Cultural Pluralism in the World War II Years." *Journal of American Ethnic History* 22, 3 (2003): 3–33.

Cavell, Richard, ed. *Love, Hate, and Fear in Canada's Cold War*. Toronto: University of Toronto Press, 2004.

Cédilot, André, and André Noël. *Mafia Inc.: The Long, Bloody Reign of Canada's Sicilian Clan*. Toronto: Random House Canada, 2011.

Champion, Christian P. "Courting Our Ethnic Friends: Canadianism, Britishness, and New Canadians, 1950–1970." *Canadian Ethnic Studies* 38, 1 (2006): 23.

Chun, Wendy Hui Kyong. "Queerying Homophily." In *Pattern Discrimination*, edited by C. Apprich, W. Chun, F. Cramer, and H. Steyerl, 5998. Minneapolis: University of Minnesota Press, 2018.

Coehlo, José Mário, and Ana Fernandes-Iria. *Small Stories, Great People: Portuguese Pioneers in Canada*. Toronto: Creative 7, 2004.

Collins, Richard. *Culture, Communication, and National Identity: The Case of Canadian Television*. Toronto: University of Toronto Press, 1990.

Couldry, Nick. *Media, Society, World: Social Theory and Digital Media Practice*. Cambridge, UK: Polity, 2012.

Couldry, Nick, and Andreas Hepp. "What Should Comparative Media Research Be Comparing? Towards a Transcultural Approach to 'Media Cultures.'" In *Internationalizing Media Studies*, 46–61. London: Routledge, 2009.

–. "Conceptualizing Mediatization: Contexts, Traditions, Arguments." *Communication Theory* 23, 3 (2013): 191–202.

Coulthard, Glen. *Red Skin White Masks: Rejecting the Colonial Politics of Recognition*. Minneapolis: University of Minnesota Press, 2014.

Cunningham, Stuart, and John Sinclair, eds. *Floating Lives: The Media and Asian Diasporas*. New York: Rowman and Littlefield, 2001.

Curran, James. "Rethinking the Media as a Public Sphere." In *Communication and Citizenship: Journalism and the Public Sphere*, edited by Peter Dahlgren and Colin Sparks, 27–57. London: Routledge, 1991.

Day, Richard J.F. *Multiculturalism and the History of Canadian Diversity*. Toronto: University of Toronto Press, 2000.

Dreisziger, N.F. "The Rise of a Bureaucracy for Multiculturalism: The Origins of the Nationalities Branch, 1939–1941." In *On Guard for Thee: War, Ethnicity, and the Canadian State, 1939–1945*, edited by N. Hillmer, B. Kordan, and L. Luciuk, 1–29. Ottawa: Department of Supply and Services, 1988.

Eaman, Ross. *Channels of Influence:* CBC *Audience Research and the Canadian Public.* Toronto: University of Toronto Press, 1994.

Edwardson, Ryan. "Other Canadian Voices: The Development of Ethnic Broadcasting in Canada." In *Racism, Eh? A Critical Inter-disciplinary Anthology of Race and Racism in Canada*, edited by Charmaine Nelson and Camille Antoinette Nelson, 316–25. Concord: Captus Press, 2004.

–. *Canadian Content: Culture and the Quest for Nationhood.* Toronto: University of Toronto Press, 2008.

–. *Canuck Rock: A History of Canadian Popular Music.* Toronto: University of Toronto Press, 2009.

Engelman, Ralph. "The Origins of Public Access Cable Television, 1966–1972." *Journalism and Communication Monographs* 123 (1990).

Fan, Victor. "New York Chinatown Theatres under the Hong Kong Circuit System." *Film History: An International Journal* 22, 1 (2010): 108–26.

Fauteux, Brian. "The Development of Community Radio in Quebec: The Rise of Community Broadcasting in Late 1960s and Early 1970s Canada." *Canadian Journal of Media Studies* 3, 1 (2008): 131–51.

–. *Music in Range: The Culture of Canadian Campus Radio.* Waterloo, ON: Wilfrid Laurier University Press, 2015.

Fetherling, George. *The Rise of the Canadian Newspaper.* Toronto: Oxford University Press, 1990.

Fleras, Augie. *Racisms in a Multicultural Canada: Paradoxes, Politics, and Resistance.* Waterloo: Wilfrid Laurier University Press, 2014.

Fielding, Stephen. "Ethnicity as an Exercise in Sport: European Immigrants, Soccer Fandom, and the Making of Canadian Multiculturalism, 1945–1979." *International Journal of the History of Sport* 34, 10 (2017): 970–91.

Foreign Language Press Review Service. *Handbook.* Ottawa: Canadian Citizenship Branch, 1958.

Foy, E., E. L'Oiseau, R. Barette, and L. Boivin. "Inventing and Experimenting: Radio Centre-Ville." In *A Passion for Radio: Radio Waves and Community*, edited by Bruce Girard, 39–46. Montreal: Black Rose Books, 1992.

Fraser, Nancy. "Rethinking the Public Sphere: A Contribution to the Critique of Actually Existing Democracy." *Social text* 25/26 (1990): 56–80.

–. "From Redistribution to Recognition? Dilemmas of Justice in a 'Post-Socialist' Age." *New Left Review* 212 (1995): 68.

Fujiwara, Aya. *Ethnic Elites and Canadian Identity: Japanese, Ukrainians, and Scots, 1919–1971.* Vol. 7. Winnipeg: University of Manitoba Press, 2012.

Glasser, Theodore L. "Competition and Diversity among Radio Formats: Legal and Structural Issues." *Journal of Broadcasting and Electronic Media* 28, 2 (1984): 127–42.

Goldberg, Kim. *The Barefoot Channel: Community Television as a Tool for Social Change*. Vancouver: New Star Books, 1990.

Gomery, Douglas. "Who Killed Hollywood?" *Wilson Quarterly* 15, 3 (1991): 106–12.

–. *Shared Pleasures: A History of Movie Presentation in the United States*. Madison: University of Wisconsin Press, 1992.

Graham, Steve, and Simon Marvin. *Splintering Urbanism: Networked Infrastructures, Technological Mobilities and the Urban Condition*. London: Routledge, 2002.

Hanna, Sharron, J. R. Weston, and Clare Bolger. *The Accommodation of Language Diversity in Canadian Broadcasting*. Government of Canada, Department of Communications, 1981.

Hansen, Miriam. *Babel and Babylon*. Cambridge, MA: Harvard University Press, 1994.

Haque, Eve. *Multiculturalism within a Bilingual Framework: Language, Race, and Belonging in Canada*. Toronto: University of Toronto Press, 2012.

Harney, Nicholas DeMaria. "The Politics of Urban Space: Modes of Place-Making by Italians in Toronto's Neighbourhoods." *Modern Italy* 11, 1 (2006): 25–42.

Hayward, Mark. "'Il Caso Canadese' and the Question of Global Media." In *Beyond Monopoly: Globalization and Contemporary Italian Media*, edited by Flavia Barca, Milly Buonanno, and Renella Cere, 21–38. Toronto: Lexington Books, 2009.

–. "Ethnic Broadcasting: A History." In *Cultural Industries.ca: Making Sense of Canadian Media in the Digital Age*, edited by Ira Wagman and Peter Urquhart, 202–17. Toronto: Lorimer, 2012.

Heffernan, Kevin. *Ghouls, Gimmicks, and Gold: Horror Films and the American Movie Business, 1953–1968*. Durham, NC: Duke University Press, 2004.

Hesmondhalgh, David. *The Cultural Industries*. 3rd ed. London: Sage, 2013.

Hinther, Rhonda L. *Perogies and Politics: Canada's Ukrainian Left, 1891–1991*. Toronto: University of Toronto Press, 2017.

Horkheimer, Max, and Theodor W. Adorno. *Dialectic of Enlightenment*. Stanford, CA: Stanford University Press, 2002.

Hu, Brian. "Defenders of the Palace." In *American and Chinese-language*

Cinemas: Examining Cultural Flows, vol. 34, edited by Lisa Funnell and Man-Fung Yip, 136–51. London: Routledge, 2014.
Husband, Charles. "The Right to Be Understood: Conceiving the Multi-Ethnic Public Sphere." *Innovation: The European Journal of Social Science Research* 9, 2 (1996): 205–15.
–. "Globalisation, Media Infrastructures and Identities in a Diasporic Community." *Javnost – The Public* 5, 4 (1998): 19–33.
Iacovetta, F. *Gatekeepers: Reshaping Immigrant Lives in Cold War Canada*. Toronto: Between the Lines Press. 2006.
Iacovetta, Franca, Roberto Perin, and Angelo Principe, eds. *Enemies Within: Italian and other Internees in Canada and Abroad*. Toronto: University of Toronto Press, 2000.
Kalbfleisch, Herbert Karl. *The History of the Pioneer German Language Press of Ontario, 1835–1918*. Toronto: University of Toronto Press, 1968.
Kaplan, David H., and Wei Li, eds. *Landscapes of the Ethnic Economy*. Toronto: Rowman and Littlefield, 2006.
Kelman, Ari Y. *Station Identification: A Cultural History of Yiddish Radio in the United States*. Berkeley: University of California Press, 2009.
Kesterton, Wilfred H. *A History of Journalism in Canada*. Vol. 36. Montreal and Kingston: McGill-Queen's University Press, 1967.
Kirkconnell, Watson. *Canadian Overtones: An Anthology of Canadian Poetry Written Originally in Icelandic, Swedish, Norwegian, Hungarian, Italian, Greek and Ukrainian and Now Translated and Edited with Biographical, Historical, Critical, and Bibliographic Notes*. New York: Columbia University Press, 1935.
–. *Canadians All: A Primer of Canadian National Unity*. Issued under authority of the Minister of Public Information, 1941.
–. *The Ukrainian Poets, 1189–1962*. Published for the Ukrainian Canadian Committee by University of Toronto Press, 1963.
–. *A Slice of Canada*. Toronto: University of Toronto Press, 1967.
Kirkconnell, Watson, ed. *The North American Book of Icelandic Verse*. Vol. 1. New York: L. Carrier and A. Isles, 1930.
–. *A Golden Treasury of Polish Lyrics: Selected and Rendered into English*. Winnipeg: Polish Press, 1936.
–. *A Little Treasury of Hungarian Verse*. Washington: American Hungarian Federation, 1947.
Kirschbaum, Joseph M., ed. *Twenty-Five Years of Canada Ethnic Press Federation*. Toronto: Canada Ethnic Press Federation, 1985.
Kirschbaum, Josef M., Benedykt Heydenkorn, and Vladimir V.B. Mauko,

eds. *Twenty Years of the Ethnic Press Association of Ontario*. Toronto: Ethnic Press Association of Ontario, 1971.
Kristmanson, Mark. *Plateaus of Freedom: Nationality, Culture, and State Security in Canada, 1940–1960*. Toronto: University of Toronto Press, 2003.
Krukones, James H. "The Unspooling of Artkino: Soviet Film Distribution in America, 1940–1975." *Historical Journal of Film, Radio and Television* 29, 1 (2009): 91–112.
Kymlicka, Will. *Multicultural Citizenship: A Liberal Theory of Minority Rights*. Oxford: Oxford University Press, 1995.
Kymlicka, Will, and Kathryn Walker, eds. *Rooted Cosmopolitanism: Canada and the World*. Vancouver: UBC Press, 2012.
Lanken, Dane. *Montreal Movie Palaces: Great Theatres of the Golden Era, 1884–1938*. Waterloo: Penumbra, 1993.
Larkin, Brian. "The politics and poetics of infrastructure." *Annual Review of Anthropology* 42 (2013): 327–43.
Levendel, Lewis. *A Century of the Canadian Jewish Press, 1880s–1980s*. Nepean: Borealis Press, 1989.
Light, Ivan Hubert. *Ethnic Enterprise in America: Business and Welfare among Chinese, Japanese, and Blacks*. Berkeley: University of California Press, 1972.
Light, Ivan, and Steven Gold. *Ethnic Economies*. Cambridge, MA: Academic Press, 2000. Available at https://ssrn.com/abstract=2761931.
Lindal, W.J. *Canadian Citizenship and Our Wider Loyalties*. Winnipeg: Canada Press Club, 1947.
–. *The Icelanders in Canada*. Vol. 2. Winnipeg: National Publishers and Viking Printer, 1967.
–. *Two Ways of Life: Freedom or Tyranny*. Whitby, ON: Ryerson Press, 1940.
Longfellow, Brenda. "Bollywood/Toronto: Transnational Spectatorship." *Public* 29 (2004): 85–104.
Luconi, Stefano. "Radio Broadcasting, Consumer Culture, and Ethnic Identity among Italian Americans in the Interwar Years." *Italian Americana* 20, 2 (2002): 150–9.
Mandel, Michael. *The Jewish Hour: The Golden Age of a Toronto Yiddish Radio Show and Newspaper*. Kitchener, ON: Now and Then Books, 2016.
Mata, Fernando G. "Latin American Immigration to Canada: Some Reflections on the Immigration Statistics." *Canadian Journal of Latin American and Caribbean Studies* 10, 20 (1985): 27–42.

Margolis, Rebecca. "The Yiddish Press in Montreal, 1900–1945." *Canadian Jewish Studies/Études juives canadiennes* 16, 1 (2008): 3–6.

Marston, Sallie A., John Paul Jones, and Keith Woodward. "Human Geography without Scale." *Transactions of the Institute of British Geographers* 30, 4 (2005): 416–32.

Martynowych, Orest T. "The Ukrainian Socialist Movement in Canada: 1900–1918 (II)." *Journal of Ukrainian Studies* 2, 1 (1977): 22.

Mata, Fernando G. "Latin American Immigration to Canada: Some Reflections on the Immigration Statistics." *Canadian Journal of Latin American and Caribbean Studies* 10, 20 (1985): 27–42.

Mayer, Vicki, Miranda J. Banks, and John T. Caldwell, eds. *Production Studies: Cultural Studies of Media Industries*. London: Routledge, 2009.

Mazepa, Patricia. "Democracy of, in and through Communication: Struggles around Public Service in Canada in the First Half of the Twentieth Century." *info* 9, 2/3 (2007): 45–56.

McCarthy, Anna. "'Like an Earthquake!' Theater, Television, boxing, and the Black Public Sphere." *Quarterly Review of Film and Video* 16, 3–4 (1997): 307–23.

McKenzie, K. "Multiculturalism and the De-politicization of Blackness in Canada: the case of FLOW 93.5 FM." PhD diss., University of Toronto, 2009.

Mochoruk, Jim. "Orest T. Martynowych, the Showman and the Ukrainian Cause: Folk Dance, Film, and the Life of Vasile Avramenko." *Manitoba History* 80 (2016): 56–8.

Murray, Catherine. "Media Infrastructure for Multicultural Diversity." *Policy Options* April 2008, 63–6.

National Publications. *A Submission to the Royal Commission on Publications*. Toronto: Canada Ethnic Press Federation, 1960.

Neary, Peter. "The CBC 'Ventures in Citizenship' Broadcast of 9 November 1938." *Canadian Jewish Studies* 10 (2002): 109–22.

Nebesio, Bohdan Y. "Zaporozhets za Dunaiem (1938): The Production of the First Ukrainian-Language Feature Film in Canada." *Journal of Ukrainian Studies* 16, 1 (1991): 115.

Newman, Sydney. *Head of Drama: The Memoir of Sydney Newman*. Toronto: ECW Press, 2017.

Ng, Wing Chung. "Chinatown Theatre as Transnational Business: New Evidence from Vancouver during the Exclusion Era." *BC Studies* 148 (2005): 25–54.

Nicholson, Judith, and Mimi Sheller. "Race and the Politics of Mobility." *Transfers* 6, 1 (2016): 1–150.

O'Bryan, Kenneth G., Jeffrey G. Reitz, and Olga Kuplowska. *Non-Official Languages: A Study in Canadian Multiculturalism*. Ottawa: Minister Responsible for Multiculturalism, 1976.

Odartey-Wellington, Felix. "Broadcasting Regulation and Building the Multicultural Canadian Nation: Understanding the CRTC's Al-Jazeera Arabic Decision." *Communication Law and Policy* 18, 2 (2013): 121–54.

Pal, Leslie A. *Interests of State: The Politics of Language, Multiculturalism, and Feminism in Canada*. Montreal and Kingston: McGill-Queen's University Press, 1993.

Palmer, Howard. "Ethnic Relations in Wartime: Nationalism and European Minorities in Alberta during the Second World War." *Canadian ethnic studies/Études ethniques au Canada* 14, 3 (1982): 1–23.

Park, Robert E. *The Immigrant Press and Its Control*. New York: Harper and Brothers, 1922.

Park, Robert E., and Ernest W. Burgess. *The City*. Chicago: The University of Chicago Press, 1925.

Parks, Lisa. *Cultures in Orbit: Satellites and the Televisual*. Durham, NC: Duke University Press, 2005.

–. "Technostruggles and the Satellite Dish." *Cultural Technologies: The Shaping of Culture in Media and Society*, 64–86. London: Routledge, 2012.

Parks, Lisa, and Nicole Starosielski, eds. *Signal Traffic: Critical Studies of Media Infrastructures*. Champaign: University of Illinois Press, 2015.

Perkin, James Russell Conway, and James B. Snelson. *Morning in His Heart: The Life and Writings of Watson Kirkconnell*. Hantsport, NS: Published for Acadia University Library by Lancelot Press, 1986.

Peters, John Durham. *The Marvelous Clouds: Toward a Philosophy of Elemental Media*. Chicago: University of Chicago Press, 2015.

Polec, Patryk. *Hurrah Revolutionaries: The Polish Canadian Communist Movement, 1918–1948*. Montreal and Kingston: McGill-Queens University Press, 2015.

Principe, Angelo. *The Darkest Side of the Fascist Years: The Italian-Canadian Press, 1920–1942*. Toronto: Guernica Editions, 1999.

Prymak, Thomas Michael. *Maple Leaf and Trident: The Ukrainian Canadians during the Second World War*. North York: Multicultural History Society of Ontario, 1988.

Raboy, Marc. *Missed Opportunities: The Story of Canada's Broadcasting Policy*. Montreal and Kingston: McGill-Queen's University Press, 1990.

Razack, Sherene, ed. *Race, Space, and the Law: Unmapping a White Settler Society*. Toronto: Between the Lines Press, 2002.
Rose, Jonathan W. *Making "Pictures in Our Heads": Government Advertising in Canada*. Westport: Praeger, 2000.
Ross, Becki. *Burlesque West: Showgirls, Sex, and Sin in Postwar Vancouver*. Toronto: University of Toronto Press, 2009.
Roth, Lorna. "The Delicate Acts of 'Colour Balancing': Multiculturalism and Canadian Television Broadcasting Policies and Practices." *Canadian Journal of Communication* 23, 4 (1998): 487.
–. *Something New in the Air: The Story of First Peoples Television Broadcasting in Canada*. Vol. 43. Montreal and Kingston: McGill-Queen's University Press, 2005.
Rothenbuhler, Eric, and Tom McCourt. "Radio Redefines Itself, 1947–1962." In *Radio Reader: Essays in the Cultural History of Radio*, edited by Michele Hilmes and Jason Loviglio, 367–88. New York: Routledge, 2002.
Rutherford, Paul. *When Television Was Young: Primetime Canada, 1952–1967*. Toronto: University of Toronto Press, 1990.
Ryan, Phil. *Multicultiphobia*. Toronto: University of Toronto Press, 2010.
Saunders, Doug. *Arrival City: How the Largest Migration in History Is Reshaping Our World*. Toronto: Vintage, 2011.
Savage, Barbara Dianne. *Broadcasting Freedom: Radio, War, and the Politics of Race, 1938–1948*. Chapel Hill: UNC Press Books, 1999.
Scholz, Trebor. *Platform Cooperativism: Challenging the Corporate Sharing Economy*. New York: Rosa Luxemburg Foundation, 2016.
Sebert, John. *The Nabes: Toronto's Wonderful Neighborhood Movie Houses*. Oakville, ON: Mosaic Press, 2001.
Srnicek, Nick. *Platform Capitalism*. Cambridge, UK: Polity, 2017.
Stern, Joe. "Private Broadcasters Speak in Many Tongues." *Canadian Broadcaster and Telescreen* 14, 16 (17 August 1955): 6–8.
Straw, Will. "The Circulatory Turn." In *The Wireless Spectrum: The Politics, Practices and Poetics of Mobile Media*, edited by Barbara Crow, Michael Longford, and Kim Sawchuk, 17–28. Toronto: University of Toronto Press, 2010.
Stuebing, Douglas, John R. Marshall, and Gary Oakes. *Trudeau: A Man for Tomorrow*. Toronto: Clarke, Irwin, 1968.
Taylor, Charles. "The Politics of Recognition." In *Multiculturalism: Examining the Politics of Recognition*, edited by Amy Guttman, 25–73. Princeton: Princeton University Press, 1994.
–. *Modern Social Imaginaries*. Durham, NC: Duke University Press, 2004.

Taylor, Doug. *Toronto's Local Movie Theatres of Yesteryear: Brought Back to Thrill You Again*. Toronto: Dundurn, 2016.

Taylor, N.A. "Our Business." In *Yearbook – Canadian Motion Picture Industry*. Toronto: Film Publications of Canada, 1956.

–. "Our Business." In *Yearbook – Canadian Motion Picture Industry*. Toronto: Film Publications of Canada, 1958.

–. "Our Business." In *Yearbook – Canadian Motion Picture Industry with Television Section*. Toronto: Film Publications of Canada. 1960.

Thomas, T.J. *Monopoly and Pay TV in Canada*. Mini-Review 84-28E, Library of Parliament, Ottawa, 18 September 1984.

Thompson, John Herd. *Ethnic Minorities during Two World Wars*. No. 19. Ottawa: Canadian Historical Association, 1991.

Tolon, Kaya. "Futures Studies: A New Social Science Rooted in Cold War Strategic Thinking." In *Cold War Social Science: Knowledge Production, Liberal Science, and Human Nature*, edited by Mark Solovey and Hamilton Cravens, 45–62. New York: Palgrave Macmillan, 2012.

Turek, Viktor. *The Polish Language Press in Canada: Its History and a Bibliographical List*. Vol. 4. Toronto: Polish Alliance Press, 1962.

Van Bauwel, Sofie, Roel Vande Winkel, Philippe Meers, Iris Vandevelde, and Kevin Smets. "Between Unruliness and Sociality: Discourses on Diasporic Cinema Audiences for Turkish and Indian Films." In *Meanings of Audiences*, edited by Richard Butsch and Sonia Livingstone, 76–91. London: Routledge, 2013.

Walcott, Rinaldo. *Queer Returns: Essays on Multiculturalism, Diaspora and Black Studies*. London, ON: Insomniac Press, 2016.

Whitaker, Reginald. "Official Repression of Communism During World War II." *Labour/Le Travail* 17 (1986): 135–66.

Whitaker, Reginald, and Gary Marcuse. *Cold War Canada: The Making of a National Insecurity State, 1945–1957*. Toronto: University of Toronto Press, 1994.

Whiteoak, John. "Italian-Australian Musicians, 'Argentino' Tango Bands and the Australian Tango Band Era." *Context: Journal of Music Research* 35/36 (2010): 93–110.

Wilinsky, Barbara. *Sure Seaters: The Emergence of Art House Cinema*. Minneapolis: University of Minnesota Press, 2001.

Williams, Raymond. *Keywords*. New York: Oxford University Press, 2014.

Young, Liam Cole. *List Cultures: Knowledge and Poetics from Mesopotamia to BuzzFeed*. Amsterdam: Amsterdam University Press, 2017.

Index

Page numbers in italics indicate material in figures.

Aboriginal People's Television Network, 18
Adewumi, Olumide, 169–70
Adie, Robert, 84
advertising, 70; by ethnic agencies, 71, *71*; to ethnic audiences, 132–3; government purchasing of, 84–5, 87–94, *89*; "local" versus "national interest," 160; Mokrzycki on role of, 87–91, *89*, 132–3
African Americans, 148, 197n18
African Canadian community, 95–6
Alberta, 162, 191n30
Al-Jazeera (Qatar), 30, 145, 165
All Nations Film and Book Service, 48
"A Matter of Pride" (WKBW), 148
Americanization Studies series, 67
Americans All, 113
Angelozzi, A., 48
"Anglo-Saxon ratings," 133
anti-communism. *See* Cold War
"anti-interpretive" tendency, 8
archival material, access to, 20–5
Arena Paul-Sauvé, 48
Argentinian film, 32–3
Argentinísima II film, 32–3, 35, 44
Around the World in 80 Days, 35

"arrival cities," 41
"art house" theatres, 38–9, 44, 177n32
Artkino, 49, 179n56
assimilation goals, 67–8, 98, 110, 114, 125, 165
Association of Canadian Advertisers, 88
ATN, 156
audiences: attempts to enlarge, 40; behavior of, 53–4, *55*, 180n77; "granola," 44; ratings skewed against minorities, 111; sponsor research of, 131
audio-only cable, 136
autonomy as media infrastructure function, 9
Avon Theatre (Vancouver), 45

Baier, Karl Julius, 91
Bains, Avtar, 45
barbershops and beauty salons, 58, *59*
BBG (Board of Broadcast Governors), 120, 122–5, 128–9, 155
"bicycling" of tapes, 160
bilingualism and multilingualism, 100–2

Bizocchi, Justine, 138, 199n46
Blanding, Lee, 99
Bobby Orr Entertainment, 54
Bohaker, Heidi, 95
Bollywood films, 43, 48
Bossin, Hye, 41
Bouchard, Gérard, 13
Bowker, Geoffrey C., 15
Brighton Theatre (Toronto), 43, 46, 48
British Columbia: ethnic media in, 18; international films imported into, 23, 45–7; regional press associations, 72, 80; regional stations, 162; World View Television, 155, 159
Broadcast Act (1985), 108, 124, 154
broadcasters as community representatives, 138
Broadcasting Policy Reflecting Canada's Linguistic and Cultural Diversity, 162–3
brokered programming, 109, 139, 146, 154
Building the Future (Taylor & Bouchard), 13
Bulgarian "enemy language" ban, 184n32
Bureau of Broadcast Measurement, 132–3
"buy-through" requirements, 167, 200n81

"Cable 10 Experiment," 147
cable distribution, 4; "buy-through" requirements, 167, 200n81; community access channels, 147; early cable radio, 136–8, 140; early third-language television, 144–5, 149–50, 155–62; of FM radio stations, 136; hearings on, 145, 156; international channels and terrorism fears, 165–6; lack of regulation, 136; liability issues, 165; national distribution, 145, 149; package requirements, 168; promoting multiculturalism through, 29, 144, 149–50, 162; transition to digital, 145, 163–4, 167
Caldwell, S.W., 119, 133
Calgary, 160
Canada: cosmopolitan nationalism of, 142, 153; immigration history compared to US, 176n19
Canada Ethnic Press Federation. *See* CEPF (Canada Ethnic Press Federation)
Canada Press Club. *See* CPC (Canada Press Club)
Canadian Broadcaster, 118, 132–3
Canadian Broadcaster and Telescreen Magazine, 116
Canadian Citizenship and Our Wider Loyalties (Lindal), 76
Canadian Farmer (newspaper), 77, 86
Canadian Film Weekly, 39, 41
"Canadianism," 108
"Canadianization," 107
Canadian Jewish Chronicle (newspaper), 86
Canadian Overtones (Kirkconnell), 113
Canadians All (radio series), 75, 110, 112–15, 121
Canadian scene news agency, 72, 79, 81–4, 95–6
Cantinflas, 33
Carey, James W., 173n4
Carnegie Institute, 67
Carpino, Pasqualino, 148
CARTB (Canadian Association of Radio and Television Broadcasters), 116, 118
Castle, William, 40

Index

Cathay International Television (Fairchild), 160, 163
CBC, 109, 111–12, 114–15, 121, 149, 193n57
censorship, 24, 69–70, 75–6, 104, 184n32, 190n9
Centre Island (Toronto), 134, *135*
Centre Theatre (formerly Duchess), 32–3, 35–6, 44, 54, 175n14
CEPF (Canada Ethnic Press Federation): appearance of independence, 80–1; and Canadian scene, 84, 95; concern over English-language publications, 94; establishment of, 72; fear of foreign influence over, 87, 92; Mokrzycki participation in, 88, 90; "unity with diversity" concept, 101–2
CFAM, 119
CFCF, 123, 146
CFLP, 123
CFMB (Canada's First Multilingual Broadcaster), 111, 123–5, 130–1, 137–8, 141, 151–2
CFMT (Rogers Communication): Chinese-language service on, 159; CRTC application for, 150; Daniel Iannuzzi and, 87, 147, 150; *Ethnicity* program, 22; first multicultural broadcaster, 29; location of, 22, 64; and MTN, 156–7; Rogers' purchase of, 162–3
CFRB, 115, 118–19, 130
CFRO-FM (Vancouver Co-operative Radio), 138
CFTO, 146
Chakrabarty, Dipesh, 26
Chandrasekar, Shan, 156
Charest, Roger, 131
CHCH, Hamilton, 146, 150, 158
CHCR (Canadian Hellenic Cable Radio), 136

CHED, 119
Cheung, Francis, 147, 157, *158*
CHIN (Radio and Television), 111; annual picnic, 134–6; application for, 125, 128–31; as "continental," 129; and CRTC, 123, 133, 150–1; "Italian Day," 134–6, *135*; in Little Italy, 64; not "an ethnic station," 129; radio play on assassination, 153; signal interference by, 106–7. *See also* Lombardi, Johnny
China Theatre, 48
Chinatown News, 94
Chinavision (Fairchild), 29, 145, 147, 157–60, *158*, 163–4, 166
Chinese Canadians, 50, 159, 166
Chinese language media: and Bernard T.C. Liu, 147, 155–6, 159; Chinavision (Fairchild), 29, 145, 157–60, 163–4, 166; Chinese Art and Film Society (Vancouver), 45; films, 39, 43, 45, 46, 48, 52–3; film venues, 48, 52; and John Leung, 157; La Plaza/Acropolis/Dundas/Cinema Ellas/China Cinema/Opera House (Toronto), 50, *51*; newspapers, 86, 94; and semi-public community, 53, 57; television, 156; Tiananmen Square coverage, 163; World View, 159
CHLP, 121–2, 146
CHML, 116, *117*, 191n22
CHMS, 119
CHRS, 123
CHTO (Canadian Hellenic Toronto Radio Limited), 136
CHUM (Toronto), 116, 128, 130
Chuvalo, George, 54
CICR (Radio Italia), 136
Cine Europa (Ontario), 48
Cine Kensington (Toronto), 44

Cinema 3/Mac's Theatre (Winnipeg), 44
Cinema Colon (Toronto), 33, 52, 175n9
Cinema Lumiere (Toronto), 177n32
Cinema Riviera (Montreal), 43
Cinerama, 40
CINQ-FM (Radio Centre-Ville), 137–8
CIRV-FM, 137
Citizens All series, 115
Citizenship Act (1947), 76, 95
City-TV (Toronto), 87, 144, 149–51, 157
"civic" engineering, 4
CJMS (Montreal), 119, 122
CJOY (Ontario), 116
CJSP (Leamington), 115
CJVB (Great Pacific Broadcasting, Vancouver), 141, 151, 153, 197n19
CKAC, 122
CKFH (Toronto), 116
CKJS (Winnipeg), 141, 143, 151
CKVR, 150
Clavir, Leo, 49, 179n56
closed-circuit broadcasts, 54, 55, 144, 148
Cohen, Ben, 77
Cold War: and black press, 95; and *Canadians All* radio series, 112–15; enforcing "Canadianism," 182n8; and ethnic press, 69–72, 76–8, 87, 105; fear of communist subversion, 81–2, 94, 182n8; and liberalism, 104; and multicultural futurism, 98–9; and opposition to foreign language use, 115; replaced by global war on terror, 165
college students, 45
commonality, 172
communal spaces, 56–61, 134

communication as way of being together, 3
communists and fear of communists, 55–6, 88, 96, 101
communities and media, 9, 19, 154
community gathering places, 56–8, 57
community service, meaning of, 109, 147
community television, 147
"constitution of spaces," 60
"constrained emergence theory," 68
"container thinking," 197n8
content concerns, 23, 84–5, 142, 151, 153–4, 163–7
Continental/cosmopolitan format, 110–11, 118–19, 128, 139–40
Continental News, 77
cooking shows, 147, *148*
coordination issues, 17
Cork, Bill "The Count," 49
Corriere Canadese, 86, 95, 127, 134, 146
Corriere Italiano, 86, 146, 179n53
Couldry, Nick, 197n8
Coulthard, Glen, 14–15
counterculture and international cinema, 62
"counter-culture" radio, 137
Courier-Sud (Toronto), 91
CPC (Canada Press Club), 77; commemorative volume for, 84; formation, goals of, 71–5, 93, 99; as local branch of CPEF, 97, 99; relationship with government, 97, 99, 102, 112
CPRC (Canada Portuguese Radio Club), 137
Croatian language media, 184n32
CRTC (Canadian Radio-television and Telecommunications Commission), 65, 144–5; accused of fomenting unrest, 153; and brokered programming,

153–4; and community access channels, 147; denial of Telelatino purchase, 162; hearings on multilingual broadcasting, 150–3, 156–60; and international services, 163–4, 167; on "local" advertising, 160; and localism, 141–2; national multilingual channel, 168, 170; and official multiculturalism, 149–50; policy on third-language broadcasting, 136; RAI application, 165; Serbian assassination dramatization issue, 153; Stanczykowski hearing, 141
CTV, 149
Cultural Contributions of the Other Ethnic Groups, The, 130
cultural diversity: of "arrival cities," 41–3, 42; balancing with nationalism, 171; Charles Taylor on, 12; Gary Pieters on, 3; as goal, 98, 102, 130; infrastructure and, 11; Leon Kossar and, 151; and localism, 142–4, 155, 162–3; management of, 68–9; "managing the mosaic," 114; and RAI International, 164–5; Richard Day on, 68
Cultural Film Association (Vancouver), 45
cultural infrastructure, 9, 44, 62, 71
cultural nationalism, 111, 146
"cultural thickenings," 197n8
Czas newspaper, 77, 86

Daisons Multilingual Television, 87, 147, 150–1, 157
Daisons Publishing, 86
Darkest Side of Fascism, The, 19
Davidovich, Steve, 79, 185n48
Day, Richard, 13, 68
"death of multiculturalism," 30, 171

Defence of Canada Regulations (1939), 108, 190n9
Der Nordwesten, 72, 77, 86–7
Der Zeit, 101
Despotovich, R., 91
Dhaliwal, Arjan, 45
Diefenbaker, John, 91
digital distribution: cultural impacts of, 165; disrupting protectionism, 143; Gidilounge example, 169–71; globalization of, 145, 170–1; music streaming, 170; regulation of, 166–7; Spanish-language media, 166; of television, 29–30, 143; third-language programming, 29–30; transition to, 62, 145, 163–70
Dojacek, Frank, 77, 86
Dojack, Charles, 77, 77, 100–1, 141
"domestic" versus "foreign" broadcasting, 143, 160
Dos Yiddishe Vort (Der Kanader Yid), 72
Dreisziger, N.F., 75
dubbing, 40–1, 178n51, 199n46
Dundas, the, 50, 179n63
Dutch language media, 117, 118, 133, 195
Dworkin, Dorothy, 108

Eagleson, Alan, 54
Eastern Europe, films from, 43, 46, 49, 101
École Jeanne-Mance, 48
economic localism, 142–4, 155, 162–3
Edmonton, 119, 131, 160
educational mandate, 153
Edwardson, Ryan, 107
"electronic theatre," 65
Elliott-Haynes research, 132
El Popular newspaper, 33, 34, 44, 84, 175n8

"enemy languages" ban, 75, 184n32
England, Robert, 68
English-language material, 50, 94, 115–16, 159, 166, 200n80
Ethnic Broadcasting Policy, 163
Ethnic Channels Group, 166
ethnic economies, 35–6, 139
Ethnicity weekly program, 22
ethnic press, 71–2; circulation figures for, 182n14; concept, 13–14, 94–5, 112, 182n10; newspapers, 78–9; ownership and control of, 85, 103–4; ownership of, 85; private and government advertising in, 87–93, 89; and reader language retention, 85; relationship of with state, 97–9, 104; self-censorship by, 75–6; as tool for assimilation, 67–8. *See also* CEPF (Canada Ethnic Press Federation)
Ethnic Press Association of Ontario, 71; commemorative volumes of, 84, 97; establishment of, 72; "ethnic" versus "foreign" terminology, 79, 93; Mokrzycki and, 87, 90; origins of, 78–9; presentation before Royal Commission, 101
Ethnic Press Club of Toronto, 78
Ethnic scene, 83
"ethnic theatres," 4, 38–9, 62
"ethnic" versus "foreign," 93
ethnocultural radio format, 110. *See also* third-language programming
European immigrants, 38, 112
Evanov, Bill, 151

Fairchild (Chinavision), 29; Fairchild 2 launch, 166; financial issues, *158*, 160; Francis Cheung application for, 147, 157; international content, 164; licensing hearings, requirements, 145, 157–9; location, 64; subscription issues, 160; Tiananmen Square coverage, 163
Faith, Percy, 119–20, *120*
Fanon, Frantz, 14
Faster Pussycat Kill! Kill! (Meyer), 44
Fautaux, Brian, 138
Fenson, Mel, 77
"Festival Italiano" (Johnny Lombardi), 150
Figlia Italiana, La, 60
Films of Italy, 48
Finnish language media, 78, 151, 184n2
First World War censorship, 184n32, 190n9
Flash online music player, 169
Fleras, Augie, 10
foreign-based, foreign-born publishers, 70, 100–1
foreign films, 41; audience behavior at, 53–4; home video competition with, 63; importation of, 45–8; to increase audiences, 40; revamped movie houses for, 41; short runs, 47
'Foreign Language Press,' 79, 83, 94. *See also* ethnic press
"foreign language" radio, 152. *See also* third-language programming
"foreign," meaning of, 93, 95, 110, 143
formats: Continental/cosmopolitan, 118–19, 128, 139; as media infrastructure function, 9; multilingual radio, 110, 137–40; as recipes, 139–40
Fortier, Laval, 80
Fowler, Robert, 116
freelancers, 130, 137, 146, 156, 162

Fromm, Leonard, 32
Fromm, Miki, 32
Fromm, Wayne, 35–6, 54
Frum, Barbara, 133
Fujiwara, Aya, 20
Fulford, Ethel, 132
"The Function of Multilingual Broadcasting in Canada," 150
"fundamental terms and units" of communication, 17
Fung, Thomas, 163
future studies/futurism, 98–9

Gagliardi, Alfredo, 86, 146
German language media, 74, 118; film distribution, 48; local ads, 133; newspapers, 42, 72, 86, 95, 183n17; public anxieties regarding, 87, 101, 115, 184n32, 191n30; radio, 141
Gidilounge, 169–71
Givens, Philip, 129
Global Television, 150
Globe and Mail, 54, 55, 60, 81, 88, 89, 92, 113
Glogowski, Frank, 79
Glos Pracy newspaper, 55
Godfather, The, 34, 35
Gold, Steven, 36
Gomery, Douglas, 38
Grant, Charity, 79, 81
Greek Canadian Radio Limited, 136
Greek-language distribution: audio, 136–7; films, 43, 46, 50, 56, 57; music as disruption, 106; television, 118, 137
"grey" market distribution, 23
Griffiths, Marie, 156

Habermas, Jürgen, 13
Hamilton, Alfred, 95
Hansen, Miriam, 57
Happy Valley Investments, 163

Haque, Eve, 10, 96, 102
Harney, Nicholas, 134
healthcare, media compared to, 5
Hepp, Andreas, 197n8
Heritage Broadcasters, 151
Hirsch, Paul M., 12
Hoellige, Wilfred A., 132–3
home video: competing with theatres, 43, 46, 52, 65; introduction of, 43, 63; as legal "grey market," 23, 64–5
Hong Kong, 45–6, 48, 157, 163–4
Hu, Brian, 57
Hungarian language media: films, 48; language media, 113; publication bans, 184n32; refugee crisis, 83; television, 118
Husband, Charles, 18, 181n81

Iacovetta, Franca, 76, 95, 182n8
Iannuzzi, Daniel: as *Corriere Canadese* publisher/editor, 95, 127, 134, 146; interested in satellite distribution, 162; on local/regional/national values, 154–5; and Multilingual Television Network, 151–2, 154, 156, 159; as producer not broadcaster, 152; as publisher, 86
Icelandic Canadian publications, 76, 95, 183n17, 184n36
"identity politics," 171
Immigrant Press and Its Control, The (Parks), 16, 67–8. See also ethnic press
immigration: Canada versus United States, 176n19; from Central/South America, 33; distinguishing "good" from "bad," 69; post Depression and war, 77, 98; into suburbs, 38, 63
Indian films, 43, 45–7, 50, 58
Indigenous peoples: *Indian News*, 95–6; MTV, MTN (Multilingual

Television Network) and, 156; and politics of recognition, 14–15; print media by/for, 95
individuation of culture, 171
Industry and Identity (Murray), 17–18
infrastructure, media as, 3–4, 15–19, 69, 139, 143–4
Innis, Harold, 7
intellectual property law, 21, 25, 64
"inter-communication," 12
international services: loyalty concerns regarding, 30, 92, 163–4; radio, 130; relations with national services, 145–6, 164–7; US based, 108
interstitial media, 148–9
IODE (Imperial Order Daughters of the Empire), 79, 81, 115
Italian Canadians, 159, 192n51
Italian Film Importers, 48
Italian Journal (Hamilton), 158
Italian language media: cable television, 156; distributors of, 48; Emilio Mascia on, 65; fascist infiltration of, 92; films, 32, 43–6, 48–50, 52–3, 56, 57; *Italian Journal*, 54, 146; live theatre, 43; local ads, 133; movies as communal space, 53, 134; movie venues, 175–6n14; newspapers, 42, 86; public anxieties regarding, 30, 74, 115, 191n30; radio, 115, 117, 118–19, 136, 146, 190nn6–7; RAI International, 30, 145, 164–5; Raphael (Ralph) Pirro, 192n51; riot at *La Figlia Italiana* screening, 60; and Spanish crossover viewing, 158; television, 86–7, 146, 150, 159; and union activities, 56, 57; wealth of Italian Canadians, 159. *See also* CHIN (Radio and Television);

Lombardi, Johnny; Telelatino (Latinovision)

Japan, 74, 78
Jewish language media: audiences for, 49; films, 41; "Jewish Radio Hour," 107; and Massey Commission, 97; and multilingual broadcasting debate, 151; newspapers, 77, 86, 94–5

Kanitz, Walter, 118–19
Kaye, Vladimir J., 75–6
Keeble Cable, 147
Kensington theatre, 14, 32–3, 49, 175nn8, 177n37
King, Mackenzie, 113
Kingcrest Theatre (Vancouver), 45
King/Kino/Liberty/Studio/Shock Theatre (Toronto), 48–50, 50
King of Kensington program, 193n57
Kirkconnell, Watson, 27, 112–14, 191nn22
Kossar, Leon and Zena, 151
Kowalski, Frank J., 91–2
Kristmanson, Mark, 184n30
Krushchev, Nikita, 84

labour movement, 55–6
La Figlia Italiana, 60
Lai, James, 180n63
language as defining characteristic, 95
"language radio," 112, 118, 132. *See also* third-language programming
Lansdowne Theatre, 56, 57
La Patrie, 122
La Plaza/Acropolis/Dundas/Cinema Ellas/China Cinema/Opera House (Toronto), 50, 51
La Presse, 122
Larkin, Brian, 16

Lastman, Mel "Bad Boy," 134
Latin American culture in Canada, 33, 36, 46
Latinovision. *See* Telelatino (Latinovision)
Lavoie, Daniel, 137
Leigh Starr, Susan, 15
Lester, Robert, 49
Leung, John, 157
Levin, Slava, 166
Lezack, Leo, 77
licensing issues, 178–9n52; Al-Jazeera, 30, 165; home video, 64; international channels, 165–6; national versus regional versus local, 154–60, 168; of third-language stations, 152
Light, Ivan, 36
Lindal, Walter Jacobson, 77; background and beliefs of, 73; and Canada Press Club, 73–4, 99; *Canadian Citizenship and Our Wider Loyalties*, 76; on formation of Ethnic Press Association of Ontario, 78; political connections of, 99; remarks on ethnic press, 100–2, 114
Lingua Ads Services, 91
linguistic bias in research materials, 20
listing technique, 93–4
Little Italy (Toronto), 44, 64, 126
Liu, Bernard T.C., 147, 155–6, 159
local: defining, 143, 154–5, 160, 167; localism, 142–4, 155, 162–3; multi-local strategy, 162; relationship with national services, 158–9
Lombardi, Johnny, 106, 150–1, 194n88; application for multilingual television, 151; and CHUM (Toronto), 116, 128, 130; and "cosmopolitan"/"continental" format, 128–31, 194n88; critical of audience ratings, 111, 133; and "Festival Italiano," 150; as a promoter, 112, 123, 126, 126–9; relationship with Italian community, 128, 138; on rock and roll, 130; sponsoring annual picnic, 134–6; and Ted Rogers, 125. *See also* CFMB (Canada's First Multilingual Broadcaster); CFMT (Rogers Communication); CHIN (Radio and Television)
Lux Theatre (Vancouver), 45

Mac's Theatre/Cinema 3 (Winnipeg), 44, 177n32
Majestic Theatre (Vancouver), 45, 52
Maniatakos, Peter, 137
Manitoba: Canada Press Club, 75; foreign language press in, 72, 75; Southern Manitoba Broadcasting, 119; Winnipeg, 39, 44, 55, 72–7, 80, 86, 102
Manitoba Liberal Party, 99
Maple Leaf Gardens (Toronto), 54, 60
Marcuse, Gary, 74
Martinelli family, 45
Martyn, Stan. *See* Mokrzycki, Z.S. (Stan Martyn)
Mascia, Emilio: on "electronic theatre," 65; and Latinovision, 158; and Leon Kossar, 151; as owner and host, 54, 146; and Playhouse Theatre, 56; and Telelatino, 56
Massey, Vincent, 77, 81
Massey Commission, 97
Mastrangelo, Rocco, 65
Mauko, Vladimir, 71, 78
McGill University South Asian Student Association, 47
McLuhan, Marshall, 7, 197n9
MCTV (Metro Channel/"Multicultural Television"), 148, 150

media: as bridge to "home," 8; and formation of identity, 11; as infrastructure, 3–5, 7–9, 17–18; interconnection between, 12; mainstream versus minority, 12–13, 17; moving into general retail, 63
mediation, Charles Taylor and, 12–13
Meighen, Arthur, 81
methodological issues, 19–25
Mexican migrants to US, 176n19
Meyer, Russ, 44
Ministry for Citizenship and Immigration, 79, 82–3
minority media, 31; archival access to, 24–5; and autonomy, 9–10; and "grey" markets, 23; as infrastructure, 7, 17–18; and mainstream media, 12; minority ownership of, 162; and policy, 18
mobility of media, 8
Modern Social Imaginaries (Taylor), 12
Mokrzycki, Z.S. (Stan Martyn): background of, 78–9; and Canada Ethnic Press Federation, 90; and Daniel Iannuzzi, 151; and Ethnic Press Association of Ontario, 78, 87, 185n45; on "old" and "new" migrants, 99; and role of advertisers, 87–8, 89, 90–1, 132–3
Montreal: bilingual media infrastructure in, 47, 160; Cinema Verdi/Pagoda/Cinema Colon/New Yorker/Milieu, 52; imported international films, 43, 45, 47; north end of, 39
Moore, Paul, 178n51
Moran, Albert, 139
Moriyama, Raymond, 151

movie houses/theaters: health and safety standards, 178n37; movie experience in, 43–5; police harassment of, 60–1; vandalism of, 60; as venues for foreign-language films, 41–3, 69
MTV, MTN (Multilingual Television Network), 151, 156–7, 159, 162
multi-channel services, 166
multiculturalism: as Canadian value, 30–1, 101–2; City-TV and, 149–50; "death" of, 30, 171; and European logics of racialization, 15; as the future, 96–103; in global market, 25; good and bad of, 17, 30; groups excluded from, 95; and media, 17–18; versus multilingualism, 10; Nationalities Branch, 184n30; as official policy, 149; as political project, 140; and scale, 143–4; scholarship on, 10–11; vernacular versus official, 62
multicultural/multilingual programming. *See* third-language programming
multi-ethnic public sphere, 18, 103, 146, 181n81
Multilingual Counselling Associates, 91
multilingual radio format, 110, 137–40
Multilingual Television Network (MTV, MTN), 151, 156–7, 159, 162
multi-local services, 160, 162
Murray, Catherine, 17–18
music streaming, 169–71

Naaz Theatre (Toronto), 43, 48, 50, 51, 60, 65, 177n37
"the nabes," 41

national culture, 93, 96, 107, 168, 196n5
National Film Board, 75, 114
"national insecurity state," 74
Nationalities Branch, 75, 95, 112–13, 184n30
National Publications, 77, 100–1
national versus regional versus local, 145, 149, 154–60
nation-building through culture, 96, 107
New Canadian Publications, 72, 78–9, 87–91, 89, 99
"new Canadians": anti-communism targeting, 82; as audience for newspapers, 132; and ethnic media, 97, 106, 108; integrating, 115–16, 129, 131; media about and for, 115; as potential customers, 132–3; third-language services for, 159–60; Toronto cultural center for, 49, 50
Newcomb, Horace, 12
Newman, Sydney, 179n56
newspapers: during Cold War, 70; definition of, 181n7 (ch2), 181n85 (ch1); foreign language, 42, 42, 67, 71, 73, 75; as social institutions, 68; during World War II, 75. *See also* ethnic press
Nigerian language media, 169

Oda, Bev, 151, 157
Odyssey television, 29, 137
Olympia Theatre (Vancouver), 45
OMNI, 162, 168
Ontario, 160; archives, 22; CHML (Hamilton), 116–17; CHML, CJOY (Hamilton), 116, 117; foreign language broadcasts, 116, 118, 150; foreign language newspapers, 183n17; international films imported into, 23, 45–8; "Jewish Radio Hour" broadcasts in, 107–8; licensing issues, 64–5; Mokrzycki presentation to, 99; and NDP charges, 92; Progressive Conservatives party, 91; "radio tapes" to Chinese Canadians, 157; Telelatino in, 160; World Cup (1972) broadcast, 54. *See also* CFMT (Rogers Communication)
ownership, 36; concentration of, 142; of multilingual radio, 139; of newspapers, 85–6; separation from content, 110, 162–3

Pagoda Theatre, 48, 177n37
Pantages Theatre chain, 52
Park, Robert E., 67–8
Parks, Lisa, 16
Pavone, Rita, 60
Peoples of Canada (film), 75
Percy Faith Plays Continental Music, 119–20, 120
Peters, John Durham, 16–17
Pickersgill, J.W., 80
picnics as communal spaces, 134
Pieters, Gary, 3–4
Pirro, Raphael (Ralph), 192n51
Playhouse Theatre (Hamilton), 54, 56
policy emphasis, issues with, 18–19
Polish-language media, 19, 118; CHML (Hamilton), 116–17; communist film distribution, 55–6; *Czas* newspaper, 77, 86; film, 48; local ads, 133; newspapers, 42; radio, 133; venues, 48; and Watson Kirkconnell, 112–14, 191n22; *Zwiazkowiec* (Polish weekly), 79, 84. *See also* Mokrzycki, Z.S. (Stan Martyn); Stanczykowski, Casimir

Polish Language Press in Canada, The (Turek), 19
"politics of recognition," 11–12, 14–15, 68
Polley, Sarah, 3–5
pornography, 44
Portuguese barbershops (Montreal), 58
Portuguese language media: films, 14, 34, 35, 47–8, 175nn8; print, 58, 59; radio, 136–7, 195–6n108
postwar issues: anti-communism, 56; ban on foreign language broadcasts, 108, 121; diversity/nationalism balance, 171; ethnic press issues, 76, 103, 182n10; media environment, 20, 38–9, 110–11; migration issues, 96, 98–9, 107; US versus Canada immigration, 176n19
press associations. *See* ethnic press
press freedom and propaganda, 79–84
Principe, Angelo, 19
print. *See* newspapers
"processes of distribution," 16–17
public assembly laws, 60–1
public posters, 5, 6
public sphere: alternative versions of, 57, 155, 174n14; Charles Husband on, 18; Charles Taylor on, 12–13; expansion of, 56; multi-ethnic, 103, 181n81; postwar, 104; US black, 197n18
public transit: media compared to, 3, 5
Puliafito, Palmina, 43, 178n40

Qatar, 30, 145, 165
quasi-public/quasi-private spaces, 58–9
Quebec: cultural difference and accommodation in, 13–14; foreign language broadcasts, 118; licensing issues, 65; regional press associations, 72, 80; Sunday film screenings in, 177n30; World Cup (1972) broadcast, 54
Queen Elizabeth Playhouse (Vancouver), 45

race: master-race theory, 74, 78; as mechanism of exclusion, 10; and national culture, 93, 96; and public assembly, 60; "racist multiculturalism," 10
radical press, 72, 75–6, 105
radio, 9, 152; ad hoc regulation of, 108; cable distribution, 136–8, 140; *Canadians All* series, 75, 110, 112–15, 121; competition with television, 152, 154; "counter-culture," 137; early cable radio, 136–8, 140; early shortwave and local, 107–8; ethnocultural radio format, 110, 141; ownership issues, 139; play dramatizing assassination, 153; radio-television, 65, 137; signal reception, interference issues, 106; television competition with, 154; US formats, 109. *See also* third-language programming; *and individual stations*
Radio Centre-Ville (Montreal), 137–8
Radio City Film Exchange, 48
Radio City Video, 65
Radiotelevisione Italiana (RAI), 164
RAI International, 30, 145, 164–5
ratings, audience, 111, 131–4
ratings, content, 23, 48, 64–5
Razack, Sherene, 60, 68
"reasonable accommodation," 13
red scare. *See* Cold War
regional versus local versus national, 154–5, 160–2

religious films, 58
research scholarship: on archival material, 20–5; on ethnic press, 103; on "ethnic theatres" in United States, 38–9; on "formats," 139; on media culture, 16; on minority media, 19–20; on multiculturalism in Canada, 10–11; on post-broadcast media, 56; on the public sphere, 13; on social order and information distribution, 7
Rio Theatre (Vancouver), 45
riots caused by performances, 60
"ritual" view of communications, 173n4
Riviera (Montreal), 43
Robarts, John, 71
rock and roll, 130
Rogers, Ted (Rogers Broadcasting), 125, 162–3, 168
Rogers Cable (Toronto), 147, 150, 157
Rogers Communication, 22
Roma Film, 48
Rose, Jonathan W., 85
Roth, Lorna, 17–18
Royal Commission on Bilingualism and Biculturalism, 10, 82, 96–7, 101–2, 130
Royal Commission on Broadcasting, 116
Royal Commission on Publications, 99–100
Royal Commonwealth Society, 102
Russian language media, 48, 72, 184n32

Sampson, G.W., 113
San Carlino Theatre (Toronto), 65
satellite transmission, 143, 162, 197n9
scale and multiculturalism, 9, 143–4, 196–7n7
scotti, Arturo, 127
Second World War, 73–5; and Art House theatres, 38–9, 69; and Canada Press Club, 73–6, 112; *Canadians All* radio series, 112–13; and "constrained emergence theory," 68; and ethnic press, 79; monitoring of minority Canadians, 183n30; suspension of German-language press, 184n32. *See also* postwar issues
self-regulation by press, 104–5
semi-public community, 53, 57, 134
"semi-public"/"semi-private" spaces, 57–60
Senate Committee on Mass Media, 99
Serbian assassination dramatization, 153
Service, James, 129
settler hegemony, 15, 17, 96, 98
Shaw Cable, 163
Shori, Janki, 45, 58
signal interference, 106
Simone, V., 48
Simpson, G.W., 74
Singh, C.B, 47
slave trade, 98
Slovenska Drzava, 78
"smell-o-vision," 40
sociality, 53, 66
The Sopranos, 166
Soviet Union, films from, 46, 49, 178–9n52
space(s): common, 12, 58; cultural recoding of, 44; and individualism, 171; as media infrastructure function, 9–10, 16; policing of, 60, 68; "semi-public"/"quasi-private," 57–9, 134; versus "sphericules," 103; theaters as, 36, 53–6, 58, 61, 65, 146; virtual, 56
Spanish-language media: digital, 166; films, 14, 32–6, 34, 43–5,

49, 52, 175nn8; Latinovision, 158–9; newspapers, 33; radio-television, 65, 137. See also Telelatino (Latinovision)
Spanish-speaking community, 33
Special Broadcast Service (Australia), 139
specialty services, 136, 145, 155–6, 160–2
spectrum scarcity, 139, 168
"sphericules," 103
Sponsor magazine, 118
sporting events, 54, 55, 148, 197n18
Stanczykowski, Casimir: applying for CKJS, 141–3, 151, 155, 162, 167, 192n51; and CFMB, 137–8, 141; ownership model, 162
Stanley Cup playoffs, 106–7
Starosielski, Nicole, 16
Starr, Leigh, 15
Stars of David (Bossin), 41
St Clair Theatre (Toronto), 43, 53, 60, 65, 176n14
STELCO plant strike, 56
stereotyping of media multiculturalism, 7
St Laurent, Louis, 95
Straw, Will, 8
Studio Theatre, 48–50, 50
"sub-run" venues, 37, 40
subscription model, 65–6, 145, 155–6
subtitles, 34, 35, 49, 199n46
suburbs, 32, 38, 63–4
Sunday screenings, 40, 53, 177n30
Switzer, Phyllis, 149

Taylor, Charles, 11–15, 68
Taylor, Nathan A., 39–41
technical infrastructure of media, 4, 143
Teledomenica (television), 86, 146

Telelatino (Latinovision), *161*; broadening of programming, 166; condition of archives for, 21–2; conflict with RAI, 164; and Emilio Mascia, 56; financial issues, 162; international content for, 164; low subscription rate for, 160; national cultural policy for, 29; purchased by Shaw, 163; suburban location of, 64.
telephone distribution, 136–7
television: access to archival material, 21–4; Chinese language media, 156; community television, 147; competition with radio, 154; digital distribution, 29–30, 143; early third-language cable, 144–5, 149–50, 155–62; frequency scarcity, 146; "theatre television," 53–4. See also *individual stations*
Tenhunen, Bruno, 78, 101
Tenuto, David, 32, 35–6
theatrical runs, typical duration of, 44, 46–7
third-language programming, 107, 167–8, 171; as aid to assimilation, 124–5, 131; archival material availability and access, 23–4; Broadcast Act, 108; "brokered time" model, 146–7, 154; City-TV, 149–51; CRTC definition of, 152, 154; cultural concerns, 107, 129, 143; digital distribution, 29–30; early cable radio, 136–8, 140; early shortwave and local, 107–8; entertainment-oriented, 194n88; international providers of, 164–6, 197n19; as interstitial media, 149; Johnny Lombardi promoting, 111–12; "language radio," 112, 118, 132; legal issues, 52, 108, 111, 157; licensing for,

121–2, 157–9; as "local," 143–5, 154–5; multilingual format, 110, 137–40; multi-local stations, 161–2; ownership of, 163; producers of, 146–7; promoting integration, 131; regional broadcast concept, 155–6; "scaling up" of, 162; Serbian assassination dramatization, 153; television, 64, 66, 159; TV versus radio, 152; wartime ban on, 108. *See also individual languages, stations*
Thompson, Andrew, 88–90
Tiananmen Square coverage, 163
titles, translations of, 24
TLN, 166
Toronto: Brighton Theatre, 43, 46, 48; foreign-language movie houses, 43; foreign-language newspapers, 78; Maple Leaf Gardens, 54; regional versus local broadcasting, 162; time allotted to foreign language broadcasts, 116; west end, 39
Toronto Star, 88, 106, 127, 134
Toronto Telegram, 5, 81, 151
Tova, Theresa, 173n2
traffic network, media as a, 5
translation: of poems, 113; of printed material, 82–3, 186n69; of promotional material, 60, 72, 89
"transmission" view of communications, 173n4
transnationalism, 148–9, 163, 171
Trudeau, Pierre Elliott, 102–3, 111, 149, 188n101
Turek, Victor, 19
Turkish language ban, 184n32
TVB (Television Broadcasts Limited), 163–4
Two Ways of Life (Lindal), 73

Ubyssey ads (University of British Columbia), 45

UHF broadcasting, 144, 149, 154
Ukrainian-language media, 118; CFLP (Montreal), 123; CFMB (Montreal), 141; CHML (Hamilton), 116–17; and "enemy language" ban, 184n32; Kirkconnell and, 113; Labour-Farmer Temple (Winnipeg), 55; local ads, 133; and Massey Commission, 97; and multilingual broadcasting debate, 151, 198n41; press, 72, 79, 86, 95; prewar films, 39, 55; Winnipeg, 141. *See also* Polish-language media
Ukrainian National Information Service, 79, 185n48
Ukrayinskyi holos (Ukrainian Voice), 72
Ungerman, Irving, 54
United States, 38–9; *Americans All* series, 113; black public sphere in, 197n18; and "Canadianization," 107; Icelandic community in, 183n17; immigration history of, 67–8, 176n19; influence on Canada, 148, 164; and meaning of "continental," 119, 139; radio "formats" in, 109
Univision Canada, 166

Van Bruchem, Jan, 130–1, 141, 151, 153, 195n92, 197n19
Vancouver: Bernard T.C. Liu, 147, 155–6, 159; Chinavision, 160; CJVB (Great Pacific Broadcasting), 141, 151, 153, 197n19; foreign film in, 39, 43, 45, 52; foreign-language newspapers in, 78; foreign-language radio in, 130, 132, 138; foreign-language television in, 147; South Asian community in, 156

Vapaa Sana (weekly), 78
Ventures in Citizenship, 113
vernacular multiculturalism, 62
video. *See* home video
Vixen (Meyer), 44
Vlahos, Thomas, 179n63

Wah Shing Television, 157, 199n54
"waiting room of history," 26
Walcott, Rinaldo, 10–11, 15
war on terror, 165
Waung, Gilbert, 157
Weinstein, Leon, 149
"welfare state," 104
West, James, 149, 157
Whitaker, Reginald, 74, 182n8
Whiteoak, John, 119
Willowdale Enterprise, 106
Winnipeg, Manitoba, 39, 44, 55, 72–7, 80, 86, 102. *See also* Stanczykowski, Casimir
Winston, Milton, 157
WKBW (Buffalo, NY), 148
Wolofsky family, 86
Women's Advertising Club of Toronto, 88
Wong, Quon H., 45

Woodsworth, J.S., 68
Workers Farmers Publishing Society, 72
World Cup matches, 54, 55, 152
World View Television, 147, 155–6, 159–60

xenophobia: fear of communists, 55–6, 88, 96, 101; fear of Islamic terrorism, 165

Yearbook of the Canadian Motion Picture Industry, 39–40
Yiddish language: films, 39, 41; newspapers, 72, 86, 183n17; radio news, 108
York Theatre/the Raja (Vancouver), 43, 45
Young, Liam, 93
Yugoslav community, 95, 153
Yuzyk, Paul, 99

Zieman, Margaret, 84
Ziniak, Madeline, 23, 147
Ziniak, Marion, 189n142
Znaimer, Moses, 149
Zwiazkowiec (Polish weekly), 79, 84